ADVANCE PRAISE FOR

Reflections on Allan H. Meltzer's Contributions to Monetary Economics and Public Policy

"A nice overview of the important lifework of Allan Meltzer, one of the great monetary economists of the twentieth century."

—**Alan Greenspan**, chairman of the US Federal Reserve Board, 1987–2006

"This book succeeds in highlighting the extraordinary contributions of Allan Meltzer, sometimes with Karl Brunner, to the analysis of monetary economics, history, and policy. Anyone interested in monetary institutions should read it."

—**Paul Tucker**, Harvard Research Fellow, former central banker, and author of *Unelected Power: The Quest for Legitimacy in Central Banking and the Regulatory State*

"Allan Meltzer was a towering figure in economics who left an indelible mark on our understanding of the theory and practice of monetary policy. The concise and eloquent essays in this book describe clearly the monumental contributions he made to monetary theory, monetary history, and the economics of central banking, and why they remain vitally important today. Well worth reading for anyone with an interest in monetary matters."

—**Jeffrey M. Lacker**, Distinguished Professor, Virginia Commonwealth University

D1468660

REFLECTIONS ON
ALLAN H. MELTZER'S
CONTRIBUTIONS TO
MONETARY ECONOMICS
AND PUBLIC POLICY

EDITED BY DAVID BECKWORTH

HOOVER INSTITUTION PRESS
Stanford University Stanford, California

With its eminent scholars and world-renowned library and archives, the Hoover Institution seeks to improve the human condition by advancing ideas that promote economic opportunity and prosperity, while securing and safeguarding peace for America and all mankind. The views expressed in its publications are entirely those of the authors and do not necessarily reflect the views of the staff, officers, or Board of Overseers of the Hoover Institution.

www.hoover.org

Hoover Institution Press Publication No. 704
Hoover Institution at Leland Stanford Junior University,
Stanford, California, 94305-6003

Cover photo © Stan Franzos; used with permission.

The frontispiece photo (page ii) is from the Meltzer family photo collection.

Published in cooperation with the Mercatus Center at George Mason University.

Hoover Institution Press assumes no responsibility for the persistence or accuracy of URLs for external or third-party Internet websites referred to in this publication, and does not guarantee that any content on such websites is, or will remain, accurate or appropriate.

First printing 2019
27 26 25 24 23 22 21 20 19   9 8 7 6 5 4 3 2 1

The paper used in this publication meets the minimum requirements of the American National Standard for Information Sciences—Permanence of Paper for Printed Library Materials, ANSI/NISO Z39.48-1992. ∞

Cataloging-in-Publication Data is available from the Library of Congress.
ISBN 978-0-8179-2305-1 (pbk. : alk. paper)
ISBN 978-0-8179-2306-8 (EPUB)
ISBN 978-0-8179-2307-5 (Mobipocket)
ISBN 978-0-8179-2308-2 (PDF)

Contents

About Allan H. Meltzer

A llan Meltzer (1928–2017) was one of the greatest monetary econo-mists of his generation. During his career, he authored many books and papers that help shape the modern consensus on monetary pol-icy and the art of central banking. His work also contributed to a wider debate on the role of public policy in a capitalist system.

Meltzer's academic work on monetary policy demonstrated how central banks can sway the business cycle and why it is important to discipline this influence over economic activity. His efforts continue to inform policy making today, including his landmark books *A History of the Federal Reserve*, volumes 1 and 2 (University of Chicago Press, 2002 and 2010), and the still-ongoing and influential Carnegie-Rochester Conference Series on Public Policy that he founded along with Karl Brunner. His book *Why Capitalism?* (Oxford University Press, 2012) gives an impassioned defense of the market economy in a time when many have blamed capitalism for economic disaster, inequality, and other social ills.

Meltzer joined the faculty at Carnegie Mellon Graduate School of Industrial Administration, later named the Tepper School, in 1957 and would go on to hold a professorship in political economy there until his death. He was also a distinguished visiting fellow at the Hoover Institution as well as a visiting professor at numerous universities, including Harvard University and the University of Chicago.

Meltzer also threw his hat into the policy world by serving as a consultant for several congressional committees, the president's Council of Economic Advisers, the US Treasury Department, the Board of Governors of the Federal Reserve System, foreign governments, and various central banks. He was also a member of the President's Economic Policy Advisory Board from 1988 to 1990.

From 1986 to 2002, he was an honorary adviser to the Institute for Monetary and Economic Studies of the Bank of Japan. In 1999–2000, he served as chair of the International Financial Institution Advisory Commission, known as the Meltzer Commission, which proposed major reforms of the International Monetary Fund and the development banks.

Over the course of his career, Meltzer won many awards, including the 2003 Irving Kristol Award from the American Enterprise Institute and the 2009 Distinguished Teaching Award from the International Mensa Foundation. In 2011, he won the Bradley Award, the Harry Truman Medal for Public Policy, and the Truman Medal for Economic Policy.

Meltzer received his BA in economics from Duke University and his MA and PhD in economics from UCLA under the direction of Karl Brunner. He is survived by his wife of sixty-six years, Marilyn, as well as by three children and eight grandchildren.

Allan Meltzer had a long and productive career and the world is a better place because of it.

Introduction

DAVID BECKWORTH

A llan Meltzer was one of the leading monetary economists of the twentieth century, authoring more than a dozen books and 300 papers during his distinguished career. His work changed the fields of economics, central banking, and public policy.

Meltzer's academic work was seminal in both the theoretical and practical applications of monetary economics. He carefully showed how central banks affect broad economic activity and how that influence could, and sometimes did, end in economic disaster. His work on monetary policy, including his magisterial two-volume *A History of the Federal Reserve* and the public policy conference series he founded with Karl Brunner, is still important and relevant today.

Meltzer participated in the policy world by serving as a consultant for several congressional committees, the president's Council of Economic Advisers, the US Treasury Department, the Board of Governors of the Federal Reserve System, foreign governments, and various central banks. He also served as chair of the International Financial Institution Advisory Commission, known as the Meltzer Commission, which proposed major reforms of the International Monetary Fund and development banks in the late 1990s.

Meltzer passed away in May 2017. To commemorate his career, a conference was held on January 4, 2018, in Philadelphia, Pennsylvania. The conference, titled Meltzer's Contributions to Monetary Economics and Public Policy, was organized by the Program on Monetary Policy at the Mercatus Center at George Mason University and by the Institute for Humane Studies.

Participants at the conference spoke of three areas in which Meltzer made important contributions: the history of the Federal Reserve, the monetary transmission mechanism, and public policy more generally. Their presentations make up most of the chapters in this book. Owing to the extemporaneous nature of conference proceedings, some of the chapters in this volume have been transcribed.

Chapter 1 starts the book with an essay by John Taylor. He takes a broad look at Meltzer's career and notes that it was characterized by a desire to be holistic. This is why Meltzer spent many years developing a theory of the monetary policy transmission mechanism only to follow that with many more years working on the history and political economy of the Federal Reserve. These various endeavors complemented each other and provided a well-rounded understanding of US monetary policy. Taylor also notes that one of the inescapable lessons Meltzer drew from this work was the need for rules. That is why Meltzer became a long-time advocate for monetary policy rules.

Chapter 2 begins the section of the book that takes a closer look at Meltzer's contribution to the history of the Federal Reserve. Authoring this chapter is Michael Bordo, who reviews the broad themes in Meltzer's *History of the Federal Reserve, 1913–1986 (HFR)*. He notes that, unlike Milton Friedman and Anna Schwartz's *A Monetary History of the United States, 1867–1960*, *HFR* is not a monetary history per se but more of a biography of the institution, its leaders, and their decision-making process. A key argument of *HFR* is that had the Fed followed the quantity-theory-based classical monetary theory—as espoused by Henry Thornton, Walter Bagehot, and Irving Fisher—the Fed could have easily avoided its biggest failures: the Great Contraction of 1929–1933 and the Great Inflation of 1965–1982. Conversely, its biggest successes, the Volcker Disinflation of 1979–1982 and the Great Moderation of 1985–2001, occurred because the Fed did follow classical monetary theory.

Robert Hetzel, however, pushes back in chapter 3 against Meltzer's claims in *HFR* and elsewhere that Fed officials were capable of following the "self-evident" quantity theoretic truths from classical monetary theory and, thereby, could have avoided the Great Depression. Hetzel notes that these claims trivialize the role played by Meltzer and the other monetarists in the monetarist counterrevolution. Their efforts over many years are what led to the modern understanding of monetary policy and the role of a central bank. To believe Fed officials in the 1930s could have acted differently is to assume they had access to the body of knowledge Meltzer and the other monetarists spent a lifetime establishing.

In chapter 4, George Selgin closes out the historical portion of the book by looking at one of the fascinating stories in *HFR* and using it to shed light on current development. Specifically, he looks at the Fed's raising reserve requirements between 1936 and 1937 and compares it to the Fed introducing interest on excess reserves (IOER) at a rate higher than comparable short-term interest rates starting in late 2008. In both cases, concerns about excess reserves stoking inflation were a motivating factor, and in both cases the policy actions served to sterilize the excess reserves by increasing banks' demand for reserves. Arguably, in both cases, these actions contributed to a subsequent downturn and slow recovery. Some history lessons get repeated.

Chapter 5 starts the portion of the book that looks at Meltzer's contributions to the monetary transmission mechanism. Peter Ireland, the author of this chapter, begins by observing that Meltzer worked closely with Karl Brunner over several decades to create what became known as the Brunner-Meltzer model. This model is similar in some ways to modern macroeconomic models but differs in other ways. One key difference is that the Brunner-Meltzer model sees monetary policy working through a wide spectrum of assets prices and yields rather than through just the expected path of the short-term interest rate target. As Ireland notes, this understanding implies that the effective lower bound on short-term interest rates should not be a binding constraint on monetary policy, for other asset yields can be affected through open market operations. The Brunner-Meltzer model, therefore, can be used to justify some form of quantitative easing. More generally, as Ireland shows, the model can be used to motivate the use of monetary aggregates in modern monetary policy.

Edward Nelson notes in chapter 6 that Meltzer saw the monetary base as central to understanding the monetary transmission mechanism. Meltzer believed the growth of the monetary base helped shape the growth of broader monetary aggregates and nominal income more generally. He also believed the real monetary base could be used as a summary indicator, or index of changes, across the many asset prices that mattered for aggregate demand. Nelson explores the implications of these beliefs and resolves some seeming paradoxes they create. For example, he shows how Meltzer's focus on the liability side of the Fed's balance sheet can be reconciled with monetary policy working through changes in the mix on its asset side. Nelson shows how this understanding makes sense in light of the Fed's large-scale asset purchases and interest rate targets.

In chapter 7, Joshua Hendrickson considers what the Brunner-Meltzer model implies for US monetary policy in light of the Fed's floor system. As noted, in late 2008 the Fed introduced IOER at a level higher than comparable short-term interest rates as it vastly expanded its balance sheet. These actions turned the Fed's operating system from a corridor system to a floor system. In this new operating system, the Fed uses an administered interest rate, the IOER, to set monetary policy. Hendrickson notes, however, that the Brunner-Meltzer model implies that monetary policy works through many asset prices and yields, not just a single target interest rate like the IOER. Moreover, the floor system has intentionally divorced money from monetary policy—by raising demand for bank reserves to the perfectly elastic portion of the demand curve—and so real money balances are no longer informative about the stance of monetary policy. The Fed, therefore, may find managing monetary policy more challenging in the floor system.

In chapter 8, St. Louis Federal Reserve president James Bullard reviews Meltzer's work on the Federal Reserve's search for a nominal anchor coming out of the Great Inflation of the 1970s and early 1980s. Bullard notes that much progress has been made with the Fed's adoption of an inflation target, first de facto in the mid-1990s and then explicitly in 2012. Bullard goes on to consider whether this progress has meant the Fed is conducting something close to optimal monetary policy. He does so by looking at the disappearing Phillips curve and deviations from the price-level growth path.

Chapter 9 starts the section that looks at Meltzer's contribution to public policy thought. The author of this chapter, Gerald O'Driscoll, shares his experience working with Meltzer on the International Financial Institution Advisory Commission, known as the Meltzer Commission, which sought to reform the International Monetary Fund and development banks in light of the emerging market crises of the mid-to-late 1990s. Meltzer was the chair of the commission, and O'Driscoll was his chief-of-staff. Meltzer had six months to navigate a commission divided among Republicans and Democrats and was able to produce a bipartisan report.

In chapter 10, Robert Lucas reflects on his time working with Meltzer at Carnegie Mellon University and recalls a debate Meltzer had with Noam Chomsky. Lucas also points to the seminal work Meltzer did on theoretical money demands models, starting with his influential 1963 *Journal of Political Economy* article. Lucas notes that Meltzer's work complemented that of Friedman and Schwartz, who focused more on pure monetary history. Lucas also shows that Meltzer's early money demand work still holds up if updated to the present.

Chapter 11 closes this section with Charles Plosser recognizing the many public policy contributions made by Meltzer. They include his co-creating the Shadow Open Market Committee and the Carnegie-Rochester Conference Series on Public Policy in the 1970s. These programs continue to this day and have made many important contributions to monetary policy, including John Taylor's 1993 Carnegie-Rochester Conference paper that coined his now-famous Taylor rule. Plosser suggests that Meltzer's biggest public policy contribution was his enduring support for monetary policy rules. Plosser agrees with Meltzer's assessment that the Fed's biggest policy failures occurred in periods of excessive discretion, the Great Depression and the Great Inflation. Conversely, in periods of more rule-like behavior, such as the Great Moderation, the Fed performed the best.

The final chapter of this book is a transcript of a live interview Meltzer did for the podcast *Macro Musings*. The interview took place in November 2016, just six months before he died. It is Meltzer in his own words, one last time before he passed. I was the host of the show and was impressed with his sharp-witted insights during our conversation. We talked about how he got into economics, the monetarist counterrevolution, his work with Brunner, his reinterpretation of Keynes's work, the role of money in monetary policy analysis, and his thoughts on the Great Recession, quantitative easing, and inflation targets.

CHAPTER 1
Making the Rules and Breaking the Mold: Allan Meltzer, 1928–2017

JOHN B. TAYLOR

Allan Meltzer, who died in May 2017 at the age of eighty-nine, had a long and productive career, fundamentally affecting the fields of economics, central banking, and, more broadly, economic policy. An extraordinary scholar, he immersed himself in the practical world of policy making in many ways. He had a unique ability to understand, explain, and improve the interface between the fields of economics and economic policy.

For Meltzer, it was not enough to develop a novel theory of the economic impact of monetary policy, which he did in his research on the financial system starting with Swiss economist Karl Brunner. He also examined the institutions responsible for policy through his landmark two-volume work *A History of the Federal Reserve* (*HFR*) and the Carnegie-Rochester Conference Series on Public Policy, which he cofounded with Brunner.

For Meltzer, it was not sufficient to show empirically that policy mistakes caused poor economic performance. He also researched why the mistakes were made, including by developing, with Scott Richard and Alex Cukierman,

This chapter originally appeared in *Central Banking Journal* 23, no. 1 (June 2017). Copyright © 2017 Infopro Digital Services Limited. Reprinted with permission.

theories of political economy and decision-making. It was not enough for him to conduct research and teach at Carnegie Mellon University, where he was a professor. He also threw his hat into the ring of real-world policy making, serving on the US president's Council of Economic Advisers (CEA), chairing the Meltzer Commission on international monetary reform, writing reports for Congress, and often testifying in congressional committees on monetary policy.

It was not even enough for him to have had a profound impact on central banking; he also delved into the operations of the whole market system, asking the key question in the title of his book *Why Capitalism?* and answering that capitalism is "the only system that the world has ever known that produces both growth and freedom."

CRITICISM WAS NEVER PERSONAL

In engaging with actual policy, Meltzer never held back criticism of policy decisions and policy-making institutions when he felt strong criticism was warranted. But he avoided personal attacks or impugning people's motives. Regarding US Federal Reserve Board decisions, for example, he wrote in *HFR* that, "although I find many reasons to criticize decisions, I praise the standards and integrity of the principals" (Meltzer 2010, x).

Meltzer's views on monetary policy began to take form in his research with Brunner, whom Meltzer noted was his "teacher, dissertation supervisor, later my co-author and lifelong friend." They wrote twenty-five papers together on policy, many focused on a model of the monetary transmission process. The modeling research began in the 1960s, and the key framework was later called the Brunner-Meltzer model. Meltzer went on to develop this framework further and apply it in practice.

The model was unique in the way it incorporated the determinants of both the supply of money and the demand for money, going behind the scenes of the quantity equation of money employed by Irving Fisher and Milton Friedman. The model showed how the economic effects of changes in the money supply involved a complex channel with credit flows, wealth effects, interest rates, and asset prices. Today, many macroeconomic researchers are trying to incorporate credit into popular macro models because changes in credit flows had such a noticeable and devastating impact during the global financial crisis. Meltzer had incorporated these features into his thinking fifty years ago.

Based on this theoretical and empirical research, Meltzer came to a particular view of how to evaluate monetary policy that gave clear advantages of predictable rule-like decisions for the policy instruments, whether the interest rate or the monetary base. He then applied this framework consistently over time to actual policy, uncovering policy mistakes in the midst of policy successes. More than any other monetary economist, he looked for and examined the reasons for the mistakes, and he focused on two basic reasons: political interference with policy and mistaken beliefs about policy. This led to his recommendations about how central banks should be governed and how monetary policy should be conducted, which have had an important impact.

THE FED'S MISTAKES IN THE 1930s AND 1970s

Meltzer argued that the Great Depression of the 1930s was largely caused by a mistake made by Fed officials who allowed the money supply—currency and deposits—to fall by 28 percent. He looked for the reasons for that mistake and concluded the problem was mainly a faulty belief at the Fed about how monetary policy works. He found evidence in the Fed's own records that it had used misleading indicators, such as nominal interest rates or bank borrowings, as measures of monetary tightness, when economic theory pointed to the real interest rate and broader monetary aggregates, such as currency and deposits. For this reason, the Fed decided that open market purchases were not necessary because low member bank borrowings and low interest rates were a sign of monetary ease. Meltzer showed that the alternative, correct, view, that the central bank should control deposits and currency, was known outside the Federal Reserve system at the time but was not reflected in the Fed's decisions.

"So certain was the System about the correctness of its actions and its lack of responsibility for the collapse that I have found no evidence the Board undertook an official study of the reasons for the policy failure," he wrote in *HFR* (Meltzer 2002, 413). Meltzer also argued that the Great Inflation of the late 1960s and 1970s was due to a policy mistake—this time a large increase in money growth and a corresponding effort to keep interest rates too low. Again, Meltzer looked for the reasons for the policy mistake. One reason was the Fed's mistaken belief in the Phillips curve, which said that higher inflation would reduce unemployment permanently.

But a second reason was political. The Fed agreed to coordinate its actions with the US administration's fiscal policy, a practice that meant the Fed would try to keep interest rates low. A third reason was also political. As the 1972 election approached, Fed chair Arthur Burns became convinced that the unemployment rate required to reduce inflation would be politically unacceptable. He became the leading proponent of wage and price controls, and let money growth increase. So, both Meltzer's categories of reasons for mistakes were to blame.

VOLCKER RECAPTURES LOST FED INDEPENDENCE

The end of the Great Inflation and the start of the Great Moderation of price and output stability was a different story. There was an absence of the big mistakes and a corresponding emphasis on more predictable rule-like behavior. Meltzer stressed Fed chair Paul Volcker's reliance on a framework in which inflation is a monetary phenomenon with no long-run Phillips curve trade-off. He emphasized how Volcker recaptured much of the independence the Fed had lost during the Great Inflation and was, thereby, able to resist political interference and take the necessary steps required to restore stability.

Going deeper, Meltzer wrote how Volcker was ideally suited for preventing the mistakes. Volcker had "the background and experience to be a successful chairman. . . . Foreign central bankers and New York bankers knew him and had confidence in him. He was knowledgeable and strong-willed, and determined and committed to the task" (Meltzer 2010, 1012).

During the Great Moderation, which continued under Volcker and much of Alan Greenspan's term as chair, the Fed did not succumb to political pressures or faulty theories. Meltzer was again critical of monetary policy for its role in the global financial crisis.

He argued that it was a mistake for the Fed to depart from a rule-like policy and keep rates unusually low in the years before the crisis. The explanation for these policy mistakes appeared to be in the "mistaken beliefs" category: a mistaken view that rule-like policy was not necessary and that a return to discretion was OK. Meltzer was also critical of quantitative easing after the crisis and said that the Fed's lender-of-last-resort actions during the crisis had no clear strategy. On the political side, he argued that the Fed seemed willing to sacrifice much of the independence Volcker had restored in the 1980s.

In sum, Meltzer concluded that the Great Depression was mainly due to bad economics: mistaken beliefs about interest rates and bank borrowings; that the Great Inflation was a combination of both factors, with political pressures dominating near the end as beliefs changed but policies did not; that the Disinflation avoided big mistakes of either type as the Fed regained independence and restored basic monetary fundamentals, which continued into the Great Moderation, a period of more rule-based policy; and that the global financial crisis and its aftermath was a return to a combination of both kinds of errors. Meltzer's research, thus, led him to a clear policy conclusion, as he wrote in the second volume of *HFR*, published in 2010: "Discretionary policy failed in 1929–33, in 1965–80 and now." And it is equally clear and convincing that "the lesson should be less discretion and more rule-like behavior"

(Meltzer 2010, 1255). This considered assessment, based on years of research and study, is, perhaps, his most fundamental contribution to central banking.

HFR was itself a "monumental accomplishment," to use the words of economic historian Michael Bordo (2006, 613). Meltzer examined transcripts of meetings of the Federal Open Market Committee; notes and interviews with Fed officials; records at the New York Fed and other regional banks; papers from presidents of the United States and their assistants; and the records of Congress, the Treasury, the CEA, foreign monetary officials, academics, and journalists. He insisted that policy makers express their views and explain their decisions in their own words and, thus, frequent quotes of policy makers are found throughout *HFR*. He connected complex series of events, transforming his painstaking research into "an exceptionally clear story," as economist David Laidler described it (2003, 1256). By making so much information accessible in a readable and manageable form, he contributed greatly to economics and central banking.

CONGRESSIONAL HEARINGS

Meltzer's work over the years advising Congress and many administrations is another part of his impact on policy. There is no better way to understand this influence than to have watched him in action. I recall a 2015 hearing at the Senate Committee on Banking, Housing, and Urban Affairs about monetary reform, where he was a witness (Meltzer 2015). I sat next to him at the witness table, listening carefully. Meltzer was remarkably clear, articulate, and convincing, directly addressing senators on the committee, both Democrats and Republicans. Indeed, both sides seemed to be listening carefully, in part because he was so obviously nonpartisan. In answering a question about a lender-of-last-resort proposal by Senator Elizabeth Warren, he said, "I congratulate you, Senator Warren, for keeping this issue alive."

Meltzer spent a lot of time at this hearing explaining the merits of a bill that would require the Fed to describe its rules or strategy for monetary policy. In his opening, Meltzer said,

> We need change to improve the oversight that this committee and the House Committee exercises over the Fed. You have the responsibility. Article I, Section 8 gives that to you. But you do not have the ability to exercise authority.
>
> You are busy people. You are involved in many issues. The chairperson of the Fed is a person who has devoted his

life to monetary policy. There is not any series of questions that you can ask on the fly that they are not going to be able to brush aside. That is why you need a rule.

I agree with John Taylor about some of the reasons for the rule, but I believe one of the most important is that Congress has to fulfil its obligation to monitor the Fed, and it cannot do that now because the chairman of the Fed can come in here, as Alan Greenspan has said on occasion, Paul Volcker has said on occasion, and they can tell you whatever it is they wish, and it is very hard for you to contradict them.

So you need a rule which says, look, you said you were going to do this, and you have not done it. That requires an answer, and that I think is one of the most important reasons why we need some kind of a rule.

Later in the hearing, Senator Sherrod Brown asked, "Dr. Meltzer, be specific, if you would, about your thoughts about the audit-the-Fed proposals." Meltzer answered,

Suppose you found out that the Fed chooses its policy using a Ouija board. What would you be able to do with that? What you want to do is get something which permits you to see that the policies that are carried out, are carried [out] for the benefit of the public. . . . What I think the Congress needs to do, it needs to face up to its responsibilities. Its responsibility is to be able to say to the Fed: "You told us you were going to do this, and you didn't do it. Why?" [That's what] the rule gives you. . . . [That is] more important than any other single thing you can do. You do not have the ability now to monitor them.

THE MELTZER COMMISSION

In 1998, Meltzer was asked to chair the Congress-mandated International Financial Institution Advisory Commission, also known as the Meltzer Commission, to recommend policy and reforms. The commission recommended reforms for the US government to try to implement at the International Monetary Fund (IMF) and the World Bank, including limits on

IMF lending and greater emphasis on grants for poor countries rather than loans the countries could not pay back. The actual reforms promoted by the US administration and implemented in the years that immediately followed were heavily influenced by the commission's recommendations. I can say this with conviction because I served as undersecretary of the Treasury during this period. Examples included the greater emphasis on grants rather than loans from the World Bank and limits on lending from the IMF.

When thinking about Meltzer's important role in chairing the commission, one is reminded of his research and writings on the international side of monetary policy. In *HFR*, he covers the growing US trade deficits in the 1960s and the reluctance to deal with them in a way that might risk slowing economic growth. The result, in his view, was failed policies of capital controls and efforts to twist the yield curve by buying longer-term Treasury securities in Operation Twist. He also had many sessions on international financial institutions at the Carnegie-Rochester conferences over the years and was later president of the international Mont Pelerin Society.

ENCOURAGING ECONOMISTS

An important part of Meltzer's impact was his constructive influence on other economists, and I can say that was certainly true of me. When I was just beginning my career as an economist as an assistant professor at Columbia University in the early 1970s, he invited me to attend the Carnegie-Rochester conference in Pittsburgh, Pennsylvania, knowing that it was a city I was from and where my family still lived. He opened a window for me to see serious policy-orientated research and to meet economists and policy makers who were committed to applying this research. In November 1976, he gave me the opportunity to discuss a paper by Ed Prescott, in which Prescott explained the policy implications of time inconsistency, which he published a year later with Finn Kydland. I was working at the CEA in Washington, DC, at the time and was delighted to get up to Pittsburgh for that.

By far my biggest opportunity was his invitation to me to present a paper on the practical use of policy rules at the November 1992 Carnegie-Rochester conference in Pittsburgh. This paper turned out to be the first exposition of what would come to be called the Taylor rule.

Ben McCallum was on the advisory board for the conference series at the time and recalls the details of how the invitation came about. At that time, people were arguing that rules would have to be very complex, and this led to severe doubts about the sustainability or even possibility of policy rules in practice. Meltzer thought otherwise, however, and encouraged me to work more on the problem and present the results. If he had not invited me to give that presentation and write that paper at that time, I would likely have done other things.

Allan Meltzer never let up. Several years ago, he was offered and accepted a position as distinguished visiting fellow at the Hoover Institution, which meant that I would see and talk with him more often. In 2014, he started the new Regulation and the Rule of Law Initiative at the Hoover Institution. He told me about its launch in an email: "It is great to be starting on a new career at 86." As always, he was positive and enthusiastic.

In 2015, he suggested to me that we ask a group of economists to support a statement giving the reasons for legislation on policy rules. We did so, and Jeb Hensarling, chair of the Financial Services Committee, read the statement to Fed chair Janet Yellen at a later hearing. A few months later, we organized a similar statement of support for a broad financial reform bill called the Financial Choice Act.

In the months before he died, Allan remained involved in public policy, recommending people for leadership positions in the new administration and advising on policy reform proposals. The last time I saw him was in January 2017, at a dinner party at our house on the Stanford University campus. My wife and I hosted the dinner for Allan and his wife, Marilyn, and invited some friends. His enthusiasm about what he was doing spread over the whole dinner conversation, as we looked at what was right and what was wrong about public policy in its broadest dimensions and considered what to do about it. We already miss Allan greatly.

REFERENCES

Bordo, Michael D. 2006. Review of *A History of the Federal Reserve*, vol. 1, by Allan H. Meltzer. *Journal of Monetary Economics* 53: 633–57.

Laidler, David. 2003. Review of *A History of the Federal Reserve*, vol. 1, by Allan H. Meltzer. *Journal of Economic Literature* 41, no. 4 (December): 1256–71.

Meltzer, Allan H. 2002. *A History of the Federal Reserve*. Vol. 1, *1913–1951*. Chicago: University of Chicago Press.

———. 2010. *A History of the Federal Reserve*. Vol. 2, *1951–1986*. Chicago: University of Chicago Press.

———. 2015. "Federal Reserve Accountability and Reform." Testimony before the Senate Committee on Banking, Housing, and Urban Affairs, March 3.

CHAPTER 2
Allan Meltzer and the History of the Federal Reserve

MICHAEL D. BORDO

Allan Meltzer was one of the pioneering monetary economists of the twentieth century—along with Karl Brunner, Milton Friedman, and Anna Schwartz—and succeeded in revolutionizing thinking in the post–World War II era on the role of money and the conduct of monetary policy in the economy. Together, Meltzer, Brunner, Friedman, and Schwartz created the monetarist counterrevolution that, among other things, made use of monetary history as a way to provide evidence on the effect monetary developments have on the price level and real output under different institutional arrangements. Meltzer's major contribution to this literature was his two-volume *A History of the Federal Reserve* (*HFR*). Meltzer argues that, had the Fed followed classical monetary theory (and its modern offshoots), it could have avoided its three big failures: the Great Contraction of 1929–1933, the Great Inflation of 1965–1982, and the recent Great Financial Crisis of 2007–2008 (GFC). Moreover, the Fed's two great triumphs (Paul Volcker's successful disinflation 1979 to 1982 and the Great Moderation 1985 to 2001) reflected the pursuit of sound monetary principles.

Brunner and Meltzer (House Committee on Banking and Currency 1964) used a variant of the widely acclaimed "narrative approach," developed by Friedman and Schwartz in *A Monetary History of the United States* (1963) to identify natural experiments using historical episodes to identify unique causation in the relationship between money and income. Brunner and Meltzer's focus was examining the motivation for Federal Reserve policy actions since its establishment by delving into the official record of the discussions of Fed staff and officials associated with key policy actions.

Meltzer's contribution to monetary history preceded the publication of his critically acclaimed *HFR*, published in 2002 and 2010. Two key earlier articles that influenced my work and that of other economic historians were his 1968 *Canadian Journal of Economics* article with Brunner that attributed the Federal Reserve's failure to prevent the Great Contraction of 1929–1933 to its having followed a flawed policy doctrine, which Brunner and Meltzer referred to as the Burgess-Riefler-Strong doctrine—a variant of the real bills doctrine.[1] A second influential article, published in the *Journal of Monetary Economics* in 1976, attributed the breakdown of the interwar international monetary system to the failure of the balance of payments adjustment mechanism.

HFR follows logically from these earlier studies. Meltzer, as a pioneer monetarist, accepted the basic quantity theory of money framework, but his focus in these two volumes is less on the monetary history per se, as in Friedman and Schwartz's *A Monetary History of the United States*, and more on producing a biography of the Federal Reserve as an institution; that is, on analyzing the decision-making processes of its leaders. His analytical approach encompassed much more than the tenets of established monetary theory and included political economy, especially the complex interactions between the government (administration, Treasury, and Congress) and the Fed.

The publication of *HFR* was greeted with great acclaim. In the *Journal of Monetary Economics* (2006) I called volume 1 "a monumental achievement." David Laidler, in the *Journal of Economic Literature* (2003), praised it as "an exceptionally clear story." John Taylor, in the *Journal of Monetary Economics* (2010), said "the history is comprehensive, thorough and serious," and Thomas Cargill, in *International Finance* (2011), referred to the two volumes as "a tour de force of the history of the Federal Reserve."

To understand the book and its emphasis on flawed doctrine (and political impingement on central bank independence), it is important to read chapter 2 of volume 1 because it gives a thorough history of classical monetary doctrine as espoused by Henry Thornton, Walter Bagehot, and Irving Fisher. These economists presented the fundamentals of monetary economics and, especially, the relationship between central bank policies and the macro-economy (prices, output, and exchange rates) under fixed and floating rates, the case for rules over discretion, rules for a lender of last resort, and the distinction between nominal and real interest rates. These fundamentals were at the heart of the Fed's failures and successes.

Meltzer, along with Brunner, was a key player in the US monetary policy debate from the 1950s until Brunner's death in 1989. Meltzer has continued in the role ever since. Meltzer, along with Brunner and Schwartz, founded the Shadow Open Market Committee in 1973, and with Brunner, he founded the highly successful Carnegie-Rochester conference series, the Konstanz conference series, and the Interlaken conference series. In addition, he wrote hundreds of influential articles and many books. Throughout his career, Meltzer was a strong and vocal critic of the Fed and a tireless advocate for sound money.

This chapter provides a highly selective guided tour of *HFR* and an overall evaluation.

NARRATIVE: 1913 TO 2010

The Federal Reserve System (FRS) was founded in 1913 as an independent central bank based on the principles of the real bills doctrine and the gold standard. Monetary policy was supposed to be conducted as by the Bank of England in the pre–World War I era, with the Fed passively rediscounting eligible commercial paper at the discount rate. The FRS was a compromise between the interests of the Northeast financial centers, which wanted a European-style central bank, and the rest of the country, which wanted local reserve banks dedicated to accommodating regional credit needs. World War I changed the environment drastically. Most countries suspended the gold standard, and the Fed lost its independence to serve as the financier of the Treasury by lending at preferential rates to finance the purchase of Treasury securities. It became, instead, an engine of inflation. After the war, the Fed followed the Bank of England's approach of raising its discount rate to roll back the large run-up in inflation. The resultant political backlash to the severe recession of 1920–1921 led the Fed to look for a new form of monetary control based on open market operations.

The new approach to monetary policy was laid out in the Fed's tenth annual report, in 1923. Meltzer explains how the new approach, called the Burgess-Riefler (BR) doctrine, was a derivative of the real bills doctrine and how it became the source of serious policy errors in the succeeding years. The premise for the BR doctrine was that member banks were reluctant to turn to the discount window, and so the Fed would use its open market operations to force them to the window when the economy was in recession and to repay loans when the economy was strong. Two indicators of the stance of the economy were (1) the levels of member bank borrowing in the two key Reserve cities, New York and Chicago, and (2) the level of short-term nominal interest rates. Meltzer is critical of this approach because it assumes that banks borrow only when in need and not to make profits and because it doesn't account for the difference between nominal and real interest rates.

Volume 1 of *HFR* analyzes Fed policy actions through the lens of the BR doctrine. Meltzer shows that the doctrine did work in two minor recessions in the 1920s but failed miserably between 1930 and 1933 because the two indicators provided misleading signals that the economy was in good shape when it wasn't. Member bank borrowing was low because the economy was depressed and nominal rates were low, reflecting expectations of deflation. Meltzer also blames the Fed for creating the Depression in the first place in 1929 by using tight monetary policy to prick the Wall Street boom. This was done on the real bills doctrine grounds that asset price inflation would eventually lead to general inflation and then deflation.

A key signature of volume 1 is that, unlike Friedman and Schwartz (1963), Meltzer does not blame the Fed's failure to prevent the banking panics on deep flaws in the Fed's governance structure (the struggle between the Reserve banks and the Board) and the fact that Benjamin Strong, who led the system until 1928, had died and there was no comparable successor. He argues that Strong also followed the BR doctrine and would have made the same mistakes as the other officials did. Thus, for Meltzer, bad doctrine was the key cause of the Fed's first calamitous policy failure.

In the mid-1930s, major reforms in the Bank acts of 1933 and 1935 gave the Federal Reserve Board much more power and independence de jure, but de facto the Fed became subservient to the Treasury and followed a bond support policy to keep interest rates low to help the Treasury finance its deficits. He also shows how the monetary reflation that occurred after the end of the Great Contraction in 1933 was solely attributable to expansionary Treasury gold purchase policies and the devaluation of the dollar in 1934. The one time the Fed did take serious policy action was in 1936 and 1937 when, on the grounds of the BR doctrine, the Fed doubled member banks' reserve requirements to eliminate a buildup in excess reserves. This led to the serious recession of 1937–1938. The recovery was aided by the Treasury rescinding its sterilization of gold inflows (originally imposed in 1936 to prevent the accumulation of excess reserves).

During World War II, the Fed followed the Treasury's lead and pegged bond prices, acting, as it had in World War I, as an engine of inflation. After the war, the interest rate peg regime continued under the Treasury's control. Meltzer brilliantly documents the struggle that began in the late 1940s between the Fed and the Treasury and the administration to end the interest rate pegs and restore the Fed's independence. The Fed recovered control of monetary policy in the Federal Reserve Treasury Accord of February 1951, which ends volume 1 of *HFR*.

Volume 2 begins with William McChesney Martin becoming chair of the Fed in 1951 and the system returning to active monetary policy making. Meltzer documents how, after the Fed regained its independence, it reverted to its old procedures of focusing on money market indicators and a variant of the BR doctrine, the targeting of net free reserves (NFR, excess reserves less borrowing). As he and Brunner had pointed out decades earlier, the NFR doctrine led to serious errors in Fed policy making in the 1950s and 1960s.

Meltzer is highly critical of Martin's tutelage—for his limited understanding of monetary economics (his use of nautical terms such as "leaning against the wind"); for his conception of the Fed's independence ("independent within the government"), which meant that monetary policy was secondary to fiscal policy; and for his later acceptance of the Phillips curve and Keynesian doctrine. Meltzer disagrees with Christina and David Romer (2002) who viewed the 1950s as a period of great success for the Fed. He argues that the only reason the macroeconomy performed so well was that the Eisenhower administration and, later, the early Kennedy administration were relatively fiscally conservative and believed in balanced budgets, the importance of adhering to the Bretton Woods gold constraint, and price stability. Had they run big fiscal deficits, he believes that Martin would have accommodated them.

Meltzer then documents how the Great Inflation of 1965–1982 began under Martin in 1965. He focuses on the ascendency of Keynesian views in the Kennedy administration in the 1962 Council of Economic Advisers and then within the Federal Reserve staff and the Federal Open Market Committee (FOMC); the belief in the superior performance of fiscal policy over monetary policy; the use of fine-tuning stabilization policy; and the adoption of the Phillips curve trade-off between inflation and unemployment. The Fed followed an influential article by Paul Samuelson and Robert Solow (1960) on the Phillips curve that argued that the benefits of reducing unemployment outweighed the costs of raising inflation. This meant that the weights the Fed attached to inflation and real growth in its policy reaction function between the 1950s and the 1960s shifted away from price stability toward growth.

When Lyndon Baines Johnson became president in 1963, the administration shifted to an expansionary fiscal policy to finance burgeoning domestic programs and the Vietnam War. The Martin Fed accommodated the Treasury via the use of the "even keel" policy and by the increasing reluctance to raise rates in the face of incipient inflationary pressure for fear of thwarting the administration's plans. This set the stage for the Great Inflation.

Another important theme in both volumes of *HFR* but especially in volume 2 is the international economy. The Bretton Woods system was the international monetary regime from 1945 to 1973, and the book discusses the influence of the balance of payments and the level of US gold reserves on Fed decision-making. The decline in the US monetary gold stock became particularly worrisome after the Western European countries declared current account convertibility in late 1958. After a spike in the price of gold in October 1960 (based on the fear that when Kennedy became elected he would follow expansionary fiscal policies), the Kennedy administration and the Fed began adopting policies to preserve gold. The Fed's key policies in this period were the creation of swap lines with other central banks and Operation Twist. In the early 1960s, the FOMC, in its policy deliberations, on occasion took into account the balance of payments and gold reserves in its domestic policy decision-making. Gold and the dollar also provided a reason for a number of Fed officials to maintain price stability. But after 1965, the Fed's policy became increasingly dominated by domestic concerns. This created another factor behind the Great Inflation.

Arthur Burns succeeded Martin as Fed chair in 1970. Meltzer is especially critical of his regime, in part because, as a well-respected economist, Burns should have known to make better decisions. Meltzer describes how Burns was increasingly unwilling to tighten monetary policy to stem the rise in inflation and inflationary expectations because of his fear of the political consequences of the recession that would follow. He also was subservient to the political ambitions of both President Nixon and President Carter. The Burns era is a key example of one of the great flaws in the Fed's record in being fiscally dominated, thus the Fed usually accommodated fiscal demands with expansionary monetary policy. Burns also subscribed to the importance of nonmonetary forces (especially the two oil price shocks and labor union power), and he was instrumental in the adoption by the United States of wage price controls in the 1970s, which had disastrous consequences. Burns also was responsible for the accommodation of the two oil price shocks, which further increased inflation. In addition, Meltzer criticizes Burns for not recognizing the important distinction between nominal and real interest rates. The Fed believed that rising nominal rates were evidence of tight money when, in fact, they just incorporated expectations of rising inflation.

President Carter replaced Burns with G. William Miller in March 1978, but Miller's record of achieving price stability was even worse than Burns's, and he lasted only a bit more than a year. By 1978, the United States was in the midst of a major economic crisis: inflation was in double digits, unemployment was rising, the dollar was collapsing, and there was increased financial instability reflecting the interaction between rising inflation and financial controls like regulation Q.[2] Meltzer views that period as the consequence of disastrous policy mistakes by the Federal Reserve comparable to the Great Contraction of 1929–1933.

President Carter appointed Paul Volcker to be Fed chair in the summer of 1979, with a mandate to break the back of inflation and inflationary expectations. Meltzer praises Carter for that decision. The Volcker Disinflation began with a major monetary policy regime change in October 1979 when the Fed shifted from using interest rates as its policy instrument to using monetary aggregates (nonborrowed reserves).

Meltzer gives Volcker the highest praise for following sound monetary principles and successfully ending the Great Inflation. The process was painful. It involved two recessions and a rise in unemployment well above 10 percent. Regaining credibility for low inflation was hampered by the Carter credit controls in 1980. In addition to recognizing Volcker's astute guidance, Meltzer also praises the Reagan administration for backing Volcker's actions in sharp contrast to the political interference of the 1960s and 1970s.

Volume 2 ends after low inflation is restored in the mid-1980s and Alan Greenspan succeeds Volcker as chairman of the Fed.

In an epilogue written in 2010, Meltzer covers the period from 1986 to 2010. He gives high marks to Chairman Greenspan for following rule-like monetary policy to maintain credibility for low inflation, thereby helping to create the Great Moderation, a period with low and stable inflation and high and stable economic growth.

Meltzer criticizes the Fed for shifting back to its old ways beginning in 2001 by keeping its policy interest rate well below the Taylor rule rate in a bogus attempt to prevent the emergence of a Japan-style deflation in the United States, thereby fueling a housing price boom that led to the GFC. Meltzer views the GFC as equivalent to the two previous Federal Reserve major policy errors in the twentieth century. He criticizes the Fed under Chairman Ben Bernanke for its handling of the financial crisis: for violating Bagehot's rule, for inconsistently bailing out Bear Stearns in March 2008 and letting Lehman Brothers fail in September, for following credit policy that threatened its independence, and for shifting to discretionary policy with the adoption of quantitative easing and forward guidance in late 2008.

EVALUATION: THE BOTTOM LINE

Meltzer gives two key reasons to explain why the Fed did so poorly in its monumental failures and so well in its triumphs. These are (1) sound monetary doctrine/theory and (2) political pressure (the loss of independence from the government). Reason 1 dominated the Great Depression; reasons 1 and 2 were behind the Great Inflation. He argues that both factors also were present in the GFC.

Meltzer's key prescription for successful central bank policy is to follow rule-based monetary policy; to follow a rule-based lender of last resort policy; to focus on the medium to long term and avoid "short termism"; and to avoid fine-tuning. These are the principles posited by Thornton, Bagehot, and Fisher that Meltzer emphasizes in chapter 2 of volume 1.

Allan Meltzer had the courage and force of will to let policy makers know when they were on or off track. His reputation, earned by over seventy years of sound scholarship culminating in *A History of the Federal Reserve*, made influential people heed his advice.

NOTES

1. The real bills doctrine underlays the framing of the Federal Reserve Act passed in 1913. It posited that the Federal Reserve banks should only discount commercial paper; it was a form of "self-regulating" real bill. The Reserve banks were not supposed to discount paper issued to finance speculative activity. It was believed that if the Federal Reserve followed this doctrine there never would be too much or too little credit in the economy.

2. Regulation Q imposed a ceiling interest rate on time deposits.

REFERENCES

Bordo, Michael D. 2006. Review of *A History of the Federal Reserve*, vol. 1, by Allan H. Meltzer. *Journal of Monetary Economics* 53: 633–57.

Brunner, Karl, and Allan H. Meltzer. 1968. "What Did We Learn from the Monetary Experience of the United States in the Great Depression?" *Canadian Journal of Economics* 1, no. 2 (May): 334–48.

Cargill, Thomas. 2011. Review of *A History of the Federal Reserve*, by Allan H. Meltzer. *International Finance* 14, no. 1: 183–207.

Friedman, Milton, and Anna Jacobson Schwartz. 1963. *A Monetary History of the United States, 1867–1960*. Princeton, NJ: Princeton University Press.

House Committee on Banking and Currency, Subcommittee on Domestic Finance. 1964. *Some General Features of the Federal Reserve's Approach to Policy: A Staff Analysis*. February 10.

Laidler, David. 2003. Review of *A History of the Federal Reserve*, vol. 1, by Allan H. Meltzer. *Journal of Economic Literature* 41, no. 4 (December): 1256–71.

Meltzer, Allan H. 1976. "Monetary and Other Explanations of the Start of the Great Depression." *Journal of Monetary Economics* 2, no. 4 (November): 455–71.

———. 2002. *A History of the Federal Reserve*. Vol. 1, *1913–1951*. Chicago: University of Chicago Press.

———. 2010. *A History of the Federal Reserve*. Vol. 2, *1951–1986*. Chicago: University of Chicago Press.

Romer, Christina, and David Romer. 2002. "A Rehabilitation of Monetary Policy in the 1950s." *American Economic Association Papers and Proceedings* 92, no. 2 (May): 121–27.

Samuelson, Paul, and Robert Solow. 1960. "Analytical Aspects of Anti-inflation Policy." *American Economic Review* 50: 177–94.

Taylor, John B. 2010. Review of *A History of the Federal Reserve*, vol. 2, by Allan H. Meltzer. *Journal of Monetary Economics* 58: 183–89.

CHAPTER 3
Allan Meltzer: How He Underestimated His Own Contribution to the Modern Concept of a Central Bank

ROBERT L. HETZEL

Monetarists delivered a stinging indictment of the Federal Reserve for its role in the Great Depression, when the price level fell accompanied by a decline in the money stock. The Fed had the power to prevent the decline in money through open market purchases of government securities that would have offset increases in the currency/deposit and reserves/deposit ratios. Preventing the decline in money would have prevented the deflation and the decline in output that occurred in the Depression. This critique represents the current professional consensus about monetary policy in the Depression. But where did that critique come from? Should it have been evident to monetary policy makers in the Depression?

In his critique of Fed policy in the Depression, Allan Meltzer (2002), as well as Milton Friedman and Anna Schwartz (1963), contended that Fed policy had as an obvious alternative the policy of maintaining growth in the money stock. They express bewilderment that the Fed was so "inept" (the Friedman and Schwartz term) as to ignore this policy. "All" policy makers had to do was to read Walter Bagehot ([1873] 1962) or, as Meltzer argued, Bagehot and Henry Thornton ([1802] 1939). The "truth" was staring them in the face. However, consensus over identification of the shocks that caused the Depression would require the combination of an intellectual revolution giving to government the responsibility for economic stabilization and the appearance of events that could not be rationalized within the existing framework of real bills. Complicating the problem of identification was the human trait of rationalizing preexisting beliefs rather than admitting to mistakes that resulted in disastrous consequences. In short, to agree with Meltzer, as well as with Friedman and Schwartz, that a stabilizing monetary policy in the Depression required only that policy makers read the evident truths contained in the existing quantity-theoretic literature on central banking is to trivialize the role that they themselves played in creating the modern concept of a central bank.

Starting in the 1950s and continuing through the 1970s, the monetarists pursued a research agenda that made their story about the Depression convincing ex post. Through examination of monetary "event studies" occurring over time and across countries, they established two empirical facts. The first was an association between the behavior of money and prices. The second was an association between nominal (price) and real (output) instability. Taken in isolation, each historical event inevitably had associated with it a variety of real forces capable of acting as a third variable causing these correlations. However, across time and place, only the behavior of the central bank offered a consistent smoking gun. There is no historical episode, including the recent Great Recession, that contradicts the monetarist hypothesis that contractionary monetary policy is a prerequisite for a serious recession or that monetary policy is responsible for trend inflation.

Today, no one disputes the pivotal role played by central banks with regard to the business cycle and inflation. It is true that there still remains no consensus over whether the Fed can exercise the degree of control over the economy required to exploit Phillips curve trade-offs. The monetarist prediction is that the current attempt at running the economy "hot" in an attempt to raise inflation in a moderate, controlled way will fail. The relevant point here, however, is that monetarists exercised a profound influence on the modern conception of a central bank. That influence did not occur because they enunciated "self-evident truths." It occurred only over a long period of time in which they predicted the baleful consequences of the many disastrous monetary experiments engaged in by central banks.

First, this chapter exposits "monetary policy" in the Depression, where the term is understood using the analytical concepts standard today but which were at best only embryonic during the Depression. Second, the chapter provides a microeconomic foundation for the monetarist money supply function.

Third, I explore "money policy" in the sense that policy makers understood it during the Depression, highlighting the enormous intellectual revolution that would have had to occur for policy makers to have made the transition from the real bills environment of the Depression to an environment in which they engaged in the purposeful money creation recommended by Meltzer as well as by Friedman and Schwartz.

"MONETARY POLICY" DURING THE DEPRESSION

Figure 3-1 shows the market for bank reserves created by Fed operating procedures in the early 1920s. It shows the marginal cost of renting reserves by a member bank from a regional Reserve Bank. In the period following the Treasury-Fed Accord of 1951, when the Fed revived these procedures, they carried the appellation "free-reserves." The reserves' demand schedule is shown in the figure as vertical, in that the banking system required time to adjust assets and, as a by-product, its deposits and required reserves. The vertical section of the reserves-supply schedule represents the supply of nonborrowed reserves, which was determined by flows of gold and of currency in the hands of the public, Treasury securities, and bankers' acceptances held by the Fed, float, and Treasury deposits at the Fed. Because the Fed kept the amount of nonborrowed reserves less than reserves demanded, banks obtained the marginal dollar of reserves from the discount window.

There is a horizontal section to the reserves-supply schedule (not shown in the figures) because, for small amounts of total borrowed reserves, individual banks could play musical chairs and rotate in and out of the window for short periods of time. However, as total borrowed reserves increased (nonborrowed reserves decreased), banks, of necessity, had to have recourse to the discount window for periods long enough to violate the Fed's strictures against "continuous" borrowing and to incur administrative penalties in the form of increased oversight. As a consequence, the reserves supply schedule possessed an upward-sloping segment. The marginal cost of reserves, then, was determined as the sum of the discount rate plus an amount that varied positively with borrowed reserves.

Bank reserves represent a medium for effecting finality of payment, and they support a larger superstructure of the public's various media of exchange. Through arbitrage, the interest rate determined in this market for "money," defined as a transactions medium, controls the interest rate in the "money market"; that is, the market for short-term debt instruments. The interest rate on reserves is not a free parameter. To avoid destabilizing the economy, the Fed

Figure 3-1. The Market for Bank Reserves

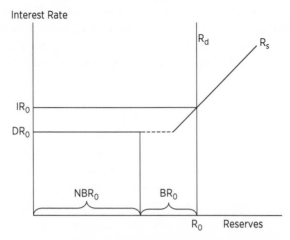

Note: R is bank reserves. R_d is the reserves demand schedule of the banking system and R_s is the reserves supply schedule of the Fed. IR is the interest rate on bank reserves. DR is the discount rate. NBR and BR are nonborrowed and borrowed reserves, respectively. The 0s denote particular values.

Figure 3-2. The Market for Bank Reserves after Fed Tightening

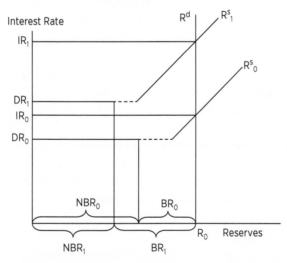

Note: See note to figure 3-1. The 0s denote the initial values and the 1s the values after tightening (lowering NBRs, raising the discount rate, and raising Fed window oversight).

needs procedures that cause the real rate of interest to track the natural rate of interest, where the latter is the interest rate that would be determined if all markets were perfectly competitive. The idea of the interest rate functioning as part of the price system to set the intertemporal price of resources and the need for procedures that would respect this functioning of the price system lay many decades in the future. Early policy makers saw the regional Reserve Banks as sources of loanable funds capable of influencing the cost and availability of credit. According to the real bills doctrine, which guided thinking about monetary policy, the role of the Reserve Banks was to keep the cost of funds high enough to avoid speculative excess and to proportion the availability of credit to the legitimate demand for credit needed to get goods and crops to market.

Figure 3-2 shows the actions taken by the Fed in 1928 and 1929 with the intention of contracting bank credit to squeeze out the lending on securities presumed responsible for the speculative excess epitomized by the soaring value of the New York Stock Exchange (NYSE). The system sold securities to force banks into the discount window. It then raised the cost of borrowing by raising the discount rate and by subjecting banks to supervisory pressures for remaining in the window. The vertical section of the reserves' supply shifted leftward, the section with the kink where the upward-sloping section started rose, and the upward-sloping section rotated upward. The marginal cost of reserves to banks rose dramatically.

A MONETARIST EXPLANATION OF THE BEHAVIOR OF THE MONEY STOCK

The resulting excess of the real rate of interest over the natural rate of interest required contraction in the money stock. Given the relatively high marginal cost of reserves (the real interest rate for banks), banks attempted to liquidate loans to obtain the reserves required to repay lending at the discount window. Bank deposits and the money stock declined as a consequence of the liquidation of bank loans. Given fractional reserve requirements, the resulting decline in bank loans and deposits was greater than the leftward shift in the reserves-demand schedule (R_d) and the decline in bank reserves (figure 3-3).

The weakening of the economy caused by monetary contraction weakened the banking system and made it susceptible to runs. A currency outflow from banks precipitated by bank panics shifted the reserves-supply schedule (R_S) leftward and forced banks into the discount window. The marginal cost of reserves (the real rate of interest) rose (see figure 3-4). Banks tried to obtain the reserves required to repay discount window lending and to build up excess

Figure 3-3. The Market for Bank Reserves: Real Rate above Natural Rate

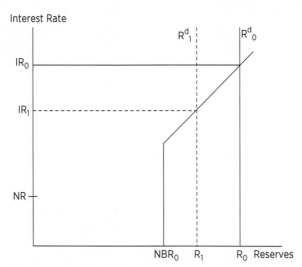

Note: R is bank reserves. R_d is the reserves demand schedule of the banking system. IR is the interest rate on bank reserves, and NR is the natural rate. NBR is nonborrowed reserves. The 0s denote the initial values and the 1s the values after tightening (lowering NBRs, raising the discount rate, and raising Fed window oversight).

Figure 3-4. The Market for Bank Reserves: Currency Outflow

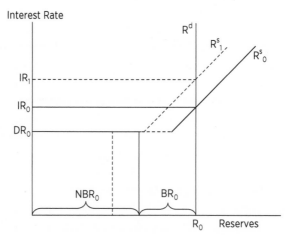

Note: See note to figure 3-3. R_s is the reserves supply schedule of the Fed. DR is the discount rate and BR is borrowed reserves.

Figure 3-5. The Market for Bank Reserves: Exogenous Reserves Supply

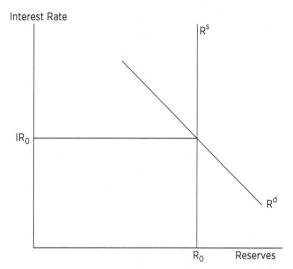

Note: R is bank reserves. R_d is the reserves demand schedule of the banking system and R_s the reserves supply schedule of the Fed. IR is the interest rate on bank reserves. The 0s denote particular values.

reserves by liquidating loans. Due to the fractional reserves characteristic of the banking system, the currency/deposit ratio rose.

Figure 3-5 shows the reserves market as of 1934, when the Treasury had taken control of monetary policy from the Fed. Now the reserves demand schedule is shown over a period long enough for banks to adjust their portfolios. Starting in 1934, the Fed held constant the size of its Treasury portfolio, while bank reserves increased due to its monetization of gold inflows, which shifted the reserves-supply schedule rightward.

Note the different implications of figures 3-1 and 3-5. With the free-reserves operating procedures of figure 3-1, the Fed set the market interest rate. Because during the Depression it set the market rate above the natural rate, the banking system contracted, along with the money stock. The resulting decline in deposits (money) shifted the reserves demand schedule leftward and lowered the market interest rate. However, the expectation of deflation created by the decline in money also lowered the nominal interest rate associated with the natural rate of interest. There was no stable equilibrium.

In contrast, with the reserves-control procedures of figure 3-5, the quantity of reserves is given and the market sets the interest rate. With reserves given, the price level is determinate. Given the price level, relative prices adjust to keep real variables equal to their natural values. In figure 3-5, the reserves demand and supply schedules intersect at a value equal to the natural rate of interest.

Early policy makers had no understanding of the real interest rate as the intertemporal price of resources (consumption) and, necessarily, no understanding of the role it played as part of the price system in keeping output moving around potential. They had no understanding of the need for the Fed to provide a nominal anchor as a prerequisite to allowing the price system to work. It is no wonder that early policy makers failed to understand the Depression in terms of a failure to abandon the procedures summarized in figure 3-1 for the procedures summarized in figure 3-5. The economy recovered after March 1933 and grew strongly with the sustained expansion of the money stock produced by the monetization of gold inflows that began in 1934. Without an analytical framework, however, policy makers learned nothing from these monetary "experiments."

The framework early policy makers possessed did not discipline their forecasts of the economy in a way that allowed its rejection. Undisciplined by a model with testable implications, they could rationalize any outcome. The human characteristic of an unwillingness to admit mistakes entailing horrific consequences only reinforced the inability of policy makers to learn. Meltzer, as well as Friedman and Schwartz, were wrong in their presumption that "truth" was staring policy makers in the face and all they had to do was to look at it. Only as the monetarists developed a framework with testable implications for the actions of central banks and organized a vast data base of experiments across time and place to test that framework did learning become possible. Similarly, only then did a consensus about the causes of the Depression and the role of a modern central bank become possible.

"MONEY POLICY" DURING THE DEPRESSION

How did early policy makers understand their world in a way that allowed them to rationalize the Depression? How did they make sense of events in terms of their real bills' view of the world organized around limiting financial intermediation to productive (legitimate) ends? They had observed in the early 1920s that any regional Reserve Bank's open market purchases would reduce member bank borrowing and lower interest rates in the New York money market. They viewed these purchases as increasing loanable funds to credit markets. Open market purchases lowered the cost and increased the availability of funds but in an indiscriminate way that did not assure their allocation to productive (nonspeculative) uses. In contrast, funds made available through the discount window and collateralized by real bills would respond to the demand for credit. The requirement that banks not be in the window continuously reinforced the presumption that the bank loans were of the self-liquidating sort associated with the movement of goods and crops to market.

During the Depression, policy makers paid little or no attention to the cost of credit. The discount rates of the Reserve Banks were at historically low levels. Policy makers assumed that "low" interest rates could do little to stimulate loan demand as long as a lack of confidence in the economy translated into a lack of demand for loans. Debate turned on how to manage the availability of credit. Open market purchases that increased bank reserves would lower member bank borrowing. Banks could then increase loans starting from a lower level of indebtedness at the discount window. But with minimal loan demand, it was supposed, open market purchases of government securities would force unwanted credit into markets and potentially reignite the "credit inflation" that had created the original "credit debauch."

The cyclical peak that began the Great Depression occurred in August 1929. The year 1930 was one of anticipatory waiting. Liquidation of the economic excesses presumed to have resulted from the speculative excesses manifested most obviously in the bull market in equities should have led to a strong, healthy economic recovery, as had occurred following the 1920–1921 recession. That recovery failed to occur. The year 1931 was devoted to maintaining the confidence of markets that policy makers believed was a prerequisite to economic recovery. Given their conservatism, maintaining confidence meant monetary stringency to counteract the external drain of gold and the internal drain of currency from banks. The regional Reserve Bank governors viewed the outflow of gold as threatening the gold reserves that constituted the basis of their ability to supply funds to the market when it came time to accommodate economic recovery.

The year 1932 became one of an aborted attempt to supply funds in an effort to start an economic recovery. If successful, that attempt might have changed the perceived character of the monetary regime from one of passive accommodation of credit demands in response to legitimate demands for credit to one of purposeful "credit inflation." For policy makers, it was terra incognita. Sustained open market purchases would have forced member banks out of the discount window. In the minds of the regional Reserve Bank governors, that meant fiat money creation; it would have breached the gold cover requirements and would have required backing the issue of currency with government securities.

CONCLUSION

When Meltzer began his career in the early 1960s, the intellectual environment was frozen into a massive Keynesian consensus. After the mid-1960s, faced by a society fractured by the Vietnam War, urban riots, and a militant civil rights movement, the political system demanded low unemployment as a social balm. Keynesians promised to deliver that low unemployment at a moderate cost in terms of inflation—the Phillips curve trade-off. That grand experiment failed, but the Volcker Disinflation and the Great Moderation were only possible because of the monetarist critique. Inflation is a monetary phenomenon. The price system works to stabilize the macro-economy as long as the Fed provides a stable nominal anchor and allows the price system to work. Without that critique, the United States would not today be a free-market economy. It would be plagued by inflation and on-and-off price controls.

Relevant to the point, acceptance of these monetarist insights came only decades after the disaster of the Great Depression. They required the feistiness and sustained attacks of Meltzer and his fellow monetarists.

REFERENCES

Bagehot, Walter. (1873) 1962. *Lombard Street: A Description of the Money Market.* Edited by F. C. Genovese. Homewood, IL: Richard D. Irwin.

Friedman, Milton, and Anna Jacobson Schwartz. 1963. *A Monetary History of the United States, 1867–1960.* Princeton, NJ: Princeton University Press.

Meltzer, Allan H. 2002. *A History of the Federal Reserve.* Vol. 1, *1913–1951.* Chicago: University of Chicago Press.

Thornton, Henry. (1802) 1939. *An Enquiry into the Nature and Effects of the Paper Credit of Great Britain.* Edited by F. A. v. Hayek. New York: Rinehart.

CHAPTER 4
"They Profess to Fear That for Which They Dare Not Hope": How the Fed Contributed to the Great Depression and the Great Recession by Boosting Banks' Demand for Reserves

GEORGE SELGIN

Among the most interesting stories told by Allan Meltzer, in his superb two-volume book *A History of the Federal Reserve* (*HFR*), is one concerning the Fed's decision during the Great Depression to double banks' minimum reserve requirements—a decision that, according to many, helped bring the US economy's incipient post-1933 recovery to an abrupt halt by triggering the "Roosevelt Recession" of 1937–1938.

Because *HFR* comes to a close some years before the subprime crisis, it does not draw any parallels between that crisis and previous ones, including the one of the 1930s. Still, the Fed's conduct during the most crucial phase of the subprime crisis parallels its conduct during the latter 1930s in ways that are too eerily striking to go unremarked. This chapter explores those parallels, by first summarizing Meltzer's account of the Fed's actions in 1936 and 1937 and then comparing those actions to ones taken by the Fed in the last months of 2008.

1937–1938

No sooner had the US economy begun to show signs of recovery from the first onslaught of the Great Depression, in mid-1933, than Fed officials began worrying about inflation. As the economy began to grow again, Fed officials worried, much as they have more recently—and much as if they already subscribed in those days to the idea of a Phillips curve—that the growth heralded a rise in prices.

The immediate consequence of this concern was a reluctance on the part of Fed officials to have the Fed continue, as FDR had been encouraging them to do, the open market purchases of government securities it had begun making following the March 1933 Bank Holiday. Concerning further purchases, then Fed governor George Harrison, expressing a view that was common within the Fed at the time, told Henry Morganthau, then the governor of the Federal Farm Board, that another round of purchases "would not do any good" because it would "be only another factor of uncertainty, tending toward inflation" (Meltzer 2002, 441). This was in November 1933, when the unemployment rate was still above 20 percent.

Yet, as can be seen in figure 4-1, when Harrison voiced this objection to further Fed purchases, the US price level (here measured by the Consumer Price Index [CPI]), having risen previously owing mainly to FDR's having taken the country off the gold standard and allowing the dollar to float, was both well below its pre-1929 level and stable. According to Meltzer, Fed officials' concern about inflation "was more closely related to the real bills doctrine than to the fact that the price level was 25 percent below its 1929 level" (2002, 441). According to the now-discredited real bills doctrine, any expansion of bank credit not based on short-term commercial bills, including expansion based on the Fed's open market security purchases, was ipso facto inflationary.[1]

But the real bills doctrine was only one of several factors informing the Fed's stand. Another was banks' post-holiday accumulation of excess reserves, the extent of which is shown in figure 4-2.

As early as August 10, 1933, Harrison informed then secretary of the Treasury William Woodin (whom Morganthau would replace upon Woodin's death in 1934) that the Federal Open Market Committee (FOMC) was opposed to additional purchases in part because banks were then holding $500 million in cash reserves and might choose to let go of them at any moment, putting upward pressure on prices. Just why some further increase in prices, following the tumble they'd taken since 1929, was to be dreaded, Harrison and his like-minded colleagues didn't say. As Keynes quipped at the time,

Figure 4-1. US Consumer Price Index, 1928–1936

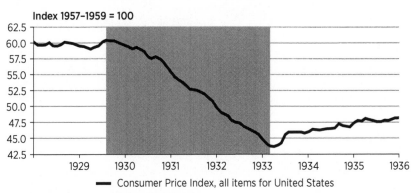

Source: National Bureau of Economic Research.
Note: Shaded area indicates US recession.

Figure 4-2. Total Bank Reserves as a Percentage of Required Reserves, 1929–1939

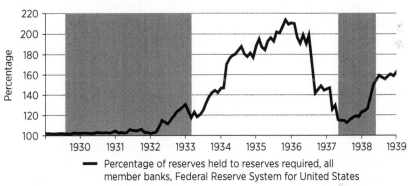

Source: National Bureau of Economic Research.
Note: Shaded areas indicate US recessions.

Fed officials "professed to fear that for which they dared not hope" (Hughes 1986, 539).

Whereas until 1935 Fed officials were content merely to resist further open market bond purchases as much as they could, by that year, and despite the fact that prices were still low compared to 1929 levels, banks' rising excess reserve holdings convinced them to take active steps to counter what they regarded as an emergent threat of inflation. After considering various alternatives, and

Table 4-1. Bank Reserve Requirements, 1936–1937

Date	Demand Deposits (%)			
	Central Reserve City	Reserve City	Country	Time
Before 8/15/36	13.00	10.00	7.00	3.00
8/15/36 to 3/1/37	19.50	15.00	10.50	4.50
3/1/37 to 5/1/37	22.75	17.50	12.25	5.25
On 5/1/37	26.00	20.00	14.00	6.00

Source: Meltzer 2002, 509.

taking advantage of the extended control the Banking Act of 1935 had given them over bank reserve requirements, they ultimately settled on the solution of raising banks' required reserve ratios to "sterilize" outstanding excess reserves by converting them to required reserves. Doing so would, Fed officials reasoned, eliminate the risk that a decline in banks' demand for reserves would translate, first, into increased bank lending, then into increased spending, and, finally, into higher prices.

As table 4-1, reproduced from Meltzer (2002, 509), shows, the Fed took full advantage of its new powers by doubling bank reserve requirements in three steps between August 1936 and May 1937. The first step, which went into effect on August 15, 1936, when the unemployment rate was still 17 percent, raised minimum ratios by 50 percent. Fed staff hoped that this first increase alone would absorb $1.45 billion excess reserves.

This initial increase in reserve requirements "had no perceptible effect on the economy" (Meltzer 2002, 503), which continued to expand rapidly, though it was still, according to estimates by Lauchlin Currie (a Treasury economist and author of the 1935 Banking Act), generating only 65 to 70 percent of its potential real income.

Encouraged by these results, the FOMC decided to implement a further 50 percent increase in bank reserve requirements, to take place in two steps. The first of these, taken in early March 1937, increased reserve requirement ratios by a third of prevailing levels. On this occasion, however, banks responded very differently than they had after the first increase, by clamping down on credit in an effort to replenish their excess reserves. Consequently, the Fed's action, instead of merely guarding against inflation as Fed officials had intended, raised the specter of a renewed outbreak of deflation.

Seeing what had happened, Governor Marriner Eccles, who had succeeded Harrison in 1934, realized that the Fed had miscalculated and that any further increase in reserve requirements was likely to have similar consequences. Yet, though the FOMC considered the possibility of canceling that last increase, it decided to go through with it anyway. According to Meltzer, apart from several committee members' continuing, albeit ill-founded, concerns about inflation, the main argument against cancellation was "concern about the embarrassment of reversing a policy that had been announced." In other words, the FOMC was simply unwilling "to appear to have made an error" (Meltzer 2002, 515).

So, on May 1, 1937, the third and final increase in reserve requirement ratios went into effect. All told, the 1936–1937 changes sterilized $3.1 billion in former excess bank reserves, or about 28 percent of the total reserves outstanding in mid-June 1936 (Meltzer 2002, 518). That, so far as Fed officials were concerned, was the good news. The bad news was that, instead of actually reducing the total quantity of excess reserves outstanding, the Fed's actions served only to encourage banks to curtail their lending enough to replace the excess reserves the Fed had taken away. Indeed, as table 4-2, reproduced from Meltzer (2002), shows, banks did not just restore their excess reserve cushions; by 1938, they had raised them beyond the amounts held before the Fed began raising their reserve requirements. Consequently, the Fed not only contributed to a severe contraction of bank lending, but it did so in a manner that left Fed officials with as much reason as ever to fear a future outbreak of inflation!

The Fed's doubling of bank reserve requirements coincided with the outbreak of the so-called "Roosevelt Recession" of 1937–1938, during which—as figure 4-3 shows—US GNP declined by 10 percent, while unemployment rose by 8 percent. Although several other policy developments have also been blamed for that downturn, including the undistributed profits tax enacted as

Table 4-2. Estimated and Actual Excess Reserves, 1937–1938, Millions of Dollars

Date	Total	New York	Other
1937			
June 14	902	156	745
September 14	800	70	720
December 14	1,150	360	800
1938			
March 14	1,400	500	900
June 14	2,730	1,040	1,690
September 14	3,150	1,480	1,670
December 14	3,520	1,850	1,670

Source: Meltzer 2002, 520.

Figure 4-3. US GNP and Unemployment, Annual Rates of Change, 1920–1940

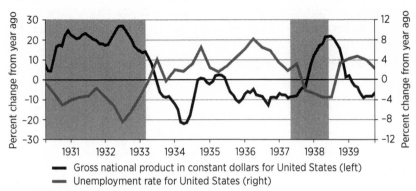

- ▬ Gross national product in constant dollars for United States (left)
- ▬ Unemployment rate for United States (right)

Source: National Bureau of Economic Research.
Note: Shaded areas indicate US recessions.

part of the Revenue Act of 1936 and the Treasury Department's decision to sterilize gold inflows from December 1936 until February 1938 (Velde 2009; Irwin 2012), most authorities agree with Meltzer in holding the Fed at least partly to blame for it.[2]

2008–2009

In defense of their actions starting in the autumn of 1936, Fed officials could at least claim that, although the price level was still quite low and the rate of inflation was stable, both stock prices and the economy more generally were swiftly regaining lost ground. In 2008, in contrast, Fed authorities could offer no comparable justification for taking steps to encourage banks to hoard excess reserves. Yet that is precisely what Fed officials did, in October 2008, by beginning for the first time in the Fed's history to pay interest on bank reserves. If it is true, as Meltzer (2002, 441) claims, that by doubling reserve requirements in the latter 1930s "Fed officials appear to have learned nothing from the experience of 1929–1933," then one might say with equal justice that Fed officials' October 2008 decision suggested that they'd learned nothing from the experience of 1936–1938.

In what ways did the 2008 decision resemble the Fed's decision to double reserve requirements in the latter 1930s? In what ways did the episodes differ? In both instances, the economy was operating at less than capacity. In 2008, it was in the midst of a recession that began, officially, in December 2007, whereas in early 1936 it was recovering from a depression that began in 1929.

And in both cases, the Fed was determined to avoid an outbreak of inflation. Thus, in mid-summer 2008, the FOMC concluded that "although the downside risks to growth remain, they appear to have diminished somewhat, and the upside risks to inflation and inflation expectations have increased" (FOMC Statement, June 25, 2008).

Yet, as was the case in 1936, there was no compelling evidence that inflation was on the horizon. As figure 4-4 shows, both the core Personal Consumption Expenditures (PCE) index and the core CPI inflation rate had been remarkably stable and very close to the Fed's 2 percent target in the years leading to the Fed's October 2008 action. Headline CPI inflation, on the other hand, had risen sharply during the summer of 2008; and it was that sharp increase that had some officials worried. Yet economists distinguish between core and headline inflation measures, where the former exclude food and energy components, precisely because of the notorious volatility of food and energy prices, which make headline inflation an especially unreliable indicator of the stance of monetary policy. As it happened, between July 2008 and July 2009, headline inflation declined dramatically, even turning negative for the first half of 2009. Core inflation also declined, though less dramatically, falling from around 2 percent to half that level.

Because they feared an outbreak of inflation otherwise, Fed officials were determined as of early October 2008 to maintain the 2 percent fed funds rate

Figure 4-4. Personal Consumption Expenditures, Core Consumer Price Index, and Headline Consumer Price Index, 2006–2011

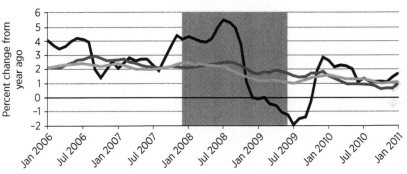

— Personal Consumption Expenditures excluding food and energy (chain-type price index)

— Core Consumer Price Index for all urban consumers: All items

— Headline Consumer Price Index for all urban consumers: All items less food and energy

Source: Bureau of Economic Analysis; Bureau of Labor Statistics.
Note: Shaded area indicates US recession.

Figure 4-5. Federal Reserve Assets, 2008

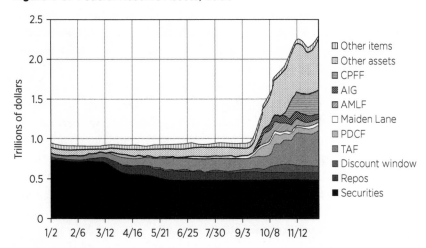

Source: Federal Reserve System, Factors Affecting Reserve Balances—H.4.1., https://www.federalreserve.gov/releases/h41/.

Note: CPFF = Commercial Paper Funding Facility, AIG = American International Group, AMLF = Asset-Backed Commercial Paper Money Market Mutual Fund Liquidity Facility, PDCF = Primary Dealer Credit Facility, TAF = Term Auction Facility.

target that was in place at the time. However, doing that was proving challenging, owing to the Fed's emergency lending, the volume of which had expanded greatly after Lehman Brothers' mid-September collapse. Unless the Fed did something to counter the tendency, new excess reserves created in connection with the Fed's emergency lending programs would find their way into the fed funds market, where they would put downward pressure on the fed funds rate, driving it below its target.

Until Lehman Brothers failed, the Fed had been able to counter that tendency by "sterilizing" its emergency loans with an equal value of open market security sales. Together, as figure 4-5 shows, these operations left the overall size of the Fed's balance sheet, and the quantity of bank reserves, unchanged. But the increased scale of the Fed's emergency lending after Lehman Brothers' failure, together with the fact that its Treasury security holdings had been largely depleted by then, forced the Fed to adopt a new strategy.

That strategy was interest on bank reserves, and especially on banks' excess reserve holdings. By paying a sufficiently high rate of interest on excess reserves (IOER), the Fed could get banks to accumulate reserves that came their way instead of offering them in the interbank market. In that way, despite not being "sterilized" by offsetting open market sales, the Fed's emergency lending, instead of putting downward pressure on the Fed's policy rate, would lead to corresponding growth in banks' excess reserve balances.

We thus arrive at the most obvious difference between the 2008 and the 1936–1937 episodes. In the earlier episode, banks had accumulated excess reserves without any deliberate encouragement by the Fed, and Fed officials were anxious to prevent them from triggering inflation, and doing so independently of any increase in the Fed's balance sheet, by deciding to rid themselves of the excess. In 2008, in contrast, the Fed wanted to encourage banks to accumulate excess reserves, to prevent growth in its balance sheet from triggering inflation. In both instances, the chosen solution consisted of measures aimed at boosting banks' demand for reserves. In the first, a doubling of reserve requirements was supposed to convert a voluntary and presumably temporary increase in reserve demand into a permanent increase. In the second, the establishment of a positive IOER rate, and one that was higher than going wholesale lending rates, was supposed to make it worthwhile for banks to accumulate as many excess reserves as came their way.

In retrospect, as almost everyone now understands, monetary policy was too tight in the fall of 2008. Paying interest on excess reserves at that time—the device the Fed resorted to so as to maintain that tight policy—was therefore a mistake. As figure 4-6 shows, as the Fed put its new policy into effect, nominal spending, as measured by both nominal GDP and Final Sales to Domestic Purchasers, was plummeting, deepening the real recession. In 2008, as in the

Figure 4-6. US Nominal Spending and Core Inflation, 1993–2013

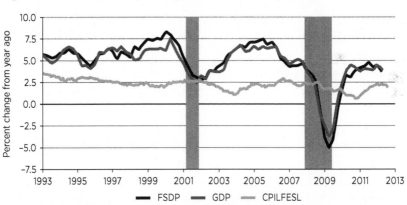

Source: FRED (Federal Reserve Economic Data), St. Louis Federal Reserve, https://fred.stlouisfed.org/.
Note: Shaded areas indicate US recessions. FSDP = Final Sales to Domestic Purchasers; GDP = Gross Domestic Product, 1 Decimal; CPILFESL = Consumer Price Index for All Urban Consumers: All Items Less Food & Energy.

latter 1930s, instead of heading off inflation, the Fed's decision to boost banks' demand for reserves helped bring about a deflationary crisis.

What few may appreciate is that in the more recent episode, as in the earlier one, the Fed might have avoided overtightening had it taken sufficient heed of signals it was getting while its reserve-boosting experiment was underway. Recall that, after noting the results of its first two rounds of reserve requirement increases, the Fed had all the reason it needed to reverse course or, at least, to discontinue further increases. Yet it went ahead anyway. Likewise, by October 6, 2008, when it actually announced that it would soon begin paying banks to hoard reserves, Fed officials were already beginning to realize that monetary policy was too tight. For that reason, the FOMC decided at last to lower the fed funds target from 2 percent to 1.5 percent. Yet the Fed still chose to go ahead with the IOER experiment, and clung obstinately to it afterward, even as it became evident that disinflation, if not deflation, was the real threat.

What made the Fed's decision particularly perverse was the fact that, by making it costless for banks to hoard reserves, it made large-scale asset purchases the Fed's only means for achieving any sort of monetary stimulus: once the opportunity cost of reserves falls to zero, either because short-term market rates fall to zero or because the IOER rate is set above those other rates, the conventional monetary transmission mechanism, with causation running from Fed reserve creation to increased bank lending to increased spending, breaks down, leaving the economy in a liquidity trap. Usually liquidity traps are not a threat so long as short-term rates are positive. But a positive, above-market IOER rate creates a corresponding, above-zero liquidity trap. The presence of such a trap is evident in figure 4-7, which shows how growth in the monetary base (bank reserves plus currency in the hands of the public) was matched by almost identical growth in banks' excess reserve balances, notwithstanding the fact, seen in figure 4-8, that wholesale and other short-term interest rates remained consistently above zero.

Was the Fed's insistence on sticking to its IOER policy even as the economy dove deeper into the Great Recession another decision driven, like that to keep raising reserve requirements in 1937, by Fed officials' "concern about the embarrassment of reversing a policy that had been announced"? The possibility ought not to be dismissed lightly, especially since something that can be called "technocratic momentum" may also have played a part. This refers to authorities' natural reluctance, after securing hard-won new powers, to admit that the economy would have fared better had the powers never been granted.

Figure 4-7. The Monetary Base and Excess Reserves, 2007–2013

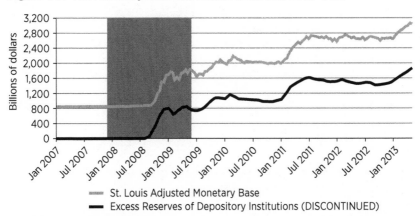

St. Louis Adjusted Monetary Base
Excess Reserves of Depository Institutions (DISCONTINUED)

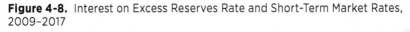

Sources: FRED (Federal Reserve Economic Data), St. Louis Federal Reserve, https://fred.stlouisfed.org/.
Note: Shaded area indicates US recession.

Figure 4-8. Interest on Excess Reserves Rate and Short-Term Market Rates, 2009–2017

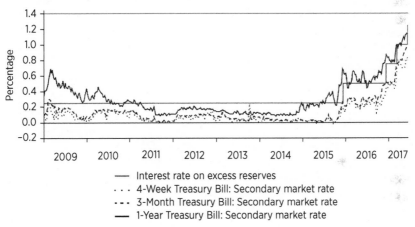

Interest rate on excess reserves
· · · 4-Week Treasury Bill: Secondary market rate
- · - 3-Month Treasury Bill: Secondary market rate
1-Year Treasury Bill: Secondary market rate

Source: Board of Governors of the Federal Reserve System.

NOTES

1.   Richard Timberlake (2007) provides and an excellent discussion of the real bills doctrine and its influence on the Fed's policy.

2.   For dissenting views see Charles Calomiris, Joseph Mason, and David Wheelock (2011) and Haelim Park and Patrick Van Horn (2015).

REFERENCES

Calomiris, Charles W., Joseph R. Mason, and David C. Wheelock. 2011. "Did Doubling Reserve Requirements Cause the Recession of 1937–1938? A Microeconomic Approach." Federal Reserve Bank of St. Louis Working Paper 2011-002A (January).

Federal Reserve Open Market Committee (FOMC). FOMC Statement. June 25, 2008.

Hughes, Jonathan. 1986. *The Vital Few: The Entrepreneur and American Economic Progress.* New York: Oxford University Press.

Irwin, Douglas A. 2012. "Gold Sterilization and the Recession of 1937–1938." *Financial History Review* 19, no. 3 (December): 249–67.

Meltzer, Allan H. 2002. *A History of the Federal Reserve.* Vol. 1, *1913–1951.* Chicago: University of Chicago Press.

Park, Haelim, and Patrick Van Horn. 2015. "Did the Reserve Requirement Increases of 1936–37 Reduce Bank Lending? Evidence from a Quasi-experiment." *Journal of Money, Credit and Banking* 47, no. 5 (August): 791–818.

Timberlake, Richard H. 2007. "Gold Standards and the Real Bills Doctrine in U.S. Monetary Policy." *Independent Review* XI, no. 3 (Winter): 325–54.

Velde, François R. 2009. "The Recession of 1937—a Cautionary Tale." *Federal Reserve Bank of Chicago Economic Perspectives* (4th quarter): 16–37.

CHAPTER 5
Allan Meltzer's Model of the Transmission Mechanism and Its Implications for Today

PETER N. IRELAND

A llan Meltzer developed his model of the monetary transmission mechanism in a series of papers written, mostly with Karl Brunner, over a period of decades. Key contributions include Brunner and Meltzer (1968, 1972, 1976) and the additional articles collected in Brunner and Meltzer (1989). Brunner, Alex Cukierman, and Meltzer (1980, 1983) stand out, too, for bringing the ideas introduced in those earlier papers into direct contact with the rational expectations revolution.

Since Brunner and Meltzer (1990, 1993) and Meltzer (1995) have already surveyed this work, it would be redundant to simply summarize one or more of the papers in great depth here. Instead, this discussion is aimed at highlighting a few major themes that emerge from Meltzer's writing and research and drawing out some implications for monetary policy making today.

The time seems right for a review of this kind. As the lingering effects of the Great Recession of 2007–2009 fade, Federal Reserve officials now face the challenge of designing and implementing new monetary policy strategies to replace and improve upon those adopted under duress during the financial crisis and the unexpectedly long period of zero short-term interest rates that followed. This was a big part of Meltzer's research program, too: looking back at history and identifying, with the help of monetary theory, lessons from the past that could be put to good use in the future.

THE BRUNNER-MELTZER MODEL

Underlying the Brunner-Meltzer model of the transmission mechanism is a broader worldview that all monetarists share: that the capitalist system, whatever its flaws, remains the most effective one for allocating scarce resources. According to this view, market prices adjust, in the long run, to keep the economy moving efficiently along a balanced growth path. Economic theory emphasizes, however, that market prices are relative prices. The central bank's principal role and obligation within this system is to pin down the absolute level of nominal prices. The central bank accomplishes this by exploiting its monopoly over the supply of base money: currency in circulation plus bank reserves.

Anyone who recognizes the practical relevance of these basic ideas— known collectively as the classical dichotomy—is well on his or her way toward understanding the fundamental message of the Brunner-Meltzer model. As Robert Hetzel (2017) usefully points out, the finer details of this monetarist view find their clearest exposition in the New Keynesian model's "divine coincidence," according to which, by achieving and maintaining credibility for a policy aimed at stabilizing the aggregate price level first, the central bank also creates the most favorable environment within which the market economy can respond efficiently to shocks. The Brunner-Meltzer model has this implication, too, but differs from the New Keynesian framework in at least two important ways.

First, instead of a more mechanical scheme for staggered nominal price or wage setting, the slowdown of adjustment in nominal prices that allows monetary policy to have real effects in the Brunner-Meltzer model stems from agents' imperfect information about the sources and persistence of shocks and the precise way those shocks propagate through decentralized goods, labor, and asset markets. Meltzer (1995, 49–50) summarizes this view as follows:

> For a monetarist or classical economist, long-run neutrality of nominal impulses is an implication of rational behavior. However, before impulses are fully absorbed, relative prices and real output respond to monetary impulses.

The reason is that households and businesses fail to anticipate or perceive correctly all of the future implications of
past and current actions. From a monetarist perspective,
one principal reason for the misperceptions that give rise
to relative price changes is that time is required to distinguish permanent and transitory impulses and real and
nominal impulses. These delays in correctly perceiving the
duration or type of change are part of the costs of acquiring information. Contracting in nominal terms is one
response to these uncertainties.

Thus, Meltzer's view of the nominal rigidities that underlie, for example, the
statistical Phillips curve relation that reflects short-run monetary nonneutral-
ity combines elements of Robert Lucas's (1972) misperceptions model with
those of N. Gregory Mankiw and Ricardo Reis's (2002) sticky information
setup. From the passage above it is clear, however, that, for Meltzer, real-world
informational frictions are more widespread and complex than they appear to
be in either of those models or in other, more stylized models.

Second, Meltzer emphasized repeatedly throughout all his work that the
monetary transmission mechanism involves the gradual but inevitable adjustment of many relative prices across many decentralized markets. He stressed
this point, partly, by criticizing more popular Keynesian and New Keynesian
models, which focus exclusively on the role of short-term interest rates in
transmitting the effects of monetary policy through the economy. Along those
lines, Meltzer (1995, 51–52) wrote,

To a monetarist economist, this view of the transmission
mechanism is overly restrictive and mechanical. A monetary impulse that alters the nominal and real stocks of
money does more than change a single short-term interest
rate or borrowing cost. Monetary impulses change actual
and anticipated prices on a variety of domestic and foreign
assets. Intermediation, the term structure of interest rates,
borrowing and lending, and exchange rates respond. . . .
The use of a single short-term interest rate . . . is a poor
metaphor for the classical response of relative prices following a monetary impulse and the further adjustments
that restore neutrality.

The central role that Brunner and Meltzer assigned to patterns of relative price adjustment and the underlying problems of imperfect information suggests that the intellectual exchanges the two had with Armen Alchian—mentioned in Meltzer (2015, 12)—must have influenced strongly their work on the transmission mechanism as well as their theory of monetary exchange exposited in Brunner and Meltzer (1971).

In Meltzer's view, a complete and more correct analysis of the monetary transmission mechanism requires detailed consideration of both the money and capital markets. Thus, in Brunner and Meltzer (1990) and Meltzer (1995), the effects of monetary policy actions such as open market operations are analyzed by manipulating two curves in a diagram, reproduced in the top panel of figure 5-1, that measure the nominal interest rate along one axis and the real price of capital along the other. The MM curve describes combinations of these two relative prices consistent with equilibrium in the money market, while the CM curve does the same for the capital market. The MM curve slopes up because an increase in the interest rate decreases the demand for money; with money supply unchanged, equilibrium can be maintained only if the price of capital rises, thereby lowering the expected return on capital and bringing the quantity of money demanded back in line with supply. Conversely, the CM curve slopes down because an increase in the interest rate increases the demand for bonds, and with the supply of bonds unchanged, equilibrium can be maintained only if the price of capital falls, raising the expected return on capital and bringing the quantity of bonds demanded back in line with supply.

The bottom panel of figure 5-1 shows the initial effects of an open market purchase in the Brunner-Meltzer model. The MM curve shifts to the right; some combination of a lower interest rate and a higher price of capital is needed to induce market participants to hold the additional base money that is being supplied. At the same time, the CM curve shifts to the left. Because the central bank is buying up previously-issued government bonds, some combination of a lower interest rate and a lower price of capital is needed to make market participants willingly sell those bonds. The open market operation unambiguously lowers the nominal interest rate. Its effect on the price of capital is ambiguous in sign but assumed by Brunner and Meltzer to be positive since "empirical studies suggest that open market purchases raise the asset price level" (Meltzer 1995, 55).

Thus, Brunner and Meltzer's analytic framework captures a richer set of behavioral responses according to which market participants substitute, not only between money and bonds but across a much wider range of capital assets, following an open market operation. Through these substitution effects,

Figure 5-1. Open Market Operations in the Brunner-Meltzer Model

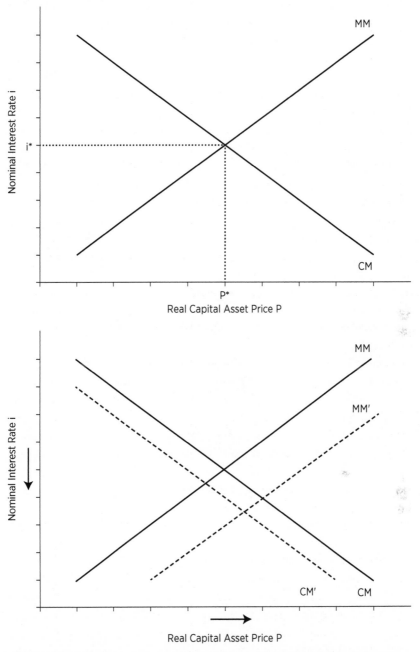

Note: In the top panel, the upward-sloping MM curve and the downward-sloping CM curve intersect to determine the equilibrium nominal interest rate i* and real price of capital assets P*. In the bottom panel, an open market operation shifts the MM curve to the right and the CM curve to the left, lowering the interest rate and increasing the asset price.

the monetary policy action triggers changes in a spectrum of asset prices, not just the short-term interest rate, all of which spill over to the goods and labor markets, generating changes in real aggregate spending and employment in the short run and in nominal prices and wages in the long run.

The Brunner-Meltzer model, therefore, has implications that differ along many dimensions from those of more basic Keynesian and New Keynesian specifications. In both Keynesian and New Keynesian models, for example, William Poole (1970) and Peter Ireland (2000) show that the central bank can insulate output and the price level from stocks to money demand by supplying reserves elastically to peg the short-term nominal interest rate. Brunner and Meltzer (1990, 390–91) emphasize that this result does not carry over to their richer model. First, if the central bank increases the monetary base to hold the interest rate steady in the face of a shock that increases money demand, capital asset prices, nevertheless, fall, with a negative impact on aggregate demand.

Figure 5-2 illustrates this result. In the top panel, the initial shock to money demand works to shift the MM curve to the left, putting upward pressure on the interest rate and downward pressure on asset prices. To stabilize the interest rate, the central bank must conduct an open market purchase that, in the bottom panel of figure 5-2, shifts the MM curve back to the right but also moves the CM curve to the left. The interest rate holds steady, but capital asset prices still fall.

What's more, shocks to the demand for credit in the Brunner-Meltzer model also require an increase in base money to prevent the nominal interest rate from rising, but an open market purchase following a shock of that kind works also to increase equity prices, with an expansionary effect on aggregate demand. In the top panel of figure 5-3, this shock—equivalent to an increase in the supply of bonds—works initially to shift the CM curve to the right, putting upward pressure on the interest rate and asset prices. Once again, an open market purchase is needed to stabilize the interest rate, but as shown in the bottom panel of figure 5-3, this amplifies the previous increase in the capital asset price. Depending on the magnitudes of various elasticities of demand and on the relative size and frequency of the two types of financial-sector shocks, a policy strategy based on interest rate targeting via the elastic supply of base money may either stabilize or destabilize the economy.

Most importantly, by emphasizing that open market operations affect a wide range of relative prices in the money, bond, and capital markets, the Brunner-Meltzer model downplays the importance of the Keynesian liquidity trap and its modern reincarnation, the zero lower bound on nominal interest rates. In the Brunner-Meltzer model, expansionary open market operations

Figure 5-2. Money-Demand Shocks and Interest Rate Stabilization in the Brunner-Meltzer Model

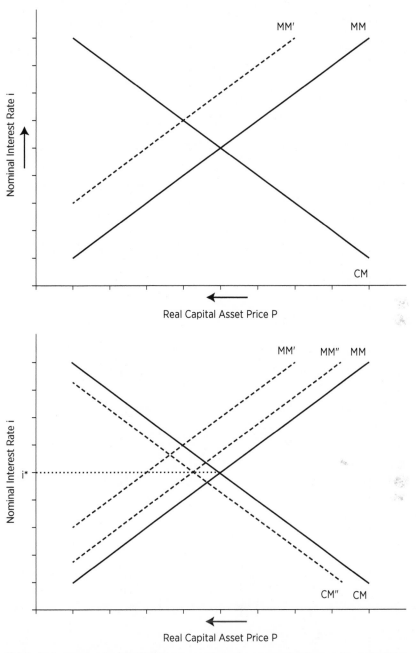

Note: In the top panel, a shock that increases money demand puts upward pressure on the nominal interest rate and downward pressure on the asset price. In the bottom panel, the central bank conducts an open market operation to stabilize the interest rate, but the asset price still falls.

Figure 5-3. Credit-Demand Shocks and Interest Rate Stabilization in the Brunner-Meltzer Model

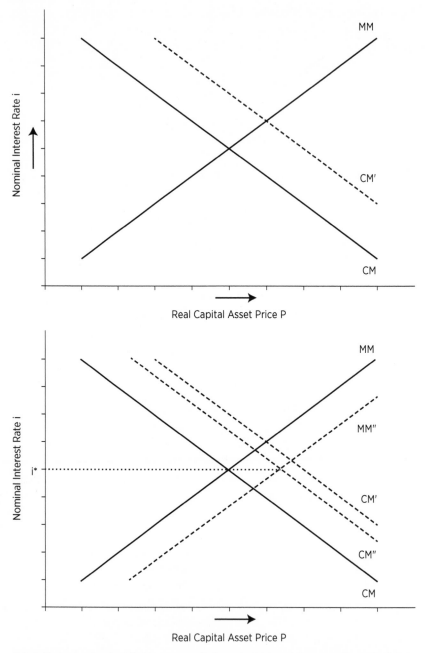

Note: In the top panel, a shock that increases credit demand puts upward pressure on the nominal interest rate and the asset price. In the bottom panel, the central bank conducts an open market operation to stabilize the interest rate but, by doing so, amplifies the initial increase in the asset price.

still work to increase other capital asset prices, even after the short-term interest rate reaches its zero lower bound. And through those additional channels, monetary policy continues to affect aggregate output and employment in the short run and the aggregate price level in the long run. Meltzer (1995, 56) explains:

> In Keynesian theory, a liquidity trap eliminates the effect of monetary impulses on the real economy. Once the interest rate reaches a minimum value, monetary policy becomes impotent; changes in the stock of money are absorbed by money holders at an unchanged interest rate. But this implication is false in monetarist analysis. Market interest rates are only one of the relative prices affected by monetary impulses. An increase in the monetary base would not lower the interest rate, but asset prices would increase. Relative price changes and their effects on spending would not be eliminated by a liquidity trap for interest rates.

Meltzer (2001) elaborates by distinguishing the real and nominal effects of these policy-induced changes in relative prices at the zero lower bound from the more traditional Haberler-Pigou-Patinkin real balance effect studied, for example, in a modern cash-in-advance framework by Ireland (2005). Meltzer (2001) also provides evidence that these effects were operative during several key episodes of US monetary history, especially the recessions of 1937–1938 and 1948–1949, when changes in the money supply had their predicted effects despite the persistence of very low nominal interest rates and spells of outright deflation. Meltzer (2001, 115) provides another brief but convincing argument that monetary policy actions must have effects through their impact on a wider range of variables beyond money market interest rates, crediting Brunner with the simple observation that

> monetary policy actions are effective and powerful in the less developed countries of Africa, Latin America, or Asia where there is no money market. Relative prices respond to monetary impulses in countries without central banks, and without money markets. There is more to the transmission mechanism than the models recognize. (Meltzer 2001, 115)

IMPLICATIONS FOR TODAY

Thus, the Brunner-Meltzer model provides at least a partial rationale for some of the actions that the Federal Reserve took during and immediately after the financial crisis of 2007–2008. According to the model, it makes sense that, after the federal funds rate reached the zero lower bound in December 2008, Federal Reserve officials shifted their attention to longer-term bond rates, mortgage rates, and equity prices to gauge the effects their policy actions were having on the US economy.

But the Brunner-Meltzer model can also be used to critique important aspects of the Fed's "unconventional" policy actions during and since the crisis. Crucially, while the model implies that the central bank can affect other asset prices while short-term interest rates are at their zero lower bound, it does not suggest that the central bank should deliberately tailor its open market purchases as to influence the prices of specific capital assets, which would be determined more efficiently in the free market. The Federal Reserve, as the US central bank, is responsible for the conduct of monetary policy: control of the aggregate nominal price level through the open market exchanges of base money for US Treasury debt. Fiscal policy, including decisions about the maturity structure of government securities held by the public and the actions, if any, that require direct intervention in private credit and capital markets, should remain the responsibility of Congress, in consultation with the president and the Treasury secretary.

The Brunner-Meltzer model is very clear on this. It implies that the Fed could and should have continued to use conventional open market operations—purchases of Treasury securities using newly created base money—to provide additional monetary stimulus during the financial crisis and the severe recession that followed, with the specific aim of preventing the aggregate price level from falling persistently below the levels prescribed by the central bank's previously announced 2 percent inflation target. Thus, to the extent that the Fed's three rounds of "quantitative easing" were directed at increasing the monetary base to prevent inflation from falling too far below target, those actions are fully justified by the model. Indeed, Meltzer (2015, 11) himself viewed the effects of quantitative easing (QE) as providing evidence consistent with the Brunner-Meltzer model's implications:

> As the QE programs at the Federal Reserve and other
> central banks showed, zero short-term interest rate did
> not prevent monetary expansion. The Federal Reserve
> purchased medium and long-term debt. Asset prices

rose and the exchange rate depreciated, as our conclusion about liquidity traps implied. The so-called zero lower bound turned out to bind very little other than very short-term rates.

As implemented, however, QE also took on the features of a fiscal, or credit market, intervention, especially when the Fed expanded its purchases to include mortgage-backed securities. At that point, the Fed stopped acting like a central bank and started behaving more like a private financial institution, issuing its own short-term liabilities to make long-term loans, specifically in the housing markets. And, likewise, the Fed's decision in September 2011 to "twist" the yield curve by selling short-term assets and buying long-term bonds with no resulting change in base money accomplished nothing more than the US Treasury could have done on its own simply by modifying the composition of its outstanding debt. At the time, Meltzer (2012, 255) observed,

> Purchasing more than $1 trillion of long-term mortgages is credit allocation. . . . Selling Treasury securities to finance mortgage of other purchases is a fiscal operation. The monetary base doesn't change, and the purchase reduces the interest payment made to the Treasury. Selling two-year Treasuries to finance purchases of longer-term bonds also doesn't change reserves or money. It is debt management and should be left to the Treasury.

Meanwhile, the beneficial pure monetary effects that its QE programs might have had were curtailed, to a large extent, by the Fed's 2008 decision to begin paying interest on bank reserves at rates at, or even above, those offered by securities with similar risk and maturity characteristics. As the analysis in Ireland (2014) makes clear, paying interest on reserves at any positive rate shifts the curve linking banks' demand for reserves to the federal funds rate outward to the right. In theory, it acts as a shock to money demand, sending deflationary impulses through the economy. In the Brunner-Meltzer model, as noted above and shown in figure 5-2, this holds true even if the central bank fully accommodates the increase in reserves demand with a corresponding increase in supply. In retrospect, the Fed's interest-on-reserves policy was a mistake, which reinforced the deflationary pressures set off by flight-to-quality dynamics during and after the financial crisis, which similarly increased both banks' and the public's demand for safe and highly liquid monetary assets. As Meltzer (2014b, 148) explains,

> By paying interest on excess reserves, policy encouraged the reserve accumulation. . . . The Federal Reserve made a traditional error, an error repeated many times. They equated monetary expansion to the first-round effects on interest rates, exchange rates, and asset prices. They ignored any subsequent effects from growth of money and credit. A better policy would have expanded money and credit growth more and excess reserves less. That would have provided more stimulus and avoided the problem posed by more than $2 trillion of excess reserves.

In hindsight, one must acknowledge that few people, if anyone, anticipated the depth and duration of the Great Recession of 2007–2009, or the prolonged period of time during which Fed interest rate policy would be constrained by the zero lower bound. Many features of QE, as well as other aspects of the Fed's policy response, had to be improvised under stress, within an environment marked by both political and economic turmoil. Looking forward, however, Federal Reserve officials now have the chance to design, more deliberately, a robust set of strategies that will help the central bank achieve its monetary policy goals more effectively, in both good times and bad. In general, the Brunner-Meltzer model points to a need for the Fed to delineate more clearly the boundaries between monetary and credit policies, along the lines suggested by Marvin Goodfriend (2014), working with Congress to clarify what the Fed can and cannot do to stabilize the economy and the financial system during the economic crisis. In particular, the Fed should return to a "Treasuries only" policy, according to which it eschews direct interventions allocating credit to any specific sector of the economy and focuses, instead, on its traditional monetary policy role of using open market operations to maintain a credible regime of stable prices in the long run.

The Brunner-Meltzer model also points to the possibility that the Fed could minimize future disruptions to its policy procedures caused by the zero lower bound through institutional arrangements that would allow it to use its control over the monetary base to exert greater influence on the growth rate of broader monetary aggregates. Reconsidering or modifying its interest on reserves policies and the associated reverse repurchase agreement programs it established for nonbank financial intermediaries could help in this regard. Along the same lines, it should be noted that the Federal Reserve has, for many decades, largely ignored information about the effects of its policies conveyed by the monetary aggregates. In Meltzer's (2014a, 525) view, "monetary policy without money is a serious mistake." But this is a mistake that might easily be corrected if, as suggested by Michael Belongia and Ireland (2017), the Fed adopted a "two-pillar" strategy like the European Central Bank's. During normal times, the growth rates of broad monetary aggregates could serve as a cross check against the more conventional macroeconomic analyses conducted at the Federal Reserve Board and in the research departments at the Federal Reserve banks, to ensure that the Fed's interest rate policies remain consistent with its commitment to long-run price stability. But then, in times of crisis, when interest rate policy may again be constrained by the zero lower bound, money growth could take on a bigger role, as a focal point for open market purchases intended to achieve the same, unchanging goals.

THE ENDURING CASE FOR MONETARY POLICY RULES

Any discussion of Meltzer's model of the transmission mechanism would be incomplete without mention of the need for the Fed to adopt and announce a specific monetary policy rule to guide its meeting-by-meeting decisions. Meltzer's arguments in support of rules leaned heavily on his view that the rigidities that allow monetary policy to have real effects in the short run reflect private agents' imperfect information about the economy. But they also drew on the related observation, made more forcefully in Meltzer (1987), that policy makers, too, lack the full and timely knowledge that they would need to successfully fine tune the economy through purely discretionary policy actions. In more detail, Meltzer (1995, 69) argues that

> support for rules is related to five monetarist propositions: 1) neither the central bank nor private forecasters can predict output, employment, inflation or other variables with sufficient accuracy to damp fluctuations on average; 2) lags are not constant; neither government nor private forecasters can distinguish between permanent and transitory disturbances to levels and growth rates until sometime after they occur; 3) the response of particular relative prices to monetary and other impulses in any cycle may differ from previous cycles depending on initial conditions, the nature of the shocks and the policy rule that is followed;

4) the private sector damps fluctuations and returns to stability if undisturbed by unanticipated policy impulses; and

5) rules that are easily monitored reduce costs of information.

Meltzer (1987) describes a rule that, unlike Milton Friedman's (1960) prescription for constant money growth and more akin to the John Taylor (1993) rule for setting the federal funds rate, adjusts the growth rate of the monetary base in response to changes in output growth and monetary velocity. Like both Friedman and Taylor, however, Meltzer emphasizes the benefits that would accrue if the Fed conducted policy with reference to any sensible rule that would make its actions more predictable and easier for the public to understand and would allow policy makers to focus their attention on intermediate-term developments instead of short-term noise. With specific reference to the Taylor rule, for example, Meltzer (2014a, 535) notes that

> the years when Volcker was chairman are one of the few periods in which the Federal Reserve was less influenced by short-term events. Volcker followed the successful disinflation by relying for guidance on a Taylor rule after 1985. His successor, Alan Greenspan, continued that policy until 2003. This produced the longest period in Fed history of price stability with relatively stable growth, and short, mild recessions. The period is known as the "Great Moderation." I believe that the reduction in fluctuations is mainly the result of a rule-based policy that focused more attention in the medium-term than on current data.

"History has an important message for theory and policy," he went on to say (Meltzer 2014a, 535). The message is that nothing prevents the Fed from recreating the conditions for stable inflation and robust economic growth, today and in the future. The first and most important step in doing so is for the central bank to announce and consistently follow a specific monetary policy rule.

REFERENCES

Belongia, Michael T., and Peter N. Ireland. 2017. "Circumventing the Zero Lower Bound with Monetary Rules Based on Money." *Journal of Macroeconomics* 54 (December): 42–58.

Brunner, Karl, Alex Cukierman, and Allan H. Meltzer. 1980. "Stagflation, Persistent Unemployment and the Permanence of Economic Shocks." *Journal of Monetary Economics* 6, no. 4 (October): 467–92.

———. 1983. "Money and Economic Activity, Inventories and Business Cycles." *Journal of Monetary Economics* 11, no. 3: 281–319.

Brunner, Karl, and Allan H. Meltzer. 1968. "Liquidity Traps for Money, Bank Credit, and Interest Rates." *Journal of Political Economy* 76, no. 1 (January–February): 1–37.

———. 1971. "The Uses of Money: Money in the Theory of an Exchange Economy." *American Economic Review* 61, no. 5 (December): 784–805.

———. 1972. "Money, Debt, and Economic Activity." *Journal of Political Economy* 80, no. 5 (September-October): 951–77.

———. 1976. "An Aggregative Theory for a Closed Economy." In *Monetarism*, edited by Jerome L. Stein, 67–103. Amsterdam: North-Holland.

———. 1989. *Monetary Economics.* Oxford: Basil-Blackwell.

———. 1990. "Money Supply." In *Handbook of Monetary Economics*, edited by B. M. Friedman and F. H. Hahn, 1:357–98. Amsterdam: North-Holland.

———. 1993. *Money and the Economy: Issues in Monetary Analysis.* Cambridge: Cambridge University Press.

Friedman, Milton. 1960. *A Program for Monetary Stability.* New York: Fordham University Press.

Goodfriend, Marvin. 2014. "Lesson from a Century of Fed Policy: Why Monetary and Credit Policies Need Rules and Boundaries." *Journal of Economic Dynamics and Control* 49 (December): 112–20.

Hetzel, Robert L. 2017. "A Proposal to Clarify the Objectives and Strategy of Monetary Policy." *Journal of Macroeconomics* 54 (December): 72–89.

Ireland, Peter N. 2000. "Interest Rates, Inflation, and Federal Reserve Policy since 1980." *Journal of Money, Credit and Banking* 32 (August): 417–34.

———. 2005. "The Liquidity Trap, the Real Balance Effect, and the Friedman Rule." *International Economic Review* 46 (November): 1271–301.

———. 2014. "The Macroeconomic Effects of Interest on Reserves." *Macroeconomic Dynamics* 18 (September): 1271–312.

Lucas, Robert E., Jr. 1972. "Expectations and the Neutrality of Money." *Journal of Economic Theory* 4 (April): 103–24

Mankiw, N. Gregory, and Ricardo Reis. 2002. "Sticky Information versus Sticky Prices: A Proposal to Replace the New Keynesian Phillips Curve." *Quarterly Journal of Economics* 117 (November): 1295–328.

Meltzer, Allan H. 1987. "Limits of Short-Run Stabilization Policy: Presidential Address to the Western Economic Association, July 3, 1986." *Economic Inquiry* 25, no. 1 (January): 1–14.

———. 1995. "Monetary, Credit and (Other) Transmission Processes: A Monetarist Perspective." *Journal of Economic Perspectives* 9, no. 4 (Fall): 49–72.

———. 2001. "The Transmission Process." In *The Monetary Transmission Process: Recent Developments and Lessons for Europe*, edited by Deutsche Bundesbank, 112–30. New York: Palgrave.

———. 2012. "Federal Reserve Policy in the Great Recession." *Cato Journal* 32, no. 2 (Spring/Summer): 255–63.

———. 2014a. "Current Lessons from the Past: How the Fed Repeats Its History." *Cato Journal* 34, no. 3 (Fall): 519–39.

———. 2014b. "A Slow Recovery with Low Inflation." In *Across the Great Divide: New Perspectives on the Financial Crisis*, edited by Martin Neil Baily and John B. Taylor, 145–61. Stanford, CA: Hoover Institution Press.

———. 2015. "Karl Brunner, Scholar: An Appreciation." Economics Working Paper 15116, Hoover Institution, Stanford University, Stanford, CA, October.

Poole, William. 1970. "Optimal Choice of Monetary Policy Instruments in a Simple Stochastic Macro Model." *Quarterly Journal of Economics* 84 (May): 197–216.

Taylor, John B. 1993. "Discretion versus Policy Rules in Practice." *Carnegie-Rochester Conference Series on Public Policy* 39 (December): 195–214.

CHAPTER 6
The Monetary Base in Allan Meltzer's Analytical Framework

EDWARD NELSON

Two quotations shape the following analysis of Allan Meltzer's research in monetary economics.

The first is Benjamin Friedman's (1988, 205) remark: "Allan Meltzer, throughout his voluminous corpus of writings (often coauthored with Karl Brunner), has consistently emphasized the role of fluctuations of the monetary base." The second is Meltzer's (1999) observation: "Monetary policy works by changing relative prices. There are many, many such prices. Some economists erroneously believe monetary policy works only by changing a single short-term interest rate."

Both of these quotations convey crucial aspects of Meltzer's analytical framework. But because one emphasizes quantities and the other stresses prices, the two quotations, taken together, highlight the need to confront and analyze seeming paradoxes in Meltzer's thinking about monetary matters.

This chapter, originally presented as a speech at the Meltzer's Contributions to Monetary Economics and Public Policy conference (January 4, 2018; see p. 1), was published as a staff working paper in the Federal Reserve's Finance and Economics Discussion Series (FEDS) 2019-001, https://doi.org/10.17016/FEDS.2019.001. The analysis and conclusions expressed are those of the author and do not indicate concurrence by other members of the research staff, the Federal Reserve System, the Board of Governors, or the regional Federal Reserve banks.

Proceeding along these lines, the following discussion will aim to resolve five paradoxes in Meltzer's treatment of the monetary base.

Paradox 1. Brunner and Meltzer emphasized the effects that monetary policy has on a variety of asset prices, such as prices of interest-bearing securities and the price of "real capital," yet they summarized monetary policy stance using growth rates of quantities; that is, monetary aggregates, including the monetary base.

Paradox 2. Brunner and Meltzer stressed that monetary policy, in addition to changing a baseline interest rate, affected the risk or term premiums embedded in other yields on assets by altering the relative quantities of assets. Yet they often summarized policy stance using central bank liabilities, specifically the monetary base, H—usually adjusted for changes in reserve requirements—or its growth rate.

Paradox 3. Brunner and Meltzer made the money-multiplier process endogenous by modeling the components of the multiplier, other than the required-reserve ratio, but they often regarded a constant money multiplier as a good approximation for the purposes of policy analysis.

Paradox 4. Meltzer indicated that the concept of the money stock that mattered for nonbank private-sector portfolio decisions was one that included some of commercial banks' deposit liabilities—yet he often used the monetary base not only in analyzing the behavior of the money stock but also with direct reference to the behavior of aggregate nominal income, the price level, or aggregate output.

Paradox 5. Meltzer long acknowledged that a rule for the short-term nominal interest rate could, in principle, be workable and stabilizing—yet only late in his career did he grant that an interest-rate rule was a valid, and perhaps superior, alternative in practice to the use of the monetary base as the monetary policy instrument.

By concentrating on these five paradoxes, I provide an analysis that complements other retrospectives on Meltzer's view of the transmission process—including those of Michael Bordo and Anna Schwartz (2004), Peter Ireland (2017), David Laidler (1995), and my own previous work, such as Edward Nelson (2003, 2004, 2017).

SCOPE AND METHODOLOGY OF THIS ANALYSIS

In the resolution offered here of the five seeming paradoxes, no attempt will be made at an exhaustive analysis of the Meltzer canon of public statements. The canon is, in fact, nearly *in*exhaustible. Meltzer, who died in May 2017, added to "his voluminous corpus of writings" for nearly thirty years after the 1988 Benjamin Friedman remark quoted earlier. As Robert Lucas (1988, 137) put it, "It would be an act of folly . . . to review [Meltzer's body of research] in a single paper." One must also remember that Meltzer's various contributions on monetary matters appeared not only in research publications but also in congressional testimony and submissions over many years (roughly speaking, from 1960 to 2015). Furthermore, he was a prolific writer in the US and UK financial press.

Consequently, the analysis in the following sections will consider only a subset of Meltzer's work. In analyzing this subset, deductions will be made about Meltzer's analytical framework by following a recommendation Meltzer (1992, 153) made in the context of studying Keynes's monetary framework. This recommendation was to glean an economist's views from their writings by focusing on elements of "consistency, shown by repetition of ideas and thoughts." That said, important changes in Meltzer's views will be noted when these are found.

RESOLUTION OF PARADOX 1

The first seeming paradox is that Brunner and Meltzer's research emphasized the effects of monetary policy on a variety of asset prices, yet Brunner and Meltzer summarized monetary policy stance using monetary quantities or by the growth rates of these quantities.

The resolution of this paradox is as follows: Although Brunner and Meltzer saw asset prices as the link between central bank operations (for example, the central bank's open-market and discount-window transactions) and economic activity, they suggested that a monetary quantity might convey overall policy stance well.

Underlying this suggestion was the hypothesis that the private sector's spending on goods and services likely depended, among other things, on an unobserved index of interest rates, and monetary growth might have a short-run inverse relationship with that index (see especially Meltzer 2001). This position was in contrast to the argument of James Tobin (1969) that the key asset price driving private spending was an observable equity-market variable (specifically Tobin's q).

To Meltzer, monetary aggregates were also likely to be a better index of spending-relevant (and monetary-policy-sensitive) asset prices than were observed nominal market interest rates. In particular, Brunner and Meltzer's (1968b) and Meltzer's (1976, 2002, 2010a) analysis of US monetary and economic developments during the 1930s and 1960s stressed the Fisher effect—through which changes in expected inflation tended to generate changes in nominal interest rates—as a factor hindering the reliability of nominal interest rates as a measure of monetary policy stance. Meltzer observed that low short-term nominal interest rates had erroneously been taken by the US authorities in the early 1930s as implying monetary ease, while rising—and by then-historical standards, high—short-term nominal interest rates had erroneously been taken as implying monetary policy tightness in 1967 and 1968. Monetary growth, as measured by M1 or M2 (monetary aggregates), was negative in the early 1930s and was rapid in 1967 and 1968, so it gave a better indication of monetary policy stance in both episodes than did nominal market interest rates.

One might agree about the importance of the Fisher effect and about the likely dependence of spending on a multiplicity of yields yet still challenge the suggestion that monetary growth should be used as an indicator of monetary policy stance under these circumstances. Ultimately, the argument for money's usefulness being made in this instance is not one in which a monetary aggregate or its growth rate appears in the structural equation describing spending behavior. It is, instead, an argument for an indirect approach of focusing on monetary growth, real or nominal, instead of directly measuring the various spending-relevant—real—yields. Why not measure these yields directly? This question amounted to the objection voiced with regard to the monetarist position by Rudiger Dornbusch (1976) and Lars Svensson (2003).

The answer, according to Meltzer, was that there was a major problem of accurate measurement of a key asset price. In the monetarist transmission mechanism—sketched by Milton Friedman and Schwartz (1963) and explicitly modeled (mathematically, albeit not with microeconomic foundations) by Brunner and Meltzer (1973)—the nonbank private sector holds at least three assets: money, interest-bearing securities, and real capital. Yields on the latter two of these assets appeared in the IS-type equation describing real aggregate spending behavior. Securities yields may be reasonably observable; they would need to be converted into real interest rates to deliver the yield relevant for real spending, but this may be feasible. The key matter is, therefore, What is "real capital," and how should we measure its price (or yield)? Brunner and Meltzer saw severe measurement problems in this area. They strongly urged "going beyond the two-asset world" (Brunner and Meltzer 1981, 133) and including real capital in analytical models, but they were not confident about accurate empirical measurement of the extra asset price that such an expansion of a model would entail. For example, Brunner and Meltzer (1976, 178) contended that equity prices were too noisy to be used to obtain a valuable measure of the yield on capital. Meltzer (1993) tried instead using another observable price— the price of land—but the results were inconclusive.

More recent research conducted since Brunner and Meltzer's heyday may mean that the best empirical proxy for the third yield is one related to a longer-term bond rate. Perhaps a composite of government and corporate interest rates might be relevant. This composite could be constructed, and then an index of overall yields related to spending might be obtained via further aggregation of observed short- and long-term interest rates.

Consequently, it could be that improved measurement of important asset prices leads to an asset-price index that is comprehensively superior to money as an indicator of the aggregate-demand conditions put in place by monetary policy. For his part, however, Meltzer did not think this point had been reached. He contended that nominal monetary growth, Δm (or real monetary growth, $\Delta m - \Delta p$), was usually the best proxy available of the joint behavior of the yields that matter for private spending.[1] Money might proxy these yields well for two interrelated but distinct reasons: injections of money resulting from central bank operations likely affected a variety of yields, and the money demand relationship may make variations in real money balances systematically related to key yields in the economy.

RESOLUTION OF PARADOX 2

The second paradox consists of the fact that Brunner and Meltzer stressed that monetary policy, in addition to changing a baseline interest rate—such as the federal funds rate or the Treasury bill rate—affected the risk or term premiums embedded in other interest rates by altering the relative quantities of assets, yet they often summarized policy stance using central bank liabilities, specifically growth in the monetary base, usually adjusted for changes in reserve requirements.

The seeming paradox is brought out by considering this statement from Brunner and Meltzer (1966):

> No critical issues of monetary policy, debt management, or fiscal policy are raised by the size of the Federal Reserve's portfolio of securities. From the standpoint

of monetary policy, the most important items on [the] Federal Reserve's consolidated balance sheet [are] the volume and rate of change of Federal Reserve monetary liabilities—reserves plus currency, the monetary base. Unless the proposed changes in the volume of securities held by Federal Reserve banks produce changes in the monetary base, they will have no important monetary consequences for the economy.

This 1966 statement may appear jarring in view of the fact that Bank of England and Federal Reserve officials (such as King 1999; Bean 2009; and Bernanke 2002, 2012) have over the years cited Brunner and Meltzer's work as part of the basis for a policy in which purchases alter the asset composition of the central bank's balance sheet (thereby putting downward pressure on longer-term interest rates).

However, once again, a reconciliation is possible, and the seeming paradox can be resolved. The resolution is that, as long as short-term nominal interest rates were positive ($R > 0$), Brunner and Meltzer regarded x percent growth in the monetary base as giving rise to approximately x percent monetary growth, and with M being a multiple of H, most portfolio balance reactions come from monetary growth, Δm, reflecting private-sector rebalancing in response to an enhanced stock of money. These reactions involving M could swamp the portfolio balance effects resulting from the central bank asset transactions that produced the initial change in the monetary base.

However, when the short-term nominal interest rate has reached its lower bound (that is, when $R = 0$), the marginal money multiplier may be small—monetary growth is less than monetary base growth; that is, $\Delta m < \Delta h$—and the principal portfolio balance effects may be those stemming from the central bank's alteration of the stocks of debt outstanding. *How Δh comes about* (that is, what assets are purchased by the central bank) then becomes crucial in determining whether there is appreciable stimulus associated with the increase in the monetary base as well as the magnitude of this stimulus. For example, at $R = 0$, a program of open market purchases of short-term securities may generate far less in the way of increases in commercial bank deposit liabilities, asset prices, and aggregate demand than an equal-sized program of open market purchases of longer-term securities, even though the two purchase programs would deliver the same scale of increase in the monetary base.

The resolutions to both paradox 1 and paradox 2 highlight the fact that, to Meltzer, the zero lower bound is not a special case in one sense and yet is a special case in another sense. As already stressed, at the zero bound ($R = 0$), the central bank's scope to raise both asset prices and M likely rests on how it increases H. As a precondition for generating an expansion of the money stock in zero-bound conditions, the central bank first has to provide an expansion of the monetary base sufficient to accommodate the increases—associated with lower interest rates and with the uncertainty of an adverse economic and banking climate—in the commercial banking system's desired reserve/deposit ratio and the nonbank public's currency/deposit ratio.[2] Having thereby stabilized the money stock, it then has to take operations that actually boost M. At the lower bound on short-term interest rates, unconventional open market purchases that raise H can still increase M (that is, generate Δm, though it may be that $\Delta m < \Delta h$ in this case) and also stimulate nominal and real aggregate demand. This reflects the likelihood that, when $R = 0$, purchases of longer-term securities are more likely to generate asset-price rises and M expansion than purchases of riskless short-term securities.

There is, therefore, no liquidity trap in this framework, because monetary policy can always stimulate the economy.[3] But at the lower bound on short-term nominal interest rates ($R = 0$), the chosen type of open market operations becomes crucial in determining whether the monetary policy action does appreciably stimulate the economy. This was a message of Brunner and Meltzer (1968a), as acknowledged in some later analyses of the $R = 0$ case, such as Paul Wonnacott's (1974, 161) and Tim Congdon's (2011, 417).

RESOLUTION OF PARADOX 3

The third seeming paradox is that Brunner and Meltzer made the money-multiplier process endogenous by modeling the components of the multiplier—other than the required-reserve ratio—but they often regarded a constant money multiplier as a good approximation for policy analysis.

The resolution lies in the conclusions that Brunner and Meltzer drew from their multiplier analysis. Brunner and Meltzer offered models of the individual components of the money multiplier (which, for them, was usually the M1 multiplier) other than the required-reserve ratio, which was a policy variable. They, nevertheless, regarded $\Delta m = \Delta h$ as a good approximation in normal times—which might be described as conditions of positive interest rates, widespread confidence in the commercial banking system, and satisfaction by commercial banks that they have achieved appropriate amounts of liquidity in their asset structure and of equity capital in their liability structure. The condition of traditional money-multiplier analysis (see Rasche 1993)—that the marginal money multiplier equals the average multiplier—then, roughly prevails. That being so, Brunner and Meltzer saw variations in the multiplier, other than those attributable to trends, as largely comprising short-term stationary dynamics or one-time changes to the level of the multiplier—not variations that disconnected Δm from Δh over periods of a year or longer.

Hence, Brunner and Meltzer (1969, 7) concluded that "changes in the monetary base are the main determinant of longer-term changes in the stock of money." And Brunner and Meltzer (1981, 136) affirmed, "Our own work . . . shows that the multiplier approach is not incompatible with equilibrium analysis."

Brunner and Meltzer were writing in an era that largely preceded such phenomena as sweeps, interest payments on reserves, and large-scale issuance of nontraditional central bank liabilities, all of which would force major revisions to their money supply framework, even for the $R > 0$ case. Money supply theory is in a morass until these issues have been confronted satisfactorily.

The existence of these many complications does not, of course, imply the absence of any relationship, today or in the past, between the monetary base and the money stock. Nor does their existence overturn the notion that the base/multiplier approach provides, under specific conditions, a valid and useful description of the deposit-creation process. Indeed, the validity of the base/multiplier approach in certain circumstances was acknowledged even by some critics of that approach, such as M. D. K. W. Foot, Charles Goodhart, and Anthony Hotson (1979, 151–52).

Some further observations on the connection between the monetary base and central bank behavior are in order. Brunner and Meltzer (1981, 130) observed, "The central bank controls the stock of base money in a closed economy." By this, they meant that central bank operations are felt in the behavior of the monetary base. Brunner and Meltzer recognized, of course, that central banks had rarely used the monetary base as an instrument and had seldom tried to set even the total-reserves portion of the base.

Meltzer also realized that central banks cannot, in the short run, drastically reduce—or dramatically alter the path of—the monetary base without creating great disruptions. But he stressed that, over longer periods, concerted central bank policies do play an important role in shaping the path of the monetary base and that, if desired, a smooth transition to a lower base path is achievable by open market sales accompanied by temporary discount window lending.

Some critics of the base/multiplier approach (for example, Goodhart 1994) have characterized actual central banks as letting the monetary base (or total reserves) adjust to M rather than vice versa. But to Meltzer, this was not a fundamental criticism of the base/multiplier approach. It was, rather, a *description* of how central banks might be too permissive in their operations and strategy, in a way that allowed the money stock to be procyclical (see Meltzer 1967).[4] He often viewed interest-rate policies largely in terms of their implications for the trajectory of the monetary base and the associated permitted path for the money stock. From this perspective, the monetary base retains value as an indicator of what could happen to the money stock, even under conditions in which the nominal short-term interest rate is the central bank's policy instrument.

RESOLUTION OF PARADOX 4

The fourth paradox is that Meltzer indicated that the money stock that mattered in nonbank private-sector decisions included deposits issued by commercial banks—yet he often used the monetary base not only in analyzing the behavior of the money stock but also with direct reference to the behavior of nominal spending, the price level, or output.

The resolution of this paradox lies in Meltzer's (2010b, 1130) suggestion that, in times when financial innovations create distortions to deposit behavior (for example, changes that blur the distinction between M1 and non-M1 deposits, or that involve growth of deposit substitutes not included in standard measures of the money stock), monetary base growth could be superior to measured growth in the money stock as a proxy for true, underlying monetary growth. In particular, Meltzer (2010a, 2010b) largely focused on monetary base growth when analyzing money/income relations.

The notion that Δh might be a valuable stand-in for Δm under conditions of financial change is not universally applicable. One example: The relationship between the monetary base and the economy is itself affected by financial innovation—such as automatic teller machines, debit cards, sweeps, and dollarization abroad—and innovation also complicates the adjustments of the base for changes in reserve requirements. A second example: In periods of surges in commercial banks' demand for reserves in relation to their issuance of deposits, like the 1930s and the period from 2008 onward, monetary base growth is far more distorted than is measured money stock growth. Indeed, Meltzer (2002) used M1 rather than the monetary base when considering US output behavior in the early 1930s.

RESOLUTION OF PARADOX 5

The final paradox to be considered is that Meltzer long acknowledged that a short-term interest-rate rule could, in principle, be workable and stabilizing, yet only late in his career did he perceive an interest-rate instrument rule as a valid, and perhaps superior, alternative in practice to the use of the monetary base as the instrument.

The main resolution of this paradox lies in the fact that monetary policy developments and economists' research findings ultimately convinced Meltzer that interest-rate policies that were stabilizing were more achievable in practice than he had thought.[5]

In explaining this change of view, it is worth mentioning that Meltzer did not put particular stress on the discretion-versus-rules distinction as the way of framing his frequent disagreement with central banks on operating (or monetary-control) procedures. Brunner and Meltzer (1969, 19) seemed to express dissatisfaction with the "rules versus authorities" dichotomy, and Meltzer (1983, 95) would conclude that "every policy is a choice of rule." Meltzer recognized that the interest-rate policy followed by a central bank was, or could be, a rule (that is, that the central bank's interest-rate reaction function is its "rule"). He also appreciated the fact that a rule for the interest rate could, in principle, achieve control of monetary growth and inflation.

As a practical matter, however, Meltzer was, for many years, very skeptical about whether the features required for an interest-rate rule to work really existed (see Meltzer 1980a). He particularly doubted whether central banks had either sufficient information about the economy's structure or the readiness to move R sufficiently and promptly.

These matters featured prominently in US monetary policy discourse in 1979, when the debate on Federal Reserve operating procedures was at a cross-roads. Meltzer (2010b, 885–86, 897), in noting that until 1979 the FOMC used the federal funds rate to pursue Δm targets, observed that the FOMC routinely attained its desired interest-rate settings yet frequently missed the intermediate targets for monetary growth that these settings had been intended to achieve. Correspondingly, Meltzer (1979) contended that, in practice, the FOMC "just did not seem able to find the right interest target to get control of money growth." Meltzer (1981, 23) outlined his concern about a pattern observed repeatedly when the private sector's demand for credit experienced declines. Such developments put downward pressure on market interest rates. "Central banks can delay the fall by slowing money growth, and they generally do. Money growth collapses as we enter recessions, and since the error is symmetric, money growth soars during expansions."

What was needed for better monetary control, Meltzer suggested, was an arrangement in which market interest rates adjusted more promptly. For a long time, he saw the solution in the central bank stepping away from management of interest rates. Just ahead of the 1979 regime change, Meltzer (1980b) pointed to the inadequacy of "policies that move the fed funds rate an eighth of a point at a time." Meltzer's (and other monetarists') proposed alternative was that the central bank should target money using the monetary base as the instrument. The interest-rate movements consistent with control of monetary growth— and ultimately, of inflation—then occur automatically.

Meltzer recognized that, irrespective of which operating procedures were adopted, a period of a higher federal funds rate and of recession was inevitable if disinflation was to occur. He said in January 1979: "There's no way I know of to stop inflation costlessly. It's a social question of whether you're willing to take the temporary cost to stop inflation. If not, you won't get rid of inflation."[6]

Meltzer was extremely critical of both the FOMC's pre-1979 interest-rate policy and its 1979–1982 regime, which centered operating procedures on control of nonborrowed reserves. In later years, Meltzer did not recant his position that the nonborrowed reserves regime promoted fluctuations in the monetary base, the money stock, the term structure, and the economy of a magnitude that could have been avoided under a policy of direct control of the base (or by control of total reserves). But he would, in his retrospectives on the period, soften his criticisms of 1979–1982 policy, particularly the 1981–1982 portion, which he came to see as the prelude to an enlightened employment of an interest-rate reaction function during the 1980s and 1990s under Federal Reserve chairmen Paul Volcker and Alan Greenspan (see Meltzer 2010b).

Also during the early 1980s, Meltzer showed some signs of the thinking that ultimately led to his acceptance of the viability of some interest-rate rules. For example, Meltzer (1982, 230) saw that an interest-rate policy could be marshaled to establish a firm resolve against inflation. He pointed to the early Thatcher experience in the United Kingdom: "Steps taken during the past year [1980] reinforce the belief that a change in policy has occurred. These include . . . a manifest unwillingness to reduce MLR [the UK policy rate, minimum lending rate] . . . despite rising unemployment."

It must be borne in mind as well that Meltzer was exposed during the 1980s and 1990s to Bennett McCallum's (1981) favorable analysis of interest-rate rules and to the economics profession's discussion of the Taylor rule (Taylor 1993). Also notable is the fact that Meltzer (2010b, 1241) highlighted "the Woodford model" (see Michael Woodford 2003), which oriented monetary policy and price-level analysis toward the central bank's rule for the short-term policy rate.

The considerable US economic stability experienced with an interest-rate instrument in the 1990s likely swayed Meltzer still further, especially as it occurred against a background of fluctuations in monetary velocity (for the monetary base and deposit-inclusive monetary totals alike). By 2009, Meltzer's considered account was that monetarists should have put more stress on the scenario in which, when appropriately formulated, "interest-rate control would be effective and countercyclical" (Meltzer 2010b, 1017).[7]

CONCLUSION

Meltzer's interest in the monetary base reflected neither a counterfactual belief that historical monetary policy involved direct targeting of the base nor a view that base money or deposits mattered directly for spending decisions. Rather, it flowed from his hypothesis that base behavior can shed light on the implications of monetary policy actions (including those in an interest-rate policy) for asset prices, deposit creation, aggregate spending, and inflation.

However, Meltzer's enthusiasm for the monetary base as an instrument did markedly diminish in later work, as he became more persuaded of the practical feasibility of stabilizing interest-rate reaction functions.

The future of the monetary base's status as an indicator depends on a number of factors. Among them is whether complications such as nontraditional central-bank-issued bank liabilities and the payment of interest on reserves can be integrated into good empirical models linking the monetary base, the money stock, and the economy.

It also depends on whether it is the case (as is widely believed—and contrary to Meltzer's doubts) that aggregate spending can be successfully analyzed empirically without the use of quantity variables; for example, by securing improved measures of key asset prices and interest-rate spreads and by obtaining reliable estimates of the natural real rate of interest.

APPENDIX: A FURTHER POSSIBLE REASON FOR MELTZER'S CHANGE REGARDING INTEREST-RATE RULES

A second possible reason for Meltzer's shift to a more favorable outlook on interest-rate rules—in addition to the reason given in the section called Resolution of Paradox 5—was a changed view after the early 1970s of business cycle shocks and dynamics.

During the early 1970s, Brunner and Meltzer were well disposed toward viewing historical business cycles as a consequence of policy-induced monetary "impulses": basically, variations in monetary growth. Conversely, they downplayed nonmonetary shocks' inherent importance for short-run output fluctuations. Brunner and Meltzer also cast doubt on the existence of internal dynamics in output of a kind that spread over time the output effects of shocks.[8] They conveyed the impression that potential output had few fluctuations around its trend.

In the Brunner-Meltzer view, real shocks mattered for output in the short run mainly insofar as the central bank accommodated them by letting them affect nominal monetary growth. From this flowed their frequent complaint that monetary growth was procyclical. Under a constant rate of monetary growth, the short-term interest rate would vary in response to real shocks, mirroring movements in the natural rate of interest, but output would, according to this view, be largely insensitive to these shocks.

After the first oil shock of 1973–1974, however, Meltzer put more emphasis on real shocks, noting both their temporary and permanent components as drivers of real economic activity. He recognized these shocks as factors also tending to produce one-time price-level changes, implying that monetary policy governed the ongoing inflation rate but not necessarily the absolute price level (Meltzer 1977).

Through his interactions at Carnegie Mellon University and in the Carnegie-Rochester Conference Series, Meltzer was also heavily exposed to the achievements of the real business cycle (RBC) literature, including Finn Kydland and Edward Prescott (1982), in explaining cyclical fluctuations via difference equations with real shocks and to the RBC literature's challenge to monetary accounts of output variation (see, in particular, King and Plosser 1984).

McCallum's (1989, 41) assessment was that the RBC research findings made it "unlikely that many scholars today would subscribe to the proposition that all or most of the postwar fluctuation in US output has been attributable to actions of the Federal Open Market Committee." Reflecting the spirit (if not perhaps the letter) of McCallum's assessment of the change in professional opinion, Brunner and Meltzer (1988, 1993) indicated a greater recognition of the importance of real shocks and of money's role in helping shape the response of output to real shocks.

In view of this increased recognition of nonmonetary shocks' importance for output fluctuations, Meltzer may have become more receptive to a nominal interest-rate rule that responded, possibly via reactions to observable variables, to these shocks. For example, a well-specified interest-rate rule might be more successful than a constant-monetary-growth rule in keeping the actual real interest rate in line with variations in the real natural rate.

This interpretation of Meltzer's change in views should not be pushed too far. As noted, even during the period when he doubted real shocks' importance for output fluctuations, Meltzer seemed to see real shocks as producing sizable variations in the natural real rate of interest (see, for example, Meltzer 1969, 21). He viewed uncertainty regarding this natural rate as pointing toward the desirability of a monetary base instrument.

In sum, although Meltzer's view of real shocks' role changed during the 1980s and 1990s, this altered mindset may not have been crucial to his acceptance of the viability of interest-rate rules.

NOTES

1. As discussed later, monetary base growth might in some circumstances itself be the best stand-in for monetary growth, in which case the real money growth series would be $\Delta h - \Delta p$. (Here H and M are the dollar levels of the monetary base and the stock of money, respectively, while h and m refer to their natural logarithms. Changes of x percent in H and M correspond approximately to changes in value of x units in $100 \times \Delta h$ and $100 \times \Delta m$, respectively. P is the aggregate price index, so the inflation rate is Δp.)

2. The experience of the 2007–2009 financial crisis and its aftermath suggests that Meltzer's (2002, 376, 495) historical account understated the role of uncertainty, and correspondingly overstated the role of low market interest rates, in boosting US commercial banks' desire for excess reserve balances during the 1930s. Similarly, during his public commentary on current events during 2009 and 2010, Meltzer likely very seriously underestimated the increase in the reserve/deposit ratio that was due to a rise in uncertainty. This underestimation likely played a part in leading Meltzer, over this period, to make numerous erroneous predictions that a severe upsurge in US inflation would follow from the large increase in the US monetary base.

3. It deserves emphasis that, in keeping with the bulk of the twentieth-century monetary policy literature (including Meltzer's work), the term "liquidity trap" is being used here to refer to a situation in which monetary policy is unable, using any tool available, to stimulate asset prices and spending. It is not being used simply as a label for a situation in which the short-term policy interest rate is at its lower bound.

4. If one accepted this premise, one might nonetheless prefer to use the word "driver of" or "influence on" instead of "determinant of" in the Brunner-Meltzer (1969) quotation given above. Such a substitution would appropriately recognize the link between the monetary base and

the money stock, while still reserving words like "cause" or "determine" for variables that are set exogenously. Alternatively, one might maintain that the fact that the monetary base reflects monetary policy actions, even when it is endogenous, justifies use of the word "determinant."

5. The appendix in this chapter discusses a further possible reason for Meltzer's change in view: namely, a possible change in his assessment of the importance of different shocks that the US economy faced.

6. Quoted in Michael Cronk (1979).

7. The changed Federal Reserve interest-rate policy reflected not just a greater willingness to vary interest rates but also an alteration in the FOMC's approach to the appropriate goals of, and strategy for, monetary policy. Meltzer (2010b) contended that this alteration took the form of an increased weight on inflation in policy makers' objectives. This interpretation is challenged in Nelson (2012). The latter discussion argued, instead, that inflation was always rated by US policy makers as very costly, but that the late 1970s saw an increased emphasis on the responsibility of monetary policy for inflation—as the FOMC came to accept a monetary view of inflation. It was also suggested in that review that Meltzer's analysis of the 1950s through the 1970s would have benefited from a more systematic comparison with the quite different perspective offered by Christina Romer and David Romer (2002a, 2002b) on FOMC policy during those decades.

8. For example, Brunner and Meltzer (1972, 71) stated, "[We] assert that fluctuations in prices and output are most often the result of government policies, particularly monetary policies." And Brunner and Meltzer (1976, 180) criticized business cycle research that "attributes fluctuations to . . . the pervasive effects of cumulated, serially and contemporaneously correlated random disturbances."

REFERENCES

Bean, Charles. 2009. "The Great Moderation, the Great Panic and the Great Contraction." Schumpeter Lecture, Annual Congress of the European Economic Association. Barcelona, August 25.

Bernanke, Ben S. 2002. "Deflation: Making Sure That 'It' Doesn't Happen Here." Speech before the National Economics Club. Washington, DC, November 21.

———. 2012. "Opening Remarks: Monetary Policy since the Onset of the Crisis." In *The Changing Policy Landscape,* edited by Federal Reserve Bank of Kansas City, 1–22. Kansas City, MO: Federal Reserve Bank of Kansas City.

Bordo, Michael D., and Anna Jacobson Schwartz. 2004. "IS-LM and Monetarism." *History of Political Economy* 36, Suppl. 1 (December): 217–39.

Brunner, Karl, and Allan H. Meltzer. 1966. "Joint Statement by Karl Brunner and Allan H. Meltzer, Graduate School of Industrial Administration, Carnegie Institute of Technology, Pittsburgh, Pa." In *The Federal Reserve Portfolio: Statements by Individual Economists,* prepared for the US Congress Joint Economic Committee, Subcommittee on Economic Progress, 15–16.

———. 1968a. "Liquidity Traps for Money, Bank Credit, and Interest Rates." *Journal of Political Economy* 76, no. 1 (January–February): 1–37.

———. 1968b. "What Did We Learn from the Monetary Experience of the United States in the Great Depression?" *Canadian Journal of Economics* 1, no. 2 (May): 334–48.

———. 1969. "The Nature of the Policy Problem." In *Targets and Indicators of Monetary Policy,* edited by Karl Brunner, 1–26. San Francisco: Chandler.

———. 1972. "A Monetarist Framework for Aggregative Analysis." In *Proceedings of the First Konstanzer Seminar on Monetary Theory and Monetary Policy,* edited by Karl Brunner, 31–88. Berlin: Duncker & Humblot.

———. 1973. "Mr. Hicks and the 'Monetarists.'" *Economica* 40, no. 157 (February): 44–59.

———. 1976. "Monetarism: The Principal Issues, Areas of Agreement, and Work Remaining." In *Monetarism*, edited by Jerome L. Stein, 150–82. Amsterdam: North-Holland.

———. 1981. "Time Deposits in the Brunner-Meltzer Model of Asset Markets." *Journal of Monetary Economics* 7, no. 1 (January): 129–39.

———. 1988. "Money and Credit in the Monetary Transmission Process." *American Economic Review* 78, no. 2 (May): 446–51.

———. 1993. *Money and the Economy: Issues in Monetary Analysis.* Cambridge: Cambridge University Press.

Congdon, Tim. 2011. *Money in a Free Society: Keynes, Friedman, and the New Crisis of Capitalism.* New York: Encounter Books.

Cronk, Michael. 1979. "Its Cures Stir More Worry Than Inflation." *San Jose Mercury* (California), January 19, 11B.

Dornbusch, Rudiger. 1976. Comment on "An Aggregative Theory for a Closed Economy," by Karl Brunner and Allan H. Meltzer. In *Monetarism*, edited by Jerome L. Stein, 104–25. Amsterdam: North-Holland.

Foot, M. D. K. W., Charles A. E. Goodhart, and Anthony C. Hotson. 1979. "Monetary Base Control." *Bank of England Quarterly Bulletin* 19, no. 2 (June): 149–56.

Friedman, Benjamin M. 1988. "Conducting Monetary Policy by Controlling Currency Plus Noise: A Comment." *Carnegie-Rochester Conference Series on Public Policy* 29: 205–12.

Friedman, Milton, and Anna Jacobson Schwartz. 1963. *A Monetary History of the United States, 1867–1960.* Princeton, NJ: Princeton University Press.

Goodhart, Charles A. E. 1994. "What Should Central Banks Do? What Should Be Their Macroeconomic Objectives and Operations?" *Economic Journal* 104, no. 427 (November): 1424–36.

Ireland, Peter N. 2017. "Allan Meltzer's Model of the Transmission Mechanism and Its Implications for Today." Working Paper in Economics no. 938, Boston College.

King, Mervyn. 1999. "Challenges for Monetary Policy: New and Old." In *New Challenges for Monetary Policy*, edited by Federal Reserve Bank of Kansas City, 11–57. Kansas City, MO: Federal Reserve Bank of Kansas City.

King, Robert G., and Charles I. Plosser. 1984. "Money, Credit and Prices in a Real Business Cycle." *American Economic Review* 74, no. 3 (June): 363–80.

Kydland, Finn E., and Edward C. Prescott. 1982. "Time to Build and Aggregate Fluctuations." *Econometrica* 50, no. 6 (November): 1345–70.

Laidler, David. 1995. "Some Aspects of Monetarism Circa 1970: A View from 1994." *Kredit und Kapital* 28, no. 3: 323–45.

Lucas, Robert E., Jr. 1988. "Money Demand in the United States: A Quantitative Review." *Carnegie-Rochester Conference Series on Public Policy* 39: 137–68.

McCallum, Bennett T. 1981. "Price Level Determinacy with an Interest Rate Policy Rule and Rational Expectations." *Journal of Monetary Economics* 8, no. 3: 319–29.

———. 1989. "Real Business Cycle Models." In *Modern Business Cycle Theory*, edited by Robert J. Barro, 16–50. Cambridge, MA: Harvard University Press.

Meltzer, Allan H. 1967. "Money Supply Revisited: A Review Article." *Journal of Political Economy* 75, no. 2 (April): 169–82.

———. 1969. Panelist for "The Role of Money in National Economic Policy." In *Controlling Monetary Aggregates: Proceedings of a Conference Held in June, 1969*, 25–29. Conference Series No. 1. Boston: Federal Reserve Bank of Boston.

———. 1976. "Monetary and Other Explanations of the Start of the Great Depression." *Journal of Monetary Economics* 2, no. 4 (November): 455–71.

———. 1977. "Anticipated Inflation and Unanticipated Price Change: A Test of the Price-Specie Flow Theory and the Phillips Curve." *Journal of Money, Credit and Banking* 9, no. 1, part 2 (February): 182–205.

———. 1979. "A Monetarist Looks at the Federal Reserve." *New York Times*, October 14, F16.

———. 1980a. "Central Bank Policy: Some First Principles." *Annual Monetary Review* (Centre for Banking and International Finance) 2 (December): 27–33.

———. 1980b. "First Financial Forum, September 27, 1979: Allan Meltzer's Opening Statement." In *Issues in Monetary Policy: Three Financial Forums*, edited by Michael J. Hamburger, 13–14. New York: New York University.

———. 1981. "Tests of Inflation Theories from the British Laboratory." *Banker* 131, no. 665 (July): 21–27.

———. 1982. Comment on "Exchange Rates, Interest Rates and the Mobility of Capital," by Andrew Britton and Peter Spencer. In *Exchange Rate Policy*, edited by Roy A. Batchelor and Geoffrey E. Wood, 226–31. London: Macmillan.

———. 1983. "Monetary Reform in an Uncertain Environment." *Cato Journal* 3, no. 1 (Spring): 93–112.

———. 1992. "Patinkin on Keynes and Meltzer." *Journal of Monetary Economics* 29, no. 1 (February): 151–62.

———. 1993. "Some Lessons from the Great Inflation." In *Price Stabilization in the 1990s: Domestic and International Policy Requirements*, edited by Kumiharu Shigehara, 7–29. London: Macmillan.

———. 1999. "A Liquidity Trap?" Unpublished manuscript, Carnegie Mellon University. https://kilthub.cmu.edu/articles/A_Liquidity_Trap_/6703067/1.

———. 2001. "The Transmission Process." In *The Monetary Transmission Process: Recent Developments and Lessons for Europe*, edited by Deutsche Bundesbank, 112–30. London: Palgrave.

———. 2002. *A History of the Federal Reserve*. Vol. 1, *1913–1951*. Chicago: University of Chicago Press.

———. 2010a. *A History of the Federal Reserve*. Vol. 2, Book 1, *1951–1969*. Chicago: University of Chicago Press.

———. 2010b. *A History of the Federal Reserve*. Vol. 2, Book 2, *1970–1986*. Chicago: University of Chicago Press.

Nelson, Edward. 2003. "The Future of Monetary Aggregates in Monetary Policy Analysis." *Journal of Monetary Economics* 50, no. 5 (July): 1029–59.

———. 2004. "Money and the Transmission Mechanism in the Optimizing IS-LM Specification." *History of Political Economy* 36, Suppl. 1 (December): 271–304.

———. 2012. Review of *A History of the Federal Reserve*, vol. 2, by Allan H. Meltzer. *International Journal of Central Banking* 8, no. 2 (June): 241–66.

———. 2017. "Milton Friedman and Economic Debate in the United States, 1932–1972." Unpublished manuscript.

Rasche, Robert H. 1993. "Monetary Policy and the Money Supply Process." In *Monetary Policy in Developed Economies*, edited by Michele U. Fratianni and Dominick Salvatore, 25–54. Westwood, CT: Greenwood.

Romer, Christina D., and David H. Romer. 2002a. "The Evolution of Economic Understanding and Postwar Stabilization Policy." In *Rethinking Stabilization Policy*, 11–78. Kansas City, MO: Federal Reserve Bank of Kansas City.

———. 2002b. "A Rehabilitation of Monetary Policy in the 1950s." *American Economic Review (Papers and Proceedings)* 92, no. 2: 121–27.

Svensson, Lars E. O. 2003. Comment on "The Future of Monetary Aggregates in Monetary Policy Analysis," by Edward Nelson. *Journal of Monetary Economics* 50, no. 5 (July): 1061–70.

Taylor, John B. 1993. "Discretion versus Policy Rules in Practice." *Carnegie-Rochester Conference Series on Public Policy* 39 (December): 195–214.

Tobin, James. 1969. "A General Equilibrium Approach to Monetary Theory." *Journal of Money, Credit and Banking* 1, no. 1 (February): 15–29.

Wonnacott, Paul. 1974. *Macroeconomics.* Homewood, IL: R. D. Irwin.

Woodford, Michael. 2003. *Interest and Prices: Foundations of a Theory of Monetary Policy.* Princeton, NJ: Princeton University Press.

CHAPTER 7
Monetary Policy and the Interest Rate: Reflections on Allan Meltzer's Contributions to Monetary Economics

JOSHUA R. HENDRICKSON

> Knowledge of the transmission process helps to interpret observations during the nervous interlude between the time policy action is undertaken and its effects on output and inflation become visible. During this interlude, pressure on the central bank to abandon its rule, or change its policy, is often intense. Theory—knowledge of the transmission process—is required to interpret incoming data on real variables and relative prices, including interest rates and exchange rates.
>
> —*Allan Meltzer (1995, 70)*

Exactly thirty years ago, in May 1988, Allan Meltzer and Karl Brunner presented a paper at the American Economic Association meetings titled "Money and Credit in the Monetary Transmission Mechanism." In that paper, Brunner and Meltzer (1988) argue that a proper analysis of monetary policy transmission requires an integration of the supply and demand for money with credit markets. By integrating the money market with the credit market, the short-term nominal interest rate is no longer sufficient for discussing the stance or the transmission of monetary policy on economic activity. Instead, monetary policy is transmitted through both the interest rate and the price level of real assets. Any corresponding change in economic activity, therefore, depends on how individuals and firms respond to changes in these prices. In contrast, Brunner and Meltzer argued that the monetary transmission mechanism within a standard IS-LM (investment/savings-liquidity/money) framework is too simple because of its exclusive focus on the interest rate.

This theme was echoed by Meltzer throughout the remainder of his career (Meltzer 1995). Nonetheless, in recent years, monetary policy has moved toward a system in which the Federal Reserve now uses the interest rate on reserves as its preferred policy tool. This chapter discusses Meltzer's contribution to the study of the monetary transmission mechanism and the implications for current policy.

INTEREST RATES, ASSET PRICES, AND MONETARY TRANSMISSION

Brunner and Meltzer developed a macroeconomic model for a conference on monetarism in the 1970s (Brunner and Meltzer 1976). This model drew upon their earlier work but became the core model that shaped their views of monetary policy throughout the remainder of their careers. The Brunner-Meltzer model featured a goods market equilibrium and an asset market equilibrium. For simplicity, this discussion is limited to the asset market to highlight the effects of a change in the monetary base on relative asset prices.

Brunner and Meltzer began with the assumption that there is some multiplier process that relates the total supply of credit to the monetary base as well as a multiplier process that relates broad measures of the money supply to the monetary base. Unlike the rather crude versions of the money multiplier, however, they treat these multipliers as functions of other economic variables. Their view was that there was some microeconomic behavior underlying the provision of credit and the creation of money assets that could be represented in the implicit functions outlined below. In the model, the multipliers and the demand for money and credit are a function of a large number of variables. Here, the model is simplified to only the variables of interest for this chapter.

The credit market equilibrium can be written as

$$a(i, p)B = \sigma(i - \pi, p), \qquad (1)$$

where $a(\cdot)$ is the asset multiplier, $\sigma(\cdot)$ is the demand for credit, i is the short-term nominal interest rate, p is the price level of real assets, π is the rate of inflation, and B is the monetary base. If we assume that prices (or expectations about prices) are sticky, the inflation rate can be treated as exogenous in the short run. In addition, the monetary base is exogenously determined by the central bank. Brunner and Meltzer assume that a_i, $a_p > 0$, σ_i, $\sigma_p < 0$. While this is a reduced-form approach, the basic implications are not controversial. For example, higher real borrowing costs and a higher price of acquiring real assets reduce the demand for credit. Higher interest rates and higher prices of real assets, however, will increase the supply of credit. In contrast to a typical loanable funds model, the supply and demand for credit does not uniquely determine the interest rate since both interest rates and the prices of real assets are endogenous.

The money market equilibrium can be written as

$$m(i, p)B = L(i, p), \tag{2}$$

where $m(\cdot)$ is the money multiplier and $L(\cdot)$ is the demand for broad money. Brunner and Meltzer assume that m_i, m_p, $L_p > 0$, and $L_i < 0$. The basic idea here is as follows. Money is one asset that individuals can hold in their portfolios. Bonds and real assets (or claims to real assets) are also held in individuals' portfolios. As is standard, a higher interest rate on bonds will reduce the demand for money. However, the prices of real assets also affect the demand for money. When real asset prices are high, these assets are more expensive to acquire and individuals will increase their demand for money. The money multiplier is also affected by the interest rate and the price level of real assets. Higher interest rates and higher prices on real assets tend to lead to expansions of commercial bank balance sheets and, therefore, an increase in the supply of money, broadly measured.

What these basic conditions reveal is that the supply of assets in the economy and the supply of money are connected through the banking system, which "produces" money by issuing liabilities that are subject to multilateral commitment. Thus, there is an explicit connection between the supply of credit and broad measures of the money supply. Given that the monetary base is taken as given and that (in the short run) prices are sticky, it follows that equations (1) and (2) represent two equations with two unknowns: i and p. The money market and the credit market jointly determine the nominal interest rate and the price level of real assets. This has important implications for the transmission of monetary policy.

Differentiating each of these equations yields

$$a_i B di + a_p B dp + a(i, p)dB = \sigma_i di + \sigma_p dp, \tag{3}$$

$$m_i B di + m_p B dp + m(i, p)dB = L_i di + L_p dp, \tag{4}$$

which can be rewritten as

$$\frac{a_i}{a}di + \frac{a_p}{a}dp + \frac{dB}{B} = \frac{\sigma_i}{\sigma}di + \frac{\sigma_p}{\sigma}dp,$$

$$\frac{m_i}{m}di + \frac{m_p}{m}dp + \frac{dB}{B} = \frac{L_i}{L}di + \frac{L_p}{L}dp.$$

Let's refer to m_i/m as the elasticity of the money multiplier with respect to the interest rate and use $e(m, i)$ to denote this elasticity. We can then clean up the notation of these equations by writing

$$[e(a,i) - e(\sigma,i)]di + \frac{dB}{B} = [e(\sigma, p) - e(a, p)]dp, \tag{5}$$

$$[e(m,i) - e(L,i)]di + \frac{dB}{B} = [e(L, p) - e(m, p)]dp. \tag{6}$$

Suppose that in equilibrium, $dB/B = 0$. It follows that we can plot the credit market equilibrium as a downward-sloping curve in $i - p$ space. In addition, assuming that $e(L, p) > e(m, p)$, the money market equilibrium is an upward-sloping curve in $i - p$ space. These curves are illustrated in figure 7-1.

The intuition here is as follows. Suppose that the monetary base is fixed and the nominal interest rate rises. This reduces the demand for money. As individuals reduce their money holdings, they reallocate some of their portfolio to real assets (or claims to real assets), thereby bidding up these assets' prices. This is why the *MM* curve is upward-sloping. In the credit market, a higher interest rate means that borrowing costs are higher. All else being equal, banks will want to reallocate from real assets to loans, and firms will want to borrow less. The result is that the prices of real assets decline, on average. This yields the downward-sloping *CM* curve in figure 7-1. The figure also illustrates the fact that the short-term interest rate and the price level of real assets are determined by the intersection of these two curves. However, note that if the monetary base changes, this shifts each curve. It is straightforward to show that an increase in the monetary base will lower the nominal interest rate and have an ambiguous effect on the price level of real assets.

To see this, let's rewrite our conditions as

$$e(CM,i)di + \frac{dB}{B} = e(CM,p)dp, \tag{7}$$

$$e(MM,i)di + \frac{dB}{B} = e(MM,p)dp, \tag{8}$$

Figure 7-1. Brunner-Meltzer Asset Market Equilibrium

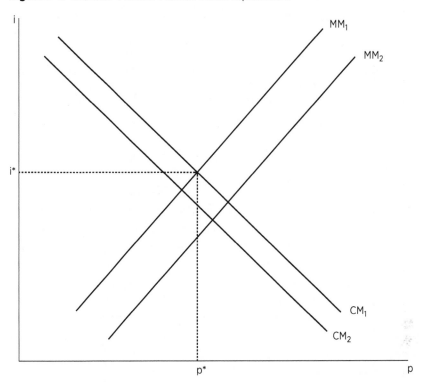

where $e(CM, i) = e(a, i) - e(\sigma, i)$ is the elasticity of the credit market to a change in the interest rate, $e(CM, p) = e(\sigma, p) - e(a, p)$ is the elasticity of the credit market to a change in the price level of real assets, $e(MM, i) = e(m, i) - e(L, i)$ is the elasticity of the money market with respect to a change in the interest rate, and $e(MM, p) = e(L, p) - e(m, p)$ is the elasticity of the money market with respect to a change in the price of real assets. From these equations, we can generate the following comparative statics:

$$\frac{di}{dB/B} = \frac{1 - e(MM, p)}{e(CM, i)e(MM, p) - e(MM, i)} < 0, \tag{9}$$

$$\frac{dp}{dB/B} = \left(\frac{e(MM, i) - e(CM, i)}{e(CM, i)e(MM, p) - e(CM, p)e(MM, p)} \right), \tag{10}$$

where the comparative static in equation (10) is positive if $e(MM, i) > e(CM, i)$. In other words, if the money market is more responsive to changes in interest rates than credit markets, then asset prices will rise. Brunner and Meltzer assumed this was the case on the basis of the empirical observation that asset prices tend to rise following a monetary injection (Meltzer 1995). This is shown in figure 7-1 by the changes to MM_2 and CM_2.

The intuition is as follows. An increase in the monetary base creates an excess supply of money. Individuals use the excess money to purchase bonds and real assets. All else being equal, this causes the interest rate to decline and the price level of real assets to rise. At the same time, the increase in the monetary base also increases in the supply of credit. At the old interest rate and price of assets, this causes an excess supply of credit. For a given price level of real assets, market clearing requires that the interest rate declines, which increases the demand for investment and, therefore, the supply of real assets. All else being equal, the increase in the supply of real assets reduces the price level of real assets. Thus, the credit market response to an increase in the monetary base is one in which the interest rate and the price level of real assets decline.

The combined effect of the money market and credit market response, therefore, leads to a decrease in the interest rate and an ambiguous effect on the price level of real assets. Whether the price of real assets rises or falls depends on the relative elasticities of the money market and credit market. In other words, the expansion of the monetary base increases both the supply of and demand for real assets. Since these changes push the price level of real assets in opposite directions, the ultimate effect on the price level of real assets depends on the relative elasticities. If, for example, the money market is more responsive to interest rates than the credit market, then the price level of real assets rises in equilibrium. Brunner and Meltzer assumed that the money market effect dominated since empirical work tended to find that monetary expansion raised asset prices. The effect on real economic activity, then, depends on how individuals respond to changes in the relative prices of real and financial assets.

As Meltzer argues, this contrasts sharply with the standard IS-LM framework in which monetary policy is transmitted entirely through the interest rate. He viewed this focus on the interest rate as "overly restrictive and mechanical" (Meltzer 1995, 51). Rather, Meltzer (1995, 51) argues,

> A monetary impulse that alters the nominal and real stocks of money does more than change a single short-term interest rate or borrowing cost. Monetary impulses change the actual and anticipated prices on a variety of domestic and foreign assets. Intermediation, the term structure of interest rates, borrowing and lending, and exchange rates respond.

The exclusive focus on the interest rate is flawed because it does not differentiate between the short-term and long-term interest rates, it ignores financial intermediation, and it fails to wrestle with the substitution between money, bonds, and other real and financial assets. In short, "Analysis of monetary policy in the IS-LM framework is deficient. A single interest rate fails to represent the problem confronting central banks and may encourage the belief that monetary policy can control interest rates" (Brunner and Meltzer 1993, 82).

This criticism is especially prescient in light of recent changes in the Federal Reserve's operating procedures. The next section considers that the workhorse model of monetary policy analysis has a number of characteristics that leave it subject to the same criticism as the IS-LM model. As a result, monetary policy is now exclusively thought to work entirely through the interest rate.

THE IMPORTANCE FOR CONTEMPORARY MODELS AND POLICY

While the profession at large has moved beyond the IS-LM model for monetary policy analysis, the modern workhorse model, the New Keynesian model, has been sold as a dynamic, forward-looking, rational-expectations version of the old IS-LM model (King 2000). Standard versions of the New Keynesian model ignore money completely.[1] Monetary policy is characterized by a feedback rule for the nominal interest rate. There are two ways to interpret this type of rule. Taken literally, the model implies that monetary policy is transmitted entirely through the short-term nominal interest rate. A higher nominal interest rate, coupled with sticky prices, leads to a higher real interest rate that reduces consumption and investment. Some scholars, however, such as Milton Friedman, have argued that the difference need not be taken literally (Roberts 2006). Friedman argued that since the Federal Reserve uses open market operations to target the nominal interest rate, the monetary transmission mechanism is the same regardless of whether the Fed is targeting monetary aggregates or an interest rate.

However, recent changes to the Federal Reserve's operating procedures are not consistent with Friedman's interpretation. The Federal Reserve now targets the interest rate on reserves rather than the federal funds rate. When the Fed targeted the federal funds rate, it had to conduct open market operations to adjust the supply of reserves such that the federal funds rate was consistent with the Fed's target. However, by switching to targeting the interest rate on reserves, the Federal Reserve no longer has to conduct open market operations to adjust its target rate. The interest rate on reserves can be adjusted by fiat.

Some have argued that the ability of the Federal Reserve to conduct policy by adjusting its target rate without using open market operations is desirable. For example, Marvin Goodfriend (2002) argues that by paying interest on reserves and sufficiently increasing the supply of reserves in the banking system, the Federal Reserve has two levers for monetary policy. The first lever is that the Federal Reserve can adjust the interest on reserves to conduct ordinary monetary policy in conjunction with its interest rate feedback rule. The second lever is that the Federal Reserve can adjust the supply of reserves in accordance with the demand for liquidity of the banking system.

Goodfriend's argument, however, is predicated on the idea that monetary policy is transmitted entirely through the interest rate. This contrasts sharply with the views of Brunner and Meltzer and other monetarists. In Brunner and Meltzer's model, it is the change in the relative supply of exogenously determined asset supplies (the monetary base and T-bills) that leads to a change in relative prices of real and financial assets and also real economic activity. By using the interest rate on reserves as the primary tool of policy, there is no need to adjust the monetary base and, therefore, policy must work entirely through changes in interest rates. Despite the widespread acceptance among policy makers, there is little empirical evidence to support an exclusive focus on the interest rate. For example, Meltzer (2001) argued that since the demand for money is a function of a wide variety of asset prices, real money balances would serve as a useful indicator of monetary policy transmission. In other words, real money balances represent a sort of index of all the relative price effects of an open market purchase (or sale). In my own work, I have found that real money balances, when measured using Divisia monetary aggregates, not only help predict changes in output: the very inclusion of money in the regression tends to eliminate any predictive power of the real interest rate (Hendrickson 2014). In addition, Michael Belongia and Peter Ireland (2015) have shown that including Divisia monetary aggregates improves the fit of vector autoregression models used to estimate monetary policy shocks. These results imply that focusing exclusively on the interest rate is misguided and that the change in operating procedures might alter the effectiveness of monetary policy in important ways.

This exclusive focus on the interest rate also raises questions about the effectiveness of recent policies adopted by the Federal Reserve. For example, Ben Bernanke (2010) argued that the Fed's large-scale asset purchases would largely work through a portfolio balance effect. His description of the portfolio balance effect is similar to Brunner and Meltzer's transmission mechanism. However, the key difference in Bernanke's discussion is that he was making this argument in the context of a regime in which the Federal Reserve pays interest on reserves.

As Dutkowsky and VanHoose (2017) have shown, using a microeconomic model of banks, that when interest is paid on all reserves (including excess reserves) there are three possible equilibria. In one equilibrium, banks do not hold excess reserves and, instead, borrow and lend reserves in the federal funds market. In another equilibrium, banks do not borrow and lend reserves but, instead, hold large amounts of excess reserves. In the third equilibrium, the economy is in an interior solution where banks hold excess reserves but also engage in interbank borrowing and lending. When the interest rate on reserves is higher than the federal funds rate, as has been the case under Federal Reserve policy, banks hold a large quantity of excess reserves and do not engage in interbank lending. In this sort of equilibrium, it is unlikely that large scale asset purchases will work through a Brunner-Meltzer mechanism. In Brunner and Meltzer's model, an open market purchase changes the composition of the exogenous supply of assets. The subsequent portfolio reallocation leads to a change in the relative prices of real and financial assets and, thereby, economic activity. In the current environment, an open market purchase leaves the banking system with greater reserve balances, but banks are content to hold these as excess reserves rather than change the composition of their balance sheet. The Brunner-Meltzer transmission mechanism is, therefore, either inoperable or sufficiently weakened in this environment. This raises questions about the monetary transmission mechanism and the effectiveness of recent large-scale asset purchases.

CONCLUDING THOUGHTS

As the quote at the beginning of this chapter indicates, Meltzer thought that an understanding of the monetary transmission mechanism was of primary importance for the conduct of monetary policy. So much of the debate about monetary policy in the contemporary literature is about what the central bank should target. However, such debates often neglect (or simply take for granted) the process through which monetary policy affects economic activity. For Meltzer, a proper understanding of the monetary transmission mechanism was not only useful for policy implementation but also for avoiding external pressure on the central bank during the time between policy implementation and its effects. In other words, without a proper understanding of monetary policy transmission, it can be difficult to determine whether policy is working as predicted. In addition, since time passes between the implementation of a policy and the actual outcomes, uncertainty about the transmission mechanism might call into question the effectiveness of the policy both within the central bank and among its critics.

If nothing else, the discussion of the Brunner-Meltzer vision of monetary policy transmission in conjunction with the discussion of contemporary policy should give a person pause about the current state of monetary policy. The Federal Reserve seems convinced that the interest rate is all that matters for monetary policy and that the current operating procedures are effective for conducting policy. However, insufficient attention has been paid to the monetary transmission mechanism. In fact, the critiques leveled by Brunner and Meltzer's early work, as well as Meltzer's later work, remain relevant criticisms of contemporary models. More work is needed on the monetary transmission mechanism, and Meltzer's work is a good place to start.

NOTE

1.   There are notable exceptions, such as Michael Belongia and Peter Ireland (2014).

REFERENCES

Belongia, Michael T., and Peter N. Ireland. 2014. "The Barnett Critique after Three Decades: A New Keynesian Analysis." *Journal of Econometrics* 18: 5–21.

———. 2015. "Interest Rates and Money in the Measurement of Monetary Policy." *Journal of Business and Economic Statistics* 33, no. 2: 255–69.

Bernanke, Ben. 2010. "The Economic Outlook and Monetary Policy." Speech at Jackson Hole, Wyoming (August).

Brunner, Karl, and Allan H. Meltzer. 1976. "An Aggregate Theory for a Closed Economy." In *Monetarism*, edited by Jerome L. Stein, 69–103. Amsterdam: North-Holland.

———. 1988. "Money and Credit in the Monetary Transmission Process." *American Economic Review* 78, no. 2 (May): 446–51.

———. 1993. *Money and the Economy: Issues in Monetary Analysis.* Cambridge: Cambridge University Press.

Dutkowsky, Donald H., and David VanHoose. 2017. "Interest on Reserves, Regime Shifts, and Bank Behavior." *Journal of Economics and Business* 91 (May): 1–15.

Goodfriend, Marvin. 2002. "Interest on Reserves and Monetary Policy." *Federal Reserve Bank of New York Economic Policy Review* 8, no. 1: 77–84.

Hendrickson, Joshua R. 2014. "Redundancy or Mismeasurement: A Reappraisal of Money." *Macroeconomic Dynamics* 18: 1437–65.

King, Robert G. 2000. "The New IS-LM Model: Language, Logic, and Limits." *Federal Reserve Bank of Richmond Quarterly Review* 86, no. 3: 45–103.

Meltzer, Allan H. 1995. "Monetary, Credit and (Other) Transmission Processes: A Monetarist Perspective." *Journal of Economic Perspectives* 9, no. 4 (Fall): 49–72.

———. 2001. "The Transmission Process." In *The Monetary Transmission Process: Recent Developments and Lessons for Europe,* edited by Deutsche Bundesbank, 112–30. London: Palgrave.

Roberts, Russ. 2006. "Milton Friedman on Money." Library of Economics and Liberty, EconTalk podcast (August 26). http://www.econtalk.org/milton-friedman-on-money/.

CHAPTER 8
Allan Meltzer and the Search for a Nominal Anchor

JAMES BULLARD

A llan Meltzer was an outstanding monetary economist with a long and distinguished career. He has been an absolute fixture on the central banking and monetary economics scene during my entire career, so much so that I have a hard time picturing that scene without him. He was also a great friend of the St. Louis Fed.

Meltzer published seven papers in the St. Louis Fed's *Review*. The first, "Controlling Money," was published in 1969. The last was published in 2005 and was a precursor to volume 2 of his monumental *A History of the Federal Reserve* (*HFR*: Meltzer 2002, 2010). I will use Meltzer's last *Review* publication as a starting point for my comments.

The paper, titled "Origins of the Great Inflation," discusses the run-up to the extraordinary inflation of the 1970s and early 1980 in the United States from a policy maker's perspective. Meltzer presents in the style later carried on in *HFR*. He quotes the views of individual members of the Federal Open

This chapter, originally presented as a speech at the Meltzer's Contributions to Monetary Economics and Public Policy conference (January 4, 2018, see p. 1), was published as a paper in the *Federal Reserve Bank of St. Louis Review* 100, no. 2 (2018): 117–26. The views expressed are those of the author and do not necessarily reflect the views of the Federal Reserve System, the Board of Governors, the regional Federal Reserve banks, or the Federal Open Market Committee.

Market Committee (FOMC), along with those of the staff, that describe what they thought they were doing in adopting particular monetary policy actions at particular times. He presents this material almost deadpan, with little judgment, to try to discern what the protagonists were thinking as the Great Inflation developed.

And, indeed, they were thinking and saying a wide variety of things. As the narrative progresses, however, it becomes quite apparent that there was little in the way of a clear framework for monetary policy during these years. Meltzer states that the committee had no common baseline, even for fundamental questions such as the causes of inflation. Ideas for the provision of a nominal anchor centered on keeping fiscal deficits low, closely regulating the growth of the money supply, or keeping interest rates sufficiently high. None of these ideas was widely accepted, and all had detractors. Some FOMC members eschewed macroeconomic theory altogether. Meltzer notes that then Board governor Sherman Maisel often exhorted the committee to spend more time on the development of a coherent model that could be used to better guide decision-making, but he had little effect. As a result of the theoretical incoherence, actual decision-making was perhaps more open to influence by other factors, such as domestic politics, which Meltzer discusses in some detail.

From this situation some five decades ago as described by Meltzer, we come to the present. Is the situation today very different? The debates in the monetary theory literature and the fiscal theory of the price level literature roll onward. Certainly, much progress has been made, but complicated arguments abound and clear resolution seems distant. Yet today, despite the remaining theoretical incoherence, inflation control has been in place in the United States for about two decades—despite the global financial crisis. If there is a problem with inflation today, it is because inflation has been lower than promised, not higher. How is it that a nominal anchor for the United States has been found without clear resolution to the puzzles posed in the academic literature?

INFLATION TARGETING

The answer to this question is surely "inflation targeting." Inflation targeting does not provide a comprehensive account of inflation dynamics or of the methods used to attain a given inflation goal over the medium term. As implemented in the United States, it is really only a credible statement of a goal and a promise to try to achieve the goal in the medium term via all means at the disposal of the FOMC. That is not enough to satisfy any modern notion of what constitutes a macroeconomic theory. Nevertheless, it has succeeded in providing the nominal anchor that so eluded the United States during the 1970s and early 1980s.

Inflation targeting came upon the global central banking scene in the 1990s. Early adopters included the Reserve Bank of New Zealand and the Bank of England, but many other central banks around the world have followed since that time. The European Central Bank was conceived and established with a formal inflation target. The Bank of Japan and the Federal Reserve did not join the club formally until fairly recently, with the United States adopting an inflation target in January 2012.

Nevertheless, in my opinion, the United States has followed a de facto inflation targeting policy from 1995 onward. As of that time, US inflation had declined to about 2 percent, and it has not deviated substantially from that target since, at least not on the scale observed during the 1970s and early 1980s. US policy makers were well aware of the trends in the international policy debate toward inflation targeting during this era, and many members of the FOMC were sympathetic to the arguments supporting inflation targeting.

Generally speaking, the evidence from around the globe is that inflation targeting has been successful in those countries that have implemented it. Inflation rates are generally lower today than in the pre-inflation-targeting era, and inflation rates are often maintained relatively close to the announced inflation target. The variance of inflation has generally been lower than in the pre-inflation-targeting era. In addition, the variance of inflation expectations has also declined, generally speaking, because financial market participants have tended to view many central bank inflation targets as relatively credible commitments. These developments are all in line with what one might expect based on theories that compare a noisy and purely discretionary monetary policy, like the one Meltzer described for the United States during the run-up to the Great Inflation, to a policy based more on a commitment by the central bank about what it intends to achieve.

What would Allan Meltzer say if he were here? My reading of his views is that he would stress that the act of naming a credible inflation target recognizes some fundamental truths—truths that were not recognized in the run-up to the Great Inflation. In particular, it assigns the responsibility for the inflation rate to the central bank. It strongly suggests that inflation is a monetary phenomenon. But it stops short of requiring an implementer of the policy to commit to any particular macroeconomic theory beyond these precepts.

I would add my own view at this point, without trying to implicate Meltzer, as I am not sure he would stress it as much as I do. The point is this: The act of naming an explicit inflation target recognizes the importance of macroeconomic expectations and future policy expectations as being paramount in the monetary policy arena. It is the expectations of future policy that can be unruly and that lead to changes in economic behavior that can, in turn, change the nature of the macroeconomic equilibrium. If expectations are the problem, then a natural way to help tie them down is to credibly commit to an inflation target. This approach has worked admirably for two decades.

One could tie private-sector expectations down still further by credibly committing to a monetary policy rule, such as a Taylor-type rule (Taylor 1993). The Taylor-type rule has the inflation target as a critical component but also specifies how the central bank should respond to various shocks to the economy. Would there be additional gains, on top of those already achieved through the naming of a credible inflation target itself, by a central bank commitment to such a rule? Meltzer thought so, and he testified to that effect before Congress (Meltzer 2015). Others have been opposed, including my long-time colleague and the now outgoing Fed chair Janet Yellen (see Yellen 2015).

TWO INDICATIONS OF MONETARY POLICY QUALITY

How can we decide whether there are additional gains that would accrue to the US economy via monetary policy makers more explicitly adopting a Taylor-type policy rule? Much has been written on this issue. Some of the issues addressed in the literature include the idea that the Taylor-type policy rule is a more model-dependent object and that its policy prescriptions will be valid only in certain model environments. A very real issue, therefore, is the substantial model uncertainty that characterizes today's policy landscape. But instead of rehashing these arguments, I wish to go in a different direction in the remainder of this chapter.[1]

I want to turn now to make an assessment about whether inflation targeting, as implemented implicitly in the United States since 1995 (and explicitly since 2012), has led US policy makers to adopt something we can view as close to optimal monetary policy. If recent monetary policy can be viewed as close to optimal, then attempts to further pin down expectations of future policy actions may be less desirable. If recent monetary policy is viewed as less close to optimal, then further monetary policy commitment may confer important benefits on the economy.

I will proceed by considering two examples. In these examples, the evidence about whether recent monetary policy is close to optimal is somewhat mixed, so the results here are broadly inconclusive. Nevertheless, it is instructive to work through these examples.

To make an assessment of this type requires a model. Since there are many models to choose from, we could simply stop here and say we do not know. But in the spirit of trying to understand a little more about the effects of inflation targeting, I will use a very simple version of a New Keynesian model. See the appendix for details about the ideas behind this model.

THE CASE OF THE DISAPPEARING PHILLIPS CURVE

The first example is the case of the disappearing Phillips curve. Here, we will begin with the empirical evidence neatly summarized in figure 8-1, adapted from the latest annual report of the Bank for International Settlements (BIS 2017; Blanchard 2016). The figure shows the coefficient on a measure of resource slack (unemployment) in a regression of price inflation on resource utilization, using the authors' preferred specification. The coefficient is estimated repeatedly in rolling fifteen-year samples, and the point estimates, along

Figure 8-1. Slope of the Phillips Curve

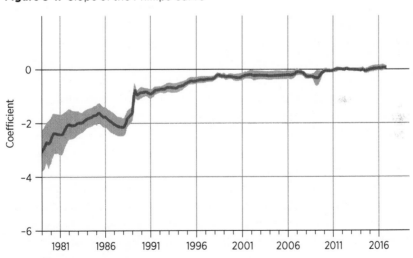

Source: Bank for International Settlements (2017).
Note: The chart shows rolling fifteen-year window estimates and confidence bands from a panel of G-7 economies.

with 90 percent confidence bands, are plotted in the figure. The sample runs from the 1980s to the present. The data are for a panel of G-7 economies, and the point estimate is a weighted average across economies.

The main idea of the figure is that the slope of the Phillips curve was once negative in the 1980s but has been drifting toward zero in the inflation targeting era since 1995. The coefficient has not been different from zero in recent years, hence the disappearing Phillips curve that has been widely discussed in financial markets and in monetary policy circles.

The empirical phenomenon documented in figure 8-1 can be related to the idea that monetary authorities have moved closer to implementing optimal monetary policy during the inflation targeting era.[2] The details of this argument can be found in the appendix, but are described here. I begin with a standard, two-equation, linearized New Keynesian model. I then assume that the monetary policy maker wishes to stabilize a quadratic function of inflation gaps and output gaps over an infinite horizon. I give the policy maker a Taylor-type linear feedback policy rule to work with. I allow the policy maker to choose just one parameter in this feedback rule to minimize the loss function. That single parameter is the coefficient on the inflation gap. We could think of this as representing the weight placed on inflation stabilization versus output stabilization in the Taylor-type rule.

In this simple exercise, the solution to the policy maker's problem is to set the value of the coefficient on the inflation gap to a very large value—technically, infinity. In this situation, optimal monetary policy would call for very low tolerance of deviations of inflation from target. The central bank reacts very aggressively to keep inflation under control.

In this simple model, we can also write out explicitly the value of the regression coefficient in regression of the inflation gap on the output gap, which is the theoretical counterpart of the slope of the Phillips curve in the BIS regression of figure 8-1. The Taylor-type rule coefficient on the inflation gap appears in this formula. As this value tends to infinity, the policy maker is following something closer and closer to optimal policy; at the same time the slope of the Phillips curve is tending toward zero.

This result is one way to state the idea that central banks have become better and better at inflation targeting and that this success has driven the Phillips curve slope to zero. The empirical evidence in figure 8-1 can, therefore, be interpreted as a signature of optimal monetary policy in observable data. Figure 8-1 is saying, in effect, that policy makers have already jumped on the Taylor rule bandwagon during the past two decades.

PRICE LEVEL TARGETING

The second example is price level targeting. I have so far argued that inflation targeting has conferred considerable benefits on the economy. And yet, within the standard New Keynesian model, optimal monetary policy is often characterized as price level targeting or its close cousin, nominal income targeting. In recent years, FOMC members (including me) have discussed both price level and nominal income targeting as a possible future of US monetary policy. A move in this direction would require considerable debate and reflection but might also confer substantial benefits on the US economy if it could be implemented effectively.

If we simply take as given that price level targeting is optimal policy within the New Keynesian construct, a signature in the US data of optimal monetary policy would be whether the price level in the United States follows a prescribed price level path. If it does, then the FOMC has been de facto price level targeting even if the committee has not officially said that it has been doing so. The hallmark of price level targeting is that periods of below-target inflation are averaged out with other periods of above-target inflation in such a way that the economy remains on a price level path consistent with a given inflation rate.

In the price level targeting world, the starting date matters. I have already argued that 1995 is the point at which the Volcker-era inflation stabilization came to full fruition, and that from that point on, the FOMC attempted to maintain a 2 percent inflation target. But did the committee do even more, implicitly attempting to keep the US economy on a 2 percent price level path?

In the fall of 2012, I argued that the FOMC had kept the United States on a 2 percent price level path since 1995 and that this was an outstanding achievement given the global financial crisis during the intervening years (Bullard 2012a, 2012b). Again, at least as of 2012, the actual implementation of US monetary policy could be viewed as optimal. By itself, this would suggest there would be little to be gained from additional monetary policy commitments by the central bank. However, as figure 8-2 illustrates, in the past five years, the United States has fallen off the 2 percent price level path established in 1995. The deviation from the path is now fairly substantial, about 4.6 percent on the low side. Recent FOMC forecasts do not seem to anticipate enough inflation to return the economy to the 2 percent path. Therefore, we will have to conclude that monetary policy has not been optimal from this perspective.

Figure 8-2. The US Price Level Path

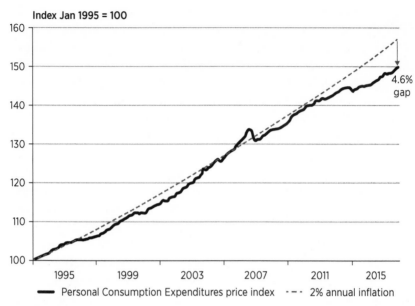

Sources: Bureau of Economic Analysis and author's calculations. Last observation: November 2017.
Note: De facto price level targeting occurred from the mid-1990s to 2012, but the actual price level has since fallen off the price level path.

SUMMARY AND CONCLUSION

I have ruminated on Allan Meltzer's excellent career by casting it in terms of a search for a nominal anchor for the United States. I took as a starting point Meltzer's last article for the St. Louis Fed's *Review*, "Origins of the Great Inflation." That article, a precursor to Meltzer's much larger work, volume 2 of *HFR*, suggests that during the period of the run-up to the Great Inflation there was no coherent monetary policy framework. This lack of coherence may have left monetary policy susceptible to influences other than those from monetary science, such as the influence of politics.

Today, some five decades later, there remains a great deal of theoretical and empirical uncertainty about the effects of monetary policy on the economy. And yet, despite this uncertainty, the United States and many other countries have been able to achieve low and stable inflation and, if anything, have faced a problem of inflation being lower than promised instead of higher than promised, as in the 1970s and early 1980s. How was the nominal anchor found, and what was it?

My answer is that it has been inflation targeting, practiced either implicitly or explicitly. This may not have been the answer many economists were expecting during the earlier portions of the postwar era; ideas then revolved around constant money growth, low fiscal deficits, or the level of short-term nominal interest rates. Inflation targeting has worked well because it deals more directly with the coordination of macroeconomic expectations than do other approaches. By committing to an inflation target, policy makers have generally kept inflation lower and less variable, and inflation expectations have also been less variable. This has been a major achievement of US monetary policy and one to which Meltzer made an outsized contribution.

If the naming of a credible inflation target coordinates expectations and helps inform the macroeconomic equilibrium, then perhaps further coordination can be achieved by being even more explicit about the future actions of monetary policy makers. One method of doing this would be for the central bank to commit to using a Taylor-type monetary policy rule. Whether this would confer added benefits would depend on whether one thinks there are, in fact, additional gains to be had for the economy by more tightly buttoning down future expectations of monetary policy.

Such questions cannot really be answered without the assistance of a macroeconomic model. But if we go ahead with a popular and simple version of the New Keynesian model, we can consider two examples of what optimal policy would look like and how it compares to actual monetary policy outcomes during the inflation targeting era. The example of the disappearing Phillips curve example suggests that actual US monetary policy has tended to be closer and closer to optimal in the past two decades, and that this has, in fact, killed off the Phillips curve correlation previously apparent in the data. The price level targeting example suggests that US monetary policy was close to optimal between 1995 and 2012 but has since fallen away somewhat.

Whether we can do better than these two examples suggest, or whether the available gains have largely accrued already via the commitment to inflation targeting implicitly made in the United States in the 1990s, remains an important question for future research. I am sure that research will continue to be influenced by the enormous contributions of Allan Meltzer.

APPENDIX

Consider the linearized equations of the standard New Keynesian model:[3]

$$y_t = E_t Y_{t+1} - \frac{1}{\sigma}[i_t - (\rho + \varepsilon_t) - E_t \pi_{t+1}],$$

$$\pi_t = \kappa y_t + \beta E_t \pi_{t+1} + u_t,$$

where y_t is the output gap, π_t is the inflation gap, and $(\rho + \varepsilon_t)$ is the natural real rate; ε_t and u_t are a natural rate and a cost-push shock, respectively. The two shocks are i.i.d. and have variance σ_ε^2 and σ_u^2, respectively. Monetary policy is the choice of the nominal interest rate set according to a standard Taylor-type linear feedback policy rule:

$$i_t = \rho + \phi_\pi \pi_t + \phi_y y_t.$$

Assuming that the Taylor principle is satisfied, the rational expectations equilibrium indicates that the evolution of the output gap and inflation can be represented as linear functions of the shocks, and that this evolution also depends on the policy parameters in the Taylor-type policy rule:

$$y_t = \frac{\varepsilon_t - \phi_\pi u_t}{\sigma + \phi_y + \kappa \phi_\pi},$$

$$\pi_t = \frac{\kappa \varepsilon_t + (\sigma + \phi_y) u_t}{\sigma + \phi_y + \kappa \phi_\pi}.$$

Optimal policy can be viewed in a variety of ways, but let's suppose we view constrained optimal monetary policy as the choice of the Taylor rule coefficient on the inflation gap, keeping the Taylor rule coefficient on the output gap fixed. This might be interpreted as the policy maker's degree of attention to deviations of inflation from target, relative to the degree of attention to output gap developments in the Taylor-type rule. The policy maker then chooses this coefficient optimally to minimize a loss function of the form

$$(1 - \beta) \sum_{t=0}^{\infty} \beta^t (\alpha \pi_t^2 + y_t^2),$$

where α is positive and represents the relative weight on the desirability of inflation stabilization compared to output stabilization in the eyes of the policy maker. The value of this parameter could be high or low, encompassing policy makers who might prefer more or less output stabilization versus inflation stabilization. It turns out that regardless of the value of α, the solution to this problem indicates that optimal policy requires a large coefficient on the inflation gap: that is, $\phi_\pi \to \infty$. What are the implications of this finding for the slope of the Phillips curve in such a model? The slope of the Phillips curve—that is, the coefficient on the output gap in a regression of the inflation gap on the output gap—is given by

$$\gamma = \frac{Cov(\pi_t, y_t)}{Var(y_t)} = \frac{\kappa\sigma_\varepsilon^2 - \phi_\pi(\sigma + \phi_y)\sigma_u^2}{\sigma_\varepsilon^2 + \phi_\pi^2\sigma_u^2}.$$

We can take the limit of the right-hand side of this expression to deduce that, under optimal monetary policy as described above, the Phillips curve becomes flat: $\lim_{\phi_\pi \to \infty} \gamma = 0$.

NOTES

1. For more on my views concerning the Taylor rule, see Bullard (2017).

2. Christian Gillitzer and John Simon (2015) relate the flattening of the Phillips curve in Australia to inflation targeting. Olivier Blanchard (2017) points to inflation targeting as one of the possible explanations for the disappearing Phillips curve.

3. For a textbook treatment of the standard New Keynesian model, see Woodford (2003).

REFERENCES

Bank for International Settlements. 2017. *87th Annual Report*. Basel, Switzerland: BIS, June 25.

Blanchard, Olivier. 2016. "The US Phillips Curve: Back to the 60s?" Peterson Institute for International Economics Policy Brief PB16-1, January.

———. 2017. "Should We Reject the Natural Rate Hypothesis?" Peterson Institute for International Economics Working Paper 17-14, November.

Bullard, James. 2012a. "Price Level Targeting: The Fed Has It about Right." Remarks, Economic Club of Memphis, October 4. Speech 205, Federal Reserve Bank of St. Louis.

———. 2012b. "A Singular Achievement of Recent Monetary Policy." Invited lecture, University of Notre Dame, September 20. Speech 204, Federal Reserve Bank of St. Louis.

———. 2017. "The Policy Role Debate: A Simpler Solution." President's Message in the Federal Reserve Bank of St. Louis. *Regional Economist*, First Quarter, 3.

Gillitzer, Christian, and John Simon. 2015. "Inflation Targeting: A Victim of Its Own Success." *International Journal of Central Banking* 11, Suppl. 1 (September): 259–87.

Meltzer, Allan H. 1969. "Controlling Money." *Review* (Federal Reserve Bank of St. Louis), May, 16–24.

———. 2002. *A History of the Federal Reserve*. Vol. 1, *1913–1951*. Chicago: University of Chicago Press.

———. 2005. "Origins of the Great Inflation." *Review* (Federal Reserve Bank of St. Louis) 87, no. 2, part 2 (March/April): 145–75.

———. 2010. *A History of the Federal Reserve*. Vol. 2, *1951–1986*. Chicago: University of Chicago Press.

———. 2015. "Federal Reserve Accountability and Reform." Testimony before the Senate Committee on Banking, Housing, and Urban Affairs, first session on "Examining the

Accountability of the Federal Reserve System to Congress and the American Public," March 3.

Taylor, John B. 1993. "Discretion versus Policy Rules in Practice." *Carnegie-Rochester Conference Series on Public Policy* 39 (December): 195–214.

Woodford, Michael. 2003. *Interest and Prices.* Princeton, NJ: Princeton University Press.

Yellen, Janet L. 2015. "Letter from Chair Yellen to House Speaker Ryan and House Minority Leader Pelosi." November 16. https://www.federalreserve.gov/foia/files/ryan-pelosi-letter-20151116 .pdf.

CHAPTER 9
The Meltzer Commission
GERALD P. O'DRISCOLL JR.

The International Financial Institution Advisory Commission was created by Congress as a response to a series of financial crises beginning with the Mexican Crisis of 1994–1995, followed by the Asian Crisis of 1997–1998 and the Russian Crisis of 1999. The United States Treasury and international financial institutions became involved in various official bailouts. The International Monetary Fund had to be recapitalized along the way.

The newly resurgent Republican Congress eventually went along with the bailouts, but at a price. The price was a commission to look at the role of the international financial institutions and consider reform proposals. As political processes go, the commission came together relatively quickly. Congress took time to name the commissioners, with the Republicans naming six and the Democrats five.

The Heritage Foundation played an important strategic role in the creation of the commission. I started working at Heritage in January 1999. Heritage advised on the Republican nominees. The commission was ready to be up and running in the fall of 1999. Then William E. Simon, the designated chair, had to resign for health reasons. Heritage president Ed Feulner called me into his office for advice on whom to recommend as a new member and chair, and I responded that he had the ideal candidate for chair already on the commission: Allan Meltzer. He asked me why.

I told Ed about attending the Shadow Open Market Committee as an observer. The meetings were instructive and illuminating. Aside from the substance, I marveled at Allan's performance as chair. As I told Ed, getting academics to agree on a policy directive was like herding cats. Allan had that skill, and we would need it for the commission.

The Republican side was still down a member, however. When Ed asked for a name, I suggested Lee Hoskins. Lee had recently retired from Huntington Bank and moved to the Reno, Nevada, area. It became my job to recruit Lee, and I did so successfully. Then I was called back into Ed's office to be informed that Allan had agreed to be chair on one condition: that I serve as his chief of staff. My job at Heritage was being the senior editor of the Index of Economic Freedom, and I could not be released from it. So I had talked myself into having two full-time jobs, of which only one paid.

Almost immediately Allan made one critical decision. This was to ally with Jeff Sachs to produce a bipartisan report. Jeff was one of the Democratic commissioners and soon took on a leadership role. From the beginning, the danger was that the commission would split six to five on a partisan vote and the commission's recommendations would go nowhere. An early straw vote demonstrated that this would, in fact, be the outcome if the commission operated in a partisan fashion.

Allan made a second, very important decision, and that was to hire Adam Lerrick as special adviser to the chairman. I do not know how we could have done all we did in six months without Adam's expertise and work ethic. Allan's hiring of Adam the way he did could have undermined my position as chief of staff, but Adam always kept me in the loop about what he was doing for the chair. It was a perfect working arrangement. To this day, he and I are friends.

The commission had a six-month life span, with the clock starting from its first official, public meeting. In that six months, we had to hold all our hearings, commission expert papers, and write the report. There were also a series of private, off-the-record policy dinners with senior officials from the Treasury and the international financial institutions. We had an impossible task. The only way to accomplish it was to begin writing the report as the hearings were being held, the papers rolled in, and the dinners were held.

Our task was made more difficult by the attitude of the Clinton administration. Though officially cooperative, the Clinton Treasury threw up obstacles at every turn. There was one extremely tense meeting with Larry Summers, Allan, and their respective staffs. And I had a very tense, one-on-one meeting with Tim Geithner.

My job was mainly to keep the trains running on time, though I did also testify and provide policy input. Heritage provided crucial logistical and staff support, among other contributions.

Ed Feulner was one of the commissioners, and the project was a personal and institutional priority. I had a tense meeting with Ed at one point because he and the chair were at odds over a key decision. I backed the chair, and Ed called me on the carpet over it. I told Ed I did not work for him on the commission but for the chair. Ed backed down—something he did not often do.

The dinners were mainly pleasant and productive. The official institutions sent observers to our hearings, and Adam and I established rapport with them. They slowly realized we were engaged in a serious effort and were not going to do a hatchet job, and the official institutions became cooperative.

Gradually, the commission came to be known not by its official name, but simply as the Meltzer Commission. That reflected the will and intellectual leadership of the chair. Much of the testimony was of high quality, as were the papers. All of these are preserved in the public record (Senate Committee on Foreign Relations 2000). Allan's long-time assistant, Alberta Reagan, recently arranged for the printed report and papers to be scanned.

The commission voted eight to three for the majority report. Two Democrat members, Jeff Sachs and Richard Huber, voted with the Republican majority. The Meltzer-Sachs strategy succeeded.

> The Commission also voted unanimously that (1) the International Monetary Fund, the World Bank and the regional development banks should write-off in their entirety all claims against heavily indebted poor countries (HIPC) that implement an effective economic and social strategy in conjunction with the World Bank and the regional development institutions, and (2) the International Monetary Fund should restrict its lending to the provision of short-term liquidity. The current practice of extending long-term loans for poverty reduction and other purposes should end. (Senate Committee on Foreign Relations 2000, 2)

The recommendation on HIPCs in particular gained the report a favorable reception among organizations like Oxfam (Global Policy Forum 2000). The report was also generally well received among Republicans. As was noted during the hearings, private lending and investment had already largely undermined the rationale of official development institutions. Markets have gone a long way toward eliminating extreme poverty worldwide. The World Bank at least now recognizes the crucial role of markets (see, for example the World Bank topic pages for "Poverty" [https://www.worldbank.org/en/topic/poverty] and "Markets and Competition Policy" [https://www.worldbank.org/en/topic/competition-policy]).

Whatever one's view of the commission's contribution, the majority report was largely shaped by Allan Meltzer. Indeed, the fact there was any report at all is due to his efforts.

REFERENCES

Global Policy Forum. 2000. "Reforming the IMF." https://www.globalpolicy.org/component/content/article/209/43155.html.

Senate Committee on Foreign Relations. 2000. *The Meltzer Commission: The Future of the IMF and World Bank.* May 23.

CHAPTER 10
Memories of Allan Meltzer

ROBERT E. LUCAS JR.

I want to tell one story about Allan Meltzer, and then I will get to work. Back in the heyday of the Vietnam War and the radical '70s, Noam Chomsky was invited to speak to a large audience at Carnegie Mellon University. I heard that Allan had agreed to debate him. Chomsky was a committed Marxist, as well as a spellbinding speaker, and a completely unscrupulous attacker of anyone who disagreed with him. I tried to convince Allan not to do it. "He's going to kill you! He'll say anything to make you look stupid or evil." Allan said that might be so but he thought our students should know that at least some of their teachers weren't convinced by Chomsky.

Isn't that just how we all remember Allan, concerned with what he saw as the right thing to do and not at all with his applause ratings? And, contrary to my fears, he did fine.

In those days, Allan's work was focused on time-series econometrics and monetary theory. In the 1930s, Simon Kuznets (1937) had produced time series for segments of the US economy, broken down into well-defined pieces that added up to an entire economy as well as all the earned returns that accrued to those who made it happen. These time series, called the "national income and product accounts," provided an ongoing picture of an entire economy and its components of consumption and production. After the 1929 crash, these time series were used to try to make sense of its aftermath. Keynes himself was excited by the possibilities. Jan Tinbergen, Lawrence Klein, and others

Figure 10-1. Money Supply Growth outside the US

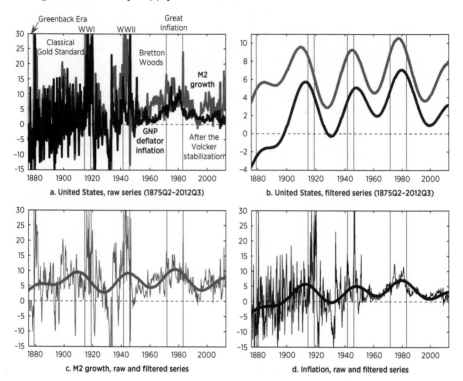

a. United States, raw series (1875Q2–2012Q3)

b. United States, filtered series (1875Q2–2012Q3)

c. M2 growth, raw and filtered series

d. Inflation, raw and filtered series

Source: Panels a and b are from Luca Benati, "Long Run Evidence on Money Growth and Inflation" (Working Paper Series No. 1027, European Central Bank, March 2009). Panels c and d are courtesy of Luca Benati.

made use of the aggregate US time series of real variables that Kuznets had created as a description of how the US economy worked over time. Until the postwar period, the only available high-quality data were Kuznets's carefully constructed series. These time series permanently changed the way we all think about economics.

But the Kuznets data had no room for the monetary forces that Milton Friedman, Phillip Cagan, Karl Brunner, and Allan Meltzer thought were important to the economy. These economists wanted to create time series on money and monetary variables that could be used alongside the Kuznets series. Cagan's 1956 studies of hyperinflations in the two world wars was and is a classic, but it involved specialized time series that were very different from the US data. Meltzer's (1959) study of French money supply had just been completed but

Figure 10-2. Different Measures of US Money Supply

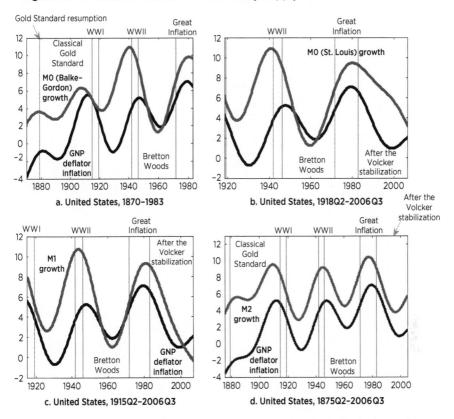

a. United States, 1870–1983

b. United States, 1918Q2–2006Q3

c. United States, 1915Q2–2006Q3

d. United States, 1875Q2–2006Q3

Source: Luca Benati, "Long-Run Evidence on Money Growth and Inflation," *Bank of England Quarterly Bulletin*, Autumn 2005, 349–55.

also was not quite what was needed for the United States. Then, in the early 1960s, Friedman and Anna Schwartz put together time series on the US money supply from the end of the Civil War through the 1950s. With the Friedman-Schwartz data, it seemed possible to put the real and nominal time series together. Brunner and Meltzer had already developed theoretical models that might do this. All that was needed was to spell out the role of money in the production process: not an easy problem, but not, you might think, an impossible one, either.

But Friedman did not want to do this. There are many valuable discussions of economic behavior in his book with Schwartz, but nothing we would call a

Figure 10-3. Various Monthly Yields and the Zero Lower Bound

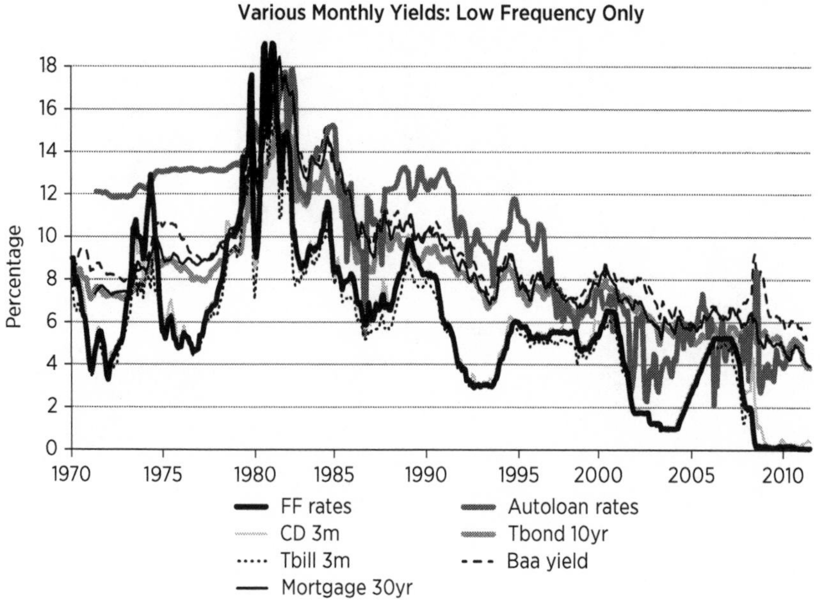

Various Monthly Yields: Low Frequency Only

Legend:
- —— FF rates
- ⋯⋯ CD 3m
- ····· Tbill 3m
- —— Mortgage 30yr
- ～～ Autoloan rates
- ▬▬ Tbond 10yr
- - - - Baa yield

Source: Updated from Hwagyun Hagen Kim, "Common and Idiosyncratic Fluctuations of Interest Rates from Various Issuers: A Dynamic Factor Approach" (PhD diss., University of Chicago, 2003). Used with permission.

theoretical model. Instead, this task was undertaken by Meltzer's 1963 article in the *Journal of Political Economy*, "The Demand for Money: The Evidence from the Time Series." This paper combined the Kuznets data on real variables with the monetary variables from Friedman and Schwartz.

Why hadn't Friedman done this himself? Meltzer's 1963 paper has a long section on this—he certainly had a deep respect for Friedman—but he was not convinced by Friedman's reasoning in this particular case. Instead, he described and defended his own quantitative vision of the demand for money. The basic formula is what we call the Baumol-Tobin model. Meltzer's contribution, as he made clear, was to define the variables involved and then to verify their stability over the 1900–1958 years of his data set.

What made his 1963 paper so distinctive is that it was a test of a specific theoretical model. The model basically required that changes in the supply of money in circulation play out as changes in inflation and not as changes in production. Obviously, this cannot be true on a day-to-day or even a year-to-year basis, but Meltzer used the years from 1900 to 1958 and found a consistent average relationship over these two variables. (I should add that in 1963 the meaning of "the supply of money" was not yet settled.) In fact, Meltzer explored a number of possibilities in his 1963 paper; this was new territory. From 1958 on, other economists have developed and extended Meltzer's data up to 1990 and beyond. Marvin Goodfriend and Bennett McCallum's (1987) paper introduced a version that many of us have adopted. There is still plenty of room for disagreement, but we have gone a long way from discussing theoretical possibilities to testing our opinions against hard evidence. Meltzer's work showed how we could do this for monetary as well as real (in Kuznets's sense) variables.

For the 100th anniversary of Brunner's birth in 2016, Meltzer wrote "An Appreciation" (Meltzer 2015) that contains many of the highlights of their joint studies of the interactions of real and monetary variables. Since I have focused here on Meltzer's early work, I thought it might be useful to see how he viewed the results of fifty more years of data. One comment that caught my eye was his belief that "economics is not the science that produces good quarterly forecasts. There is no such science. . . . Much of monthly and quarterly data is dominated by random changes." Nothing like this appears in the 1963 paper, but Meltzer liked to be close to the data, and facts are facts.

The accompanying figures, courtesy of Luca Benati, University of Bern, focus exclusively on the relation of growth of the money supply to the inflation rate at low frequencies. Figure 10-1 compares the effects of both high and low frequencies. Figure 10-2 illustrates different measures of the money supply. I think they support Meltzer's conclusion that "there is no such science" (at high frequencies). But they also show that the long-run connections of inflation and money supplies stand up well over time and space. I think, and so, I believe, did Meltzer, that it is simply foolishness to ignore these solid facts.

In the "Appreciation" paper, Meltzer wrote, "I was surprised, as I am sure Karl [Brunner] would have been, by the large volume of research on the so-called lower bound. As the QE programs at the Federal Reserve and other central banks showed, a zero short-term interest rate did not prevent monetary expansion. . . . The so-called zero lower bound turned out to bind very little other than very short-term rates."

We can see in figure 10-3 the clear distinction between the money-market rates and the rest. This distinction was something Brunner and Meltzer had often said was essential, but did they ever spell out the details? Has anyone else done so? I wish I had had the wits to ask them when they were still with us. They were always pushing us on to the hard problems that really matter.

In the remainder of this chapter, I'll discuss Meltzer's brief but remarkable 2009 testimony to the Subcommittee on Monetary Policy of the House

Committee of Financial Services (Meltzer 2009). The context was a discussion of what became the Dodd-Frank Act, made law the following year. I'm sure that everyone remembers his quip that "capitalism without failure is like religion without sin," but this testimony is no joke. You really have to read the whole thing. The writing itself is extraordinary: short, crystal-clear sentences listing historical facts and posing important questions. In just a few pages, he explains why an economy's banking system needs a lender of last resort, why the lending has to be an advanced commitment, what kind of commitments will actually be carried out under pressure and what kind will not, and why a commitment must include the failure of some banks under some conditions. He explains what can be done to avoid the spread of panic contagion to other banks. These proposals are not simply laid out on the table. There are many concrete examples drawn from his knowledge of Fed history. There are pointed questions to the reader about likely responses to proposals by Congress, banks, and lobbyists. Of course, this statement to Congress is free of economic jargon, but this is no dumbing down for the uninformed. It is easy for any economist to see the logic of the statement and, to me, this logic seemed new and promising and head-and-shoulders over the bloat of Dodd-Frank.

APPENDIX: REGULATORY REFORM AND THE FEDERAL RESERVE

Allan H. Meltzer

The Allan H. Meltzer University Professor of Political Economy and Visiting Scholar at the American Enterprise Institute

Testimony, July 9, 2009, Subcommittee on Monetary Policy, House Committee on Financial Services

Thank you for the opportunity to present my appraisal of the administration's proposal for regulatory changes. I will confine most of my comments to the role of the Federal Reserve as a systemic regulator and will offer an alternative proposal. I share the belief that change is needed and long delayed, but appropriate change must protect the public, not bankers.

During much of the past fifteen years, I have written three volumes titled *A History of the Federal Reserve*. Working with two assistants, we have read virtually all of the minutes of the Board of Governors, the Federal Open Market Committee, and the Directors of the Federal Reserve Bank of New York. We have also read many of the staff papers and internal memos supporting decisions. I speak from that perspective.

Two findings are very relevant to the role of the Federal Reserve. First, I do not know of any clear examples in which the Federal Reserve acted in advance to head off a crisis or a series of banking or financial failures. We know that the Federal Reserve did nothing about thrift industry failures in the 1980s. Thrift failures cost taxpayers $150 billion. AIG, Fannie, and Freddie will be much more costly. Of course, the Fed did not have responsibility for the thrift industry, but many thrift failures posed a threat to the financial system that the Fed should have tried to mitigate. The disastrous outcome was not a mystery that appeared without warning.

Peter Wallison, Alan Greenspan, Bill Poole, Senator Shelby, and others warned about the excessive risks taken by Fannie and Freddie, but Congress failed to legislate. Why should anyone expect a systemic risk regulator to get requisite congressional action under similar circumstances? Can you expect the Federal Reserve as systemic risk regulator to close Fannie and Freddie after Congress declines to act?

Conflicts of this kind, and others, suggest that that the administration's proposal is incomplete. Defining "systemic risk" is an essential but missing part of the proposal. Trying to define the authority of the regulatory authority when Congress has expressed an interest points up a major conflict.

During the Latin American debt crisis, the Federal Reserve acted to hide the failures and losses at money center banks by arranging with the IMF to pay the interest on Latin debt to those banks. This served to increase the debt that the governments owed, but it kept the banks from reporting portfolio losses and prolonged the debt crisis. The crisis ended after one of the New York banks decided to write off the debt and take the loss. Others followed. Later, the Treasury offered the Brady plans. The Federal Reserve did nothing.

In the dot-com crisis of the late 1990s, we know the Federal Reserve was aware of the growing problem, but it did not act until after the crisis occurred. Later, Chairman Greenspan recognized that it was difficult to detect systemic failures in advance. He explained that the Federal Reserve believed it should act after the crisis, not before. Intervention to control soaring asset prices would impose large social costs of unemployment, so the Federal Reserve, as systemic risk regulator, would be unwise to act.

The dot-com problem brings out that there are crises for which the Federal Reserve cannot be effective. Asset market exuberance and supply shocks, like oil price increases, are nonmonetary so cannot be prevented by even the most astute, far-seeing central bank.

We all know that the Federal Reserve did nothing to prevent the current credit crisis.

Before the crisis, it kept interest rates low during part of the period and did not police the use that financial markets made of the reserves it supplied. The Board has admitted that it did not do enough to prevent the crisis. It has not recognized that its actions promoted moral hazard and encouraged incentives to take risk. Many bankers talked openly about a "Greenspan put," their belief that the Federal Reserve would prevent or absorb major losses.

It was the Reconstruction Finance Corporation, not the Fed, that restructured banks in the 1930s. The Fed did not act promptly to prevent market failure during the 1970 Penn Central failure, the Lockheed and Chrysler problems, or on other occasions. In 2008, the Fed assisted in salvaging Bear Stearns. This continued the too-big-to-fail (TBTF) policy and increased moral hazard. Then without warning, the Fed departed from the course it had followed for at least thirty years and allowed Lehman to fail in the midst of widespread financial uncertainty. This was a major error. It deepened and lengthened the current deep recession.

In 1990–1991, the Fed kept the spread between short- and long-term interest rates large enough to assist many banks to rebuild their capital and surplus. This is a rare possible exception, a case in which Federal Reserve action to delay an increase in the short-term rate may have prevented banking failures.

Second, in its ninety-six-year history, the Federal Reserve has never announced a lender-of-last-resort policy. It has discussed internally the content of such a policy several times, but it rarely announced what it would do. And the announcements it made, as in 1987, were limited to the circumstances of the time. Announcing and following a policy would alert financial institutions to the Fed's expected actions and might reduce pressures on Congress to aid failing entities.

Following the rule in a crisis would change bankers' incentives and reduce moral hazard. A crisis policy rule is long overdue. The administration proposal recognizes this need.

A lender-of-last-resort rule is the right way to implement policy in a crisis. We know from monetary history that in the nineteenth century the Bank of England followed Bagehot's rule for a half-century or more. The rule committed the Bank to lend on "good" collateral at a penalty rate during periods of market disturbance. Prudent bankers borrowed from the Bank of England and held collateral to be used in a panic. Banks that lacked collateral failed.

Financial panics occurred. The result of following Bagehot's rule in crises was that the crises did not spread and did not last long. There were bank failures but no systemic failures. Prudent bankers borrowed and paid depositors cash or gold. Bank deposits were not insured until much later, so bank runs could cause systemic failures. Most bankers were prudent and held more capital and reserves in relation to their size than banks currently do, and they held more collateral to use in a crisis also.

These experiences suggest three main lessons. First, we cannot avoid banking failures, but we can keep them from spreading and creating crises. Second, neither the Federal Reserve nor any other agency has succeeded in predicting crises or anticipating systemic failure. It is hard to do, in part because systemic risk is not well defined. Reasonable people will differ, and since much is often at stake, some will fight hard to deny that there is a systemic risk.

One of the main reasons that Congress in 1991 passed FDICIA (Federal Deposit Insurance Corporation Improvement Act) was to prevent the Federal Reserve from delaying closure of failing banks, increasing losses and weakening the FDIC fund. The Federal Reserve and the FDIC have not used FDICIA against large banks in this crisis. That should change.

The third lesson is that a successful policy will alter bankers' incentives and avoid moral hazard. Bankers must know that risk-taking brings both rewards and costs, including failure, loss of managerial position and equity followed by sale of continuing operations.

AN ALTERNATIVE PROPOSAL

Several reforms are needed to reduce or eliminate the cost of financial failure to the taxpayers. Members of Congress should ask themselves and each other: Is the banker or the regulator more likely to know about the risks on a bank's balance sheet? Of course it is the banker, and especially so if the banker is taking large risks that he wants to hide. To me, that means that reform should start by increasing a banker's responsibility for losses. The administration's proposal does the opposite by making the Federal Reserve responsible for systemic risk.

Systemic risk is a term of art. I doubt that it can be defined in a way that satisfies the many parties involved in regulation. Members of Congress will urge that any large failure in their district is systemic. Administrations and regulators will have other objectives. Without a clear definition, the proposal will bring frequent controversy. And without a clear definition, the proposal is incomplete.

Resolving the conflicting interests is unlikely to protect the general public. More likely, regulators will claim that they protect the public by protecting the banks.

The administration's proposal sacrifices much of the remaining independence of the Federal Reserve. Congress, the administration, and failing banks or firms will want to influence decisions about what is to be bailed out. I believe that is a mistake. If we use our capital to avoid failures instead of promoting growth we not only reduce growth in living standards, we also sacrifice a socially valuable arrangement—central bank independence. We encourage excessive risk-taking and moral hazard.

I believe there are better alternatives than the administration's proposal.

First step: End TBTF. Require all financial institutions to increase capital more than in proportion to their increase in size of assets. TBTF is perverse. It allows banks to profit in good times and shifts the losses to the taxpayers when crises or failures occur.

My proposal reduces the profits from giant size and increases incentives for prudent banker behavior by putting losses back to managements and stockholders where they belong. Benefits of size come from economies of size and scale. These benefits to society are more than offset by the losses society takes in periods of crisis. Congress should find it hard to defend a system that distributes profits and losses as TBTF does. I believe that the public will not choose to maintain that system forever. Permitting losses does not eliminate services; failure means that management loses its position and stockholders take the losses. Profitable operations continue and are sold at the earliest opportunity.

Second step: Require the Federal Reserve to announce a rule for lender-of-last-resort. Congress should adopt the rule that they are willing to sustain. The rule should give banks an incentive to hold collateral to be used in a crisis period. Bagehot's rule is a great place to start.

Third step: Recognize that regulation is an ineffective way to change behavior. My first rule of regulation states that lawyers regulate but markets circumvent burdensome regulation.

The Basel Accord is an example. Banks everywhere had to increase capital when they increased balance sheet risk. The banks responded by creating entities that were not on their balance sheet. Later, banks had to absorb the losses, but that was after the crisis. There are many other examples of circumvention from Federal Reserve history. The reason we have money market funds was that Fed regulation Q restricted the interest that the public could earn. Money market funds bought unregulated, large certificates of deposit. For a small fee, they shared the higher interest rate with the public. Much later, Congress agreed to end interest rate regulation. The money funds remained.

Fourth step: Recognize that regulators do not allow for the incentives induced by their regulations. In the dynamic financial markets it is difficult, perhaps impossible, to anticipate how clever market participants will circumvent the rules without violating them. The lesson is to focus on incentives, not prohibitions. Shifting losses back to the bankers is the most powerful incentive because it changes the risk-return trade-off that bankers and stockholders see.

Fifth step: Either extend FDICIA to include holding companies or subject financial holding companies to bankruptcy law. Make the holding company subject to early intervention either under FDICIA or under bankruptcy law. That not only reduces or eliminates taxpayer losses, but it also encourages prudential behavior.

Other important changes should be made. Congress should close Fannie Mae and Freddie Mac and put any subsidy for low-income housing on the budget. The same should be done to other credit market subsidies. The budget is the proper place for subsidies.

Congress, the regulators, and the administration should encourage financial firms to change their compensation systems to tie compensation to sustained average earnings.

Compensation decisions are too complex for regulation and too easy to circumvent. Decisions should be management's responsibility. Part of the change should reward due diligence by traders. We know that rating agencies contributed to failures. The rating problem would be lessened if users practiced diligence of their own.

Three principles should be borne in mind. First, banks borrow short and lend long. Unanticipated large changes can and will cause failures. Our problem is to minimize the cost of failures to society. Second, remember that capitalism without failure is like religion without sin. It removes incentives for prudent behavior. Third, those that rely on regulation to reduce risk should recall that this is the age of Madoff. The Fed, too, lacks a record of success in managing large risks to the financial system, the economy and the public. Incentives for fraud, evasion, and circumvention of regulation often have been far more powerful than incentives to enforce regulation that protects the public.

REFERENCES

Cagan, Phillip. 1956. "The Monetary Dynamics of Hyperinflation." In *Studies in the Quantity Theory of Money*, edited by Milton Friedman, 25–117. Chicago: University of Chicago Press.

Goodfriend, Marvin, and Bennett McCallum. 1987. "Money: Theoretical Analysis of the Demand for Money." NBER Working Paper No. 2157, National Bureau of Economic Research, Cambridge, MA.

Kuznets, Simon. 1937. *National Income and Capital Formation, 1919–1935*. Cambridge, MA: National Bureau of Economic Research.

Meltzer, Allan H. 1963. "The Demand for Money: The Evidence from the Time Series." *Journal of Political Economy* 71, no. 3 (June): 219–46.

———. 2009. "Regulatory Reform and the Federal Reserve." Testimony before the House Committee on Financial Services, Subcommittee on Monetary Policy. American Enterprise Institute, Washington, DC, July 9. http://www.aei.org/publication/regulatory-reform-and -the-federal-reserve/.

———. 2015. "Karl Brunner, Scholar: An Appreciation." Economics Working Paper 15116, Hoover Institution, Stanford University, Stanford, CA, October.

CHAPTER 11
Allan Meltzer's Contributions to Public Policy Thought as Applied to the Federal Reserve

CHARLES I. PLOSSER

I am delighted to have the opportunity to share with you some thoughts on Allan Meltzer's contributions to public policy, particularly as they pertain to the Federal Reserve and monetary policy. I also want to express my appreciation to Scott Sumner and the Institute for Humane Studies for organizing this tribute to a scholar and friend whose interests and contributions spanned economics, philosophy, law, and political economy.

I first met Allan in the winter of 1978; he was visiting the Hoover Institution at Stanford University with his teacher, long-time friend, and collaborator, Karl Brunner. I was a young assistant professor at the Stanford Graduate School of Business. Karl, of course, was at the University of Rochester, and Allan was at Carnegie Mellon University. It was during this period that Karl, along with Robert Barro, who was also visiting Hoover, recruited me to go to Rochester. Because of Karl's close association with Allan, I was fortunate to see Allan regularly, particularly at the Carnegie-Rochester conferences.

More than many academic economists, Karl and Allan had a deep interest in policy issues. Together they created the Shadow Open Market Committee (SOMC) in 1971. It was intended as a venue to offer insights on monetary policy from a group of mostly academic economists and to make these insights accessible to the press and the broader public. They felt that scholarly work could and should inform and improve policy decisions. I was fortunate to join the SOMC some years later, and I watched and learned from Allan. Later I cochaired the group with Anna Schwartz.

But Karl and Allan's interest in public policy extended in many directions. They started the Carnegie-Rochester Conference Series on Public Policy in the early 1970s with the explicit objective of stimulating interest among academic economists in public policy issues. The work of Robert Lucas (1976) on evaluating policies in a rational expectations world and John Taylor's (1993) work on monetary policy rules were seminal contributions to policy analysis that were presented at Carnegie-Rochester conferences. Indeed, John tells the story of how Allan encouraged him to write what came to be that seminal paper on policy rules. John claims that Allan specifically asked him to write a paper on rules for the conference and gave him lots of encouragement along the way. He says it was a paper that would not have been written without Allan's prodding and encouragement.

Karl and Allan particularly wanted to engage younger economists in public policy discussions and research. They did so by continually seeking and supporting young scholars to attend and participate in various ways in the conference. Both the SOMC and the Carnegie-Rochester conferences continue to this day and are a testament to the foresight and commitment of Allan and Karl to public policy research.

Allan's work on political economy issues with Scott Richard and Alex Cukierman (Meltzer and Richard 1981; Cukierman and Meltzer 1986) further points to his theoretical interests in public policy. That work placed him squarely in the tradition of James Buchanan and others in trying to understand policy decisions as arising from policy makers making rational choices given prevailing incentives rather than from decision makers functioning as optimal social planners. This approach to understanding how policy choices are made is an important element of Allan's analysis in *A History of the Federal Reserve* (Meltzer 2002, 2010).

Allan didn't just talk about policy, its successes and its failures; he lived it. He served on President Reagan's Council of Economic Advisers for a time. He also was asked to chair the International Financial Institution Advisory Commission established by Congress in 1998. The commission focused on reforms to the International Monetary Fund and the World Bank. He was a frequent visitor to Congress, where he testified many times. He also, of course, was a frequent visitor to the Federal Reserve, and visits with the chair, other governors, district presidents, and staff were commonplace.

In this chapter, I want to talk mostly about Allan and his perspective on monetary policy. In particular, I want to focus on his view of rules and the role they should have in policy making. It was a view developed over many decades of theoretical research, observation, and study of the historical record. First, let me note that I don't claim to be an authority on Allan's work; it is much too broad and lengthy for me to absorb. Others have a much better grasp of his overall contributions and how they interact. So I will try to stick to Allan's view of rules and how I came to appreciate it as an economist and as a policy maker.

A BRIEF HISTORY OF RULES

Arguments for monetary policy rules date back to Adam Smith and were reflected in the work of Henry Thornton, David Ricardo, and others in the late eighteenth and early nineteenth centuries. In the early twentieth century, economists such as Knut Wicksell and Irving Fisher also argued for monetary policy rules (Wicksell [1898] 1936; Fisher 1922). These economists recognized that the instability in the supply of money and its value were disruptive to the functioning of commerce and, ultimately, to economic growth.

Later, Henry Simons (1936) argued that, in a democracy, policy rules were to be preferred over the discretionary use of authorities granted to a central bank. He likened the case to the importance of the rule of law in the broader context of a well-functioning society. Following the Great Depression and the development of macroeconomic models inspired by the work of John Maynard Keynes, many economists came to believe that monetary policy did not have to be a source of instability, but could and should be used to stabilize the economy in the face of outside disturbances. In such a world, so the argument went, the monetary authorities should not have their discretion constrained by rules but should be free to respond to events in such a way as to reduce the variability of the business cycle. To this day, this remains the underlying argument of many who question the case for rules.

Milton Friedman (1960), on the other hand, proposed his famous k-percent money growth rule. He believed that arbitrary and unpredictable actions by the monetary authorities remained the greater risk and that to invite or encourage central banks to exercise wide discretion was fraught with danger. The k-percent rule for money growth was intended to bring stability and limit discretion by monetary policy makers.

A more formal case for rules was developed by Finn Kydland and Ed Prescott in the late 1970s (Kydland and Prescott 1977). Their Nobel Prize–winning work demonstrated that a credible commitment by policy makers to behave in a systematic, rule-like manner over time leads to better economic outcomes than discretion. Combining this result with modern dynamic economic models has led to a framework where monetary policy is modeled as a rule. Explicit dynamic models can be used to derive optimal policies in the sense of maximizing social welfare. Thus, modern monetary theories most often formulate monetary policy as a rule. Researchers can then investigate the performance of alternative rules or seek to derive the optimal rule given the structure of the model. Policy advice derived from these modern macroeconomic models is, thus, predicated on the assumption that policy makers follow a rule. Policy recommendations from these models, then, depend on the credibility and commitment of the central bankers to follow the rule. Of course, if the policy makers' commitment to the rule is not credible, then the outcomes are not likely to follow the predictions of the model. This was a troubling aspect of the Fed's attempts at forward guidance.

MELTZER AND RULES

I think Allan's view of a rule-like approach to monetary policy evolved over a long period of time. His support for rules came mostly from his empirical analysis of monetary policy decisions, both good and bad. This perspective is, I think, apparent when reading his treatise on the Federal Reserve that has been a frequent benchmark in today's discussion. Allan's analysis of both the successes and failures of the Fed is a story about individuals and institutions as much as it is about economic theory. In Allan's view, understanding the environment in which policy makers operated was an important element in understanding policy decisions.

His was a positive analysis of their decisions. What led them to make the decisions they did? What incentives and constraints did they face? Armed with such an understanding, he could, then, consider ways to shape the environment so that better decisions were more likely. Convincing policy makers that they were Ramsey planners did not seem a fruitful avenue to pursue. It would be better to figure out ways that incentivized policy makers to behave differently.

Based on his analysis of actual Fed decision-making, Allan viewed policy failures of the Fed as arising from some combination of a faulty understanding of the way the economy worked—bad theory, if you will—and political interference with policy decisions. Policy makers given broad authorities and discretion were more likely to be pushed and pulled by the political winds into unwise, short-term, focused decisions. He believed that both these factors could be minimized with a rule-based regime that limited discretion.

Allan highlights two periods that are regarded as major failures of monetary policy. The first is the Great Recession. Allan finds that the major monetary policy mistake was the failure to counter the collapse in the supply of money. After extensive analysis of the official record and meeting minutes, he argues that the Fed relied on misleading indicators of monetary policy, including nominal interest rates and bank borrowings. According to most Fed officials at the time, these indicators signaled there was ample liquidity in the banking system. This view was predominately a result of following a faulty theory even though better approaches were available and known. The Fed thought it was correct in its actions, yet its hubris and its discretion prevented its consideration and adoption of alternative metrics.

The inflation of the 1970s is another example of a major Fed failure. Although here, too, Allan partly attributes failure to reliance on a faulty theory—a stable Phillips curve—he stresses that political interference played the dominant role in this episode. Chairman William McChesney Martin was pressured by the Johnson administration to keep interest rates low to help fund the deficits caused by the Great Society programs and the war in Vietnam. Of course, this led to excessive money creation and, ultimately, set the economy on a troubling inflationary path. Allan thought Arthur Burns was not convinced that monetary tightening was an acceptable means to reduce inflation and so argued for wage and price controls. As a result, the Fed kept interest rates low, and inflation increased. Chairman Burns and Chairman Martin squandered a great deal of the Fed's hard-earned independence.

My view is that Allan believed the record clearly showed that Fed failures were predominately driven by excessive discretion that permitted the Fed to ignore or apply economic analysis selectively combined with episodes of political interference. The success of political interference is a sign that Fed independence was and remains fragile. You might say political independence is not a sufficient condition for good policy, but it seems to be a necessary one.

The threats to independence came not just from external sources such as Congress or the executive branch: they arose internally as well. Fed leadership often encouraged or did not resist encroachment from the fiscal authorities, and sometimes initiated it. Allan suggests that some Fed chairs had doubts about independence and its appropriate role and function, and even its desirability. Both Marriner Eccles and Martin felt, to some degree, obliged to "coordinate" with Congress when it approved and authorized budget deficits. Allan also suggested that the Bernanke Fed fell into the same trap during the great recession, intentionally or not, accommodating very large budget deficits with massive quantitative easing.

Allan's analysis strengthened his view that rule-based policies were an important element of good monetary policy. However, he did not argue for rules only on theoretical grounds or because he sought the optimal policy. He thought rules would lead to better policies to be sure, but optimal policy was not the key rationale from his standpoint. The world was too uncertain to believe we could devise optimal policies. I believe Allan viewed rules as a means of reducing or limiting the discretionary authority of monetary policy makers while giving them some grounds for protecting their independence.

In my own work over the past few years, I have often stressed the political and institutional environment and its effects on policy makers. In particular, I have argued that central bank independence is an essential feature of sound monetary policy, but in a democracy, that independence must be accompanied by constraints and accountability (Plosser 2014). Rules can be an effective means of constraining discretion as well as a means of holding a central bank accountable. There are other features that can contribute to these ends. For example, I have argued that constraining the monetary authority to a single mandate or objective can help with accountability and that limiting the types of assets (such as all-treasuries) it may hold on its balance sheet reduces the ability of the monetary authority to conduct credit policy or off-budget fiscal policy. Such limitations help preserve the separation of monetary policy from fiscal policy (Plosser 2012). Including such limitations in the Federal Reserve Act raises the bar for the central bank and the fiscal authorities to act in a more predictable and systematic manner. It also makes it more difficult for fiscal authorities to engage in political interference, since the central bank is legally constrained, and it strengthens the hand of the central bank by providing the legal grounds for saying no when fiscal authorities begin to encroach on independence.

SUMMARY

Allan was convinced that a rule-based approach to monetary policy would improve economic outcomes. His analysis of monetary theory and the conduct of policy led him to this conclusion. He did not argue that rules could be chosen to achieve some optimal policy; the world was too full of uncertainty to achieve such first-best solutions. He preferred to think in terms of robust rules that performed reasonably well in a broad class of models. The value, in his eyes, of rules was to reduce the discretion of the central bank and reduce the opportunities for political interference. Since unwise discretionary actions and political interference were the most frequent reasons for major Fed failures, Allan believed that a more rule-like policy was to be preferred. For these reasons he was a vocal supporter of reform efforts that sought to force the Fed to engage in rule-like policy.

REFERENCES

Cukierman, Alex, and Allan H. Meltzer. 1986. "A Theory of Ambiguity, Credibility, and Inflation under Discretion and Asymmetric Information." *Econometrica* 54, no. 5 (September): 1099–128.

Fisher, Irving. 1922. *The Purchasing Power of Money, Its Determination and Relation to Credit, Interest and Crises.* New York: Macmillan.

Friedman, Milton. 1960. *A Program for Monetary Stability.* New York: Fordham University Press.

Kydland, Finn E., and Edward C. Prescott. 1977. "Rules Rather Than Discretion: The Inconsistency of Optimal Plans." *Journal of Political Economy* 85, no. 3: 473–92.

Lucas, Robert E., Jr. 1976. "Econometric Policy Evaluation: A Critique." *Carnegie-Rochester Conference Series on Public Policy* 1: 19–46.

Meltzer, Allan H., and Scott F. Richard. 1981. "A Rational Theory of the Size of Government." *Journal of Political Economy* 89, no. 5 (October): 914–27.

———. 2002. *A History of the Federal Reserve.* Vol. 1, *1913–1951.* Chicago: University of Chicago Press.

———. 2010. *A History of the Federal Reserve.* Vol. 2, *1951–1986.* Chicago: University of Chicago Press.

Plosser, Charles I. 2012. "Fiscal Policy and Monetary Policy: Restoring the Boundaries." Speech presented at US Monetary Policy Forum, The Initiative on Global Markets. University of Chicago Booth School of Business, New York, February 24.

———. 2014. "A Limited Central Bank." *Cato Journal* 34, no. 2: 201–11.

Simons, Henry C. 1936. "Rules versus Authorities in Monetary Policy." *Journal of Political Economy* 44, no. 1: 1–30.

Taylor, John B. 1993. "Discretion versus Policy Rules in Practice." *Carnegie-Rochester Conference Series on Public Policy* 39: 195–214.

Wicksell, Knut. (1898) 1936. *Geldzins und Güterpreise: Eine Studie über die den Tauschwert des Geldes bestimmenden Ursachen.* Published in translation as *Interest and Prices: A Study of the Causes Regulating the Value of Money,* R. F Kahn, translator. London: Royal Economic Society.

CHAPTER 12
Macro Musings: Allan Meltzer

ALLAN H. MELTZER AND DAVID BECKWORTH

O ne of Allan Meltzer's last public appearances was an interview in front of a live audience for the podcast *Macro Musings* on November 19, 2016. The interview was part of a conference titled "Rethinking Monetary Policy: Rule-Based Approaches," an event cosponsored by the Mercatus Center at George Mason University and the Institute for Humane Studies. The interview was spirited, thoughtful, and wide-ranging. This chapter provides the transcript of this conversation.

DAVID BECKWORTH: Welcome to *Macro Musings*, the podcast series where, each week, we pull back the curtain and take a closer look at the important macroeconomic issues of the past, present, and future. I'm your host, David Beckworth of the Mercatus Center. We are glad you have decided to join us.

Our guest today is Allan Meltzer. Allan is a distinguished visiting fellow at the Hoover Institution and a professor of economics at the Tepper School of Business at Carnegie Mellon University. Allan has served as a consultant for several congressional committees, the president's Council of Economic Advisers, the US Treasury Department, the Federal Reserve, and numerous central banks.

Allan's writings have appeared in numerous journals and books over the years, including the authoritative multivolume history of the Fed titled *A History of the Federal Reserve*—several volumes and over several years. Most recently he published the book *Why Capitalism?*

Allan has won numerous awards and continues to publish research. He joins us today to talk about his career and recent developments in monetary policy. Allan, welcome to the show.

ALLAN MELTZER: Thank you. Nice to be here.

DAVID: We're glad to have you on. It's a real treat. Let's begin by asking, how did you get into macroeconomics, and particularly, how did you become a monetarist?

ALLAN: Well, those are separate questions. I grew up in the 1930s. That was the period of the Great Depression. Unemployment rates were 20, 25 percent for part of that period and never got down very low. I was not alone, but a part of a generation that said, "We need to understand how things like that happened and how they can be prevented."

We went in with a very clear idea that what we were interested in was, how do we make policies? At the time, and I think still, we believe that the way you make good policy was to have good theory, so we began to work on monetary theory, and I became a monetarist.

I started life on the Left. I was a delegate to the political convention that nominated Henry Wallace for president, so that was far to the Left. I learned, gradually and over time, that that was the wrong way [laughs] to go, that people were a better judge of their own interest than anyone could be for them. And that got me interested in being a libertarian. From libertarian to monetarist is a small step.

DAVID: You were a part of the monetarist counterrevolution, where they pushed back against the dominant view of Keynesianism at the time. I was wondering if you could tell us about that experience. What was it like to go through the counterrevolution of monetarism?

ALLAN: It paid to have a tough hide because people said things about you that weren't always complimentary, but that was never a problem for me. Like many people who have strong beliefs, I thought we were right. If you were right, you would eventually convince people that you were right, and they would do things for you.

We tried to get them to do it. Karl Brunner and I, in the 1970s, after the inflation was pretty well along, were not just annoyed, but put off by the way in which the journalists discussed it on TV and radio at the time, and in the newspapers.

They saw it as a problem between those people who thought we should have price and wage controls and those people who thought we should go back on the gold standard. Brunner and I said, "That isn't what economists think or do. Let's try to get people to understand what we do."

We started the Shadow Open Market Committee. We pounded on them for the next few years and were gratified when Paul Volcker became chairman of the Fed and declared himself to be a quasi-monetarist. I think he said a *practical monetarist,* was what he called it. He set out to control money growth.

Unlike so much of what goes on now and went on then, he was smart enough, and he is very smart . . . Parenthetically, I have known him since I worked in the Kennedy administration, Treasury, in 1961. He worked there as my boss, and we used to discuss fixed and floating exchange rates.

Anyway, he became chairman of the Fed, and he declared himself to be a practical monetarist. He understood that nothing about controlling inflation was going to take place in the next week, but it was a steady problem to convince the markets that you were going to persist in what you did.

Finally, in April of, I think, the second year that he was chairman, in April of that year, with the unemployment rate at above 8 percent, he raised the interest rate. That was a body blow to the inflation because [laughs] no one before him had ever done anything like that. The market [laughs] said, "This guy is really serious. He's going to solve the inflation."

Three, four months later, the inflation rate was down to 3 or 4 percent. He convinced them. He was persistent. That was just a great thing for the country, for the world, and for monetarism. The Fed has never liked the idea of controlling money, and they got rid of the idea of monetarism as quickly as they could after that.

They make terrible mistakes, and they're making terrible mistakes in this recovery.

DAVID: Would you consider that the height of the monetarist counter-revolution, when Volcker did his thing?

ALLAN: That's the short-run high. We'll be back.

DAVID: You'll be back.

[laughter]

DAVID: Great to hear.

ALLAN: That worried the late, great Harry Johnson. He said, "Monetarism is fashionable when there's inflation and very unfashionable when there isn't." I didn't like it when he said it, but I believe it's true.

DAVID: What were the pivotal moments? Volcker is the highlight, but leading up to that, there was already momentum. Was it the 1970s experience? Was it your work with Karl Brunner? Was it Milton Friedman's work? What do you see as the pivotal moments in that revolution?

ALLAN: I think Volcker leaned heavily on the work that Friedman, [Anna] Schwartz, Brunner and I, and others had done, in a general way. That is, he understood that he had to get control of monetary aggregates and keep them from rising rapidly, and he did that.

As I said, when the time came to push up the interest rate in order to control money growth, he did it, and he did it with 8 percent unemployment. Watch the Federal Reserve policies since the 1960s. That was an unusual event.

DAVID: Yeah, I wonder if today if the central bank here could have the thick skin that he had because he received a lot of blowback, a lot of resistance from Congress, the media. You knew him then. What was it like for him to go through that?

ALLAN: Let me answer it in a slightly different way. If you compare what the Fed has done to what they've done in countries which have basically monetarist-type policies—like Switzerland, the Bundesbank before there was the ECB [European Central Bank], Singapore—here's a comparison.

The Swiss have had generally low inflation rates and rather steady policies and not a lot of fiscal intervention. Under Bretton Woods, the Swiss franc was worth 20 cents. It's now a dollar. A dollar.

As that series of events—concern about inflation, a modest fiscal policy, a series of referendum that the Swiss vote on all the time to raise tax rates or cut tax rates or raise spending, which usually get voted down . . . Did that standard policy hurt Switzerland? No. Switzerland was a poor country before World War II. It now has a per capita GDP larger than ours.

It's been a blessing for the Swiss to have relatively stable, predictable policies. Singapore fits that model very well. The Bundesbank—nothing was more monetarist than the Bundesbank. They were my friends. Karl and I started the Konstanz Seminar. We helped to train, retrain, the German economists after World War II and the Hitler period.

We brought over people like [Robert] Barro and [Rudiger] Dornbusch and [Michael] Mussa and young Americans to show them how good economics was done. They now have some very good economists, and the Konstanz Seminar has gone on. Manfred Neumann took it over after Karl and I left. Then some other people took it over after Manfred Neumann, but it still goes on.

It's had an impact on the way in which people think about and act on and do research on monetary policy. I'm not disheartened by the fact that the current Fed is one of the worst Feds in its history, and I know a fair amount about its history.

[laughter]

DAVID: You mentioned Karl Brunner, your colleague. You worked a lot together.

ALLAN: My teacher, also.

DAVID: Your teacher, and you guys are labeled monetarists. Milton Friedman, Anna J. Schwartz are also considered monetarists. What was your contribution? What did you do that was different than Friedman and Schwartz?

ALLAN: Karl Brunner was a wonderful person, I can tell you.

He and I wrote probably twenty-five papers together, not counting the introduction to all the volumes of the Carnegie-Rochester series. We never argued about who did what. We never had an argument about . . . We would talk on the phone because we were rarely in the same place together. We would talk on the phone on Wednesday night.

My teenage children hated that [laughs] because the conversation would go on for over two hours, until my arm got tired. He would take ideas from me and write them up in papers without my name on them. I would take ideas from him and write them up in papers without his name on them. We never argued about who was responsible for what. We just got along very well.[1]

We were interested in the ideas and so on. That was a great working relationship. Now, what did we do that Milton Friedman didn't do? Milton Friedman brought money back. There had been a strong monetary tradition in the '20s. The way Keynesianism was interpreted, it put that aside.

Milton Friedman brought it back, but Milton Friedman never explained how it was that, if you increase nominal money, you got real effects. The person who did that first, and that's a fundamental question, was Karl Brunner in an essay in the *JPE* in 1961.[2]

He said something which, if you think about it, you'll see how clear it is. He said, "What happens when you increase money growth is, asset prices rise. The stock market rises. Housing prices, prices of existing housing rise. These rising asset prices make it relatively cheap to invest in new production of the same assets. You get capital spending and house production."

That's a nice micro explanation of the transmission of monetary policy. It says we change the relative prices, and as the relative prices change, we get more spending on real output. That was in '61. It was not a model. It was just a couple of paragraphs in an essay. Over the next couple years, Brunner and I worked out the model.

About six years after Brunner wrote his paragraphs, Jim Tobin, in the first issue of Karl's *Journal of Money, Credit and Banking*, wrote the general equilibrium theory of money.[3] What was the transmission mechanism? It was something he called q. What was q? It was simply the relative price of assets to output.

That is the same idea that we had, but that he developed independently of what we had done. The amazing thing for me is that the Fed has always ignored that. They have played with the Phillips curve. I'm not opposed to the Phillips curve, but I have always pointed out to my students that the Phillips curve was developed by Phillips when there was a gold standard.

There was an anchor to the future price level that made that work much better than it works in periods when there isn't that close anchor. There must be hundreds of papers on the Phillips curve by this time, many of which are not very encouraging about its empirical relevance.

Here's an implication which seems to me to be important. If you took the relative price theory, our way of thinking about it, you would say that after about 2009, 2010, when you saw the excess reserves piling up on the balance sheets of the banks, you would have asked yourself, "Why is it that we're getting the asset price effects, but we're getting the output? We're not getting investment. There's not much investment.

"While there is some house-building, it's not very great. It's especially weak compared to the amount of reserves that we put into the system.

There must be something wrong. We're missing something." What they were missing, of course, was that we have a government at that point, and still, that was very antibusiness, so businesses were not investing.

They were being hit with new regulations all the time. I think it's interesting that, when the new election took place, one of the first things that happened in the stock market was that shares that were being hindered by Dodd-Frank went up because markets think Dodd-Frank will likely be modified or repealed and that regulation will come down.

I believe that that's true and that that is likely to happen under the new administration.

DAVID: You mentioned just a minute ago how Keynes was interpreted. I find that interesting because you had a 1988 book titled *Keynes's Monetary Theory: A Different Interpretation.*[4] In that, you argue the Keynesians actually got it wrong. Keynesianism as it was practiced was based on a false premise of what Keynes actually said.

Why don't you share that with us? What is your take on what Keynes actually meant in his general theory?

ALLAN: To write that book, I read just about every paper he wrote and book that he wrote from about 1920 on. The first thing I would say is, you want to think of Keynes as a Cambridge economist because that's what he was.

When he would think about what was the problem in the macroeconomy, he would begin by thinking, "Well, what is the externality that's being imposed?" He's decided that the externality is that there's too much uncertainty in the system. Uncertainty. Not risk, uncertainty. That is what, later, Don Rumsfeld called the unknown unknowns. That's the uncertainty.

As a result of that, people, he said, held more money and less capital. The problem was too little capital. What should you do? You should obviously have public investment to try to get more capital. What about the Keynesian view that you just want to do more consumption? There he is absolutely clear that no, that isn't what you want to do.

He wrote to [James] Meade, who was his colleague from Cambridge, when he was in the government, and he told them Meade was proposing to increase consumer spending during wartime Britain. Keynes wrote as if he had written or had read the permanent income theory. He said, "People have long practice habits of consumption. You don't want to interfere with them.

"You don't want to make a temporary change in those habits. You want to concentrate on investment." He was in Washington during the war when Abba Lerner, who wrote *The Economics of Control*,[5] was giving one of his first seminars on deficits and the need for big deficits, the kind of junk that Paul Krugman writes.

[laughter]

ALLAN: What did Keynes say? He was wrong in what he said, but what he said is, [laughs] "That's a bad idea. No government will ever do that." He didn't believe in large, permanent deficits. He believed in the opposite. He developed the Bretton Woods system. What is the Bretton Woods system? It was a fixed-exchange-rate system.

You can't have a fixed-exchange-rate system and have willy-nilly expansive fiscal policies all the time because you're going to have to devalue. They allowed countries to devalue, but they didn't make it easy for them to devalue. Keynes was not a believer in what is now called Keynesianism.

He was a believer in Keynes economics, which were: try to reduce uncertainty and keep trying to increase the capital stock because that's what standards of living depend upon. That's just the opposite of what these people do. It's hard to believe that they've ever read the book.

[laughter]

ALLAN: They probably haven't.

DAVID: Moving forward to the present. The standard approach to monetary economics today is a new Keynesian model in that central banks . . . they adjust short-term interest rates, they respond to output gaps, to inflation. The Taylor rule embodies that.

There is no money in monetary policy. Does that break your heart as a monetarist? Do you think there's still a need for monetary aggregates in monetary policy?

ALLAN: [laughs] My attitude towards Michael Woodford's work, which is the foundation of the idea that money and credit just don't belong in the model, is—he later modified that so that they have a little effect, but not much—is, do you have to be as smart as Michael Woodford to come up with the idea that the principal product of central banks, which are money and credit, have nothing to do with central banking? That has always seemed, to me, to be an insane idea.

The successful central banks—Switzerland, Germany before it joined the ECB, the Volcker period in the United States, countless others—control money. You want to keep inflation out, you want to control money. Milton said it correctly. Monetary inflation is always an aggregate of monetary phenomenon.

People scoff at that idea, but it's because they don't understand what it meant. What he meant was that the aggregate price level, as opposed to something like an oil shock . . . Prices rise because of an oil shock, but that's not inflation in the sense that Friedman talked about it. That's a change in relative prices.

The Shadow Committee, my Shadow Committee, in 1974 said, "You've got it wrong, Arthur Burns. This is a change in the relative price. There's no reason why you want to kill the economy by tightening money. There's no reason why you want to do that. What you want to do is, you want to let the increase in the relative prices pass through," but they didn't do that.

They tightened the economy, and then they did the same thing again later in that decade. Then by 2000 they finally got it right. They said, "Well, it's a relative price change, so we don't have to do anything about that. We'll let it pass through." That's the right answer.

When Milton [Friedman] said, "Inflation is always and everywhere a monetary phenomenon," he meant generalized increase in purchasing power, not increases in relative prices.[6]

DAVID: The last central bank to have money in its target was the ECB. They had the dual pillars. They recently dropped that. You're probably disappointed to see them do away with their dual pillars.

ALLAN: I've learned not to be disappointed but appalled by things that central bankers do.

[laughter]

ALLAN: Here's an example where Congressman Hensley, a student of economics—he was a student of Phil Gramm's in Texas—comes up with a monetary rule. He says to the Fed, "Adopt the [laughs] monetary rule of your own choosing and implement it." What do they say? "No." Why do they say that?

Is there any evidence that discretionary policy is effective, more effective than a rule? No. The best period in monetary history of one hundred years of the Fed, the two best periods, are—one was the period in the 1920s when they followed a rule, the modified gold standard. Not a rule I would pick, but that was the rule that they picked.

Then the second period in which they more or less followed a rule was the years 1986 to 2002, when Alan Greenspan had a medium-term strategy, more or less—and I emphasize more or less—following a Taylor rule. That was a period where we had low inflation, stable growth, short recessions, quick recoveries, and very little variability. Why?

People could look at what he was doing and could estimate or guess, as best they'll ever be able to guess, what the interest rate would be a year or two years from now. Compare that to what they do now. They look at the daily data and they respond to it. You don't have any idea what monetary policy is going to do.

They've been talking about [how] they're going to raise the interest rate, now, for damn near a year, and they finally are probably going to do it in December. What are we going to have? We're going to have a big quarter-point increase in interest rates. Hooray for that.

[laughter]

ALLAN: We should be way above that. What's going to happen when they finally, if they ever do, get out of this? We have a problem in the economy that we should be aware of and worry about. A lot of retirees used to finance themselves by buying CDs at the banks and rolling them over from period to period, and earning enough to live on.

With the low-interest-rate policy, they can't do that, so they've been buying bonds. Boy, how many of them are sophisticated enough to know the simple fact that when interest rates rise, bond prices sink and that they're going to lose some of their money? Are they going to be prepared to do that? Because they're retirees, they can't replace it. That's a problem.

It's a problem that is so typical of the US government. That is, you take the first step; you never think about what are the longer-term consequences of what you're doing. That's the biggest weakness of our government is that, and it shows up in beginning wars without knowing how you're going to get out of them.

I remember way back in the '60s, when John F. Kennedy was president and I was working in the Treasury. He brought in a general who would replace MacArthur in Korea. He asked him about going into Vietnam. The general said to him exactly the right thing.

He said, "Mr. President, I know how you get in, but how do you get out? Think about the consequences of what you're doing that you can see." Our government doesn't do that. The Fed doesn't do that. They look at the day-to-day numbers. The day-to-day numbers are mixtures of permanent and transitory changes.

You can't tell from looking at them whether they're permanent or transitory changes. You've got to see at least two, and maybe more, to be able to get a clear path for this. That is a foolish policy, and it has bad results.

DAVID: Let's look at some of the Fed's actions most recently. John Taylor argued in 2007 that one of the reasons we had a Great Recession is because the Fed kept rates too low for too long, so it facilitated a boom.[7] Other forces were at work, but the Fed definitely played a role.

Robert Hetzel, who would also be considered a monetarist—he argued, and Scott [Sumner] did as well, that the bust was also facilitated by the Fed.[8] The Fed was too slow to react in 2008. They were overly cautious, so things got worse. I'd like to hear your take. Did the Fed contribute both to the boom and the bust during the Great Recession?

ALLAN: Yes, I agree with those criticisms. When you say the Fed was too slow to act, the reason we have inflation is—in this country, not just now and not just in the prospect of the future, but in general, over the last forty years—is because the Fed is always too slow to act against inflation. That's why we have inflations, because it takes a while.

You're not going to stop the inflation by suddenly raising the interest rate from a quarter to a half a percent, or even from half to 1 percent. It's going to take more than that, and it's going to take time before it happens. In the Volcker period, the markets just didn't believe that he was going to persist, so it took until they became convinced he would persist.

That was more than a year of suffering by the public as unemployment rates rose. That's just a fact. There's nothing we can do to change that fact. Monetary policy works in part by changing relative prices, but in sharp part by changing people's expectations. We have no model of how that connection to expectations works.

DAVID: I want to move on, then, to the recovery stage. We've talked about the boom, the bust, and the recovery period. The Fed tried unconventional monetary policy, new experiments with QE [quantitative easing]—QE1, 2, and 3—and yet we had a very tepid recovery. It was, by historical standards, one of the weakest on record. It was slow. It was anemic. It created angst. It may explain this election to some extent.

Why didn't the Fed's QE programs do more?

ALLAN: The reason the QE programs didn't do more is because we don't have a monetary problem. First of all, let me say about QE, I think QE is an artifice that hides what was something which is shameful. That is, we had an agreement at the start of Bretton Woods, which was that because of the bad experience of the 1930s, we would not have competitive devaluations.

Bernanke broke that agreement. Calling it QE was a way of hiding the fact that he was attempting to have a relative devaluation of the dollar. That, of course, was soon followed by other countries—the ECB, Japan—that also called what they were doing QE but were also efforts to change the relative price of their currency. Now the dollar, instead of being weak, is strong.

Who gets benefit from that? Certainly not us. Who gets hurt by it? Well, as you can imagine, the countries that can't engage in that game. The weak or developing countries, as former Governor Rajan of the Bank of India pointed out, they're the people who take the heat because of the changes in the relative prices of currency.

I don't think that any model is going to tell you that it's optimal to put the costs of these things onto them without getting much benefit for ourselves.

DAVID: Even nominal measures of inflation . . . for example, the Fed's own preferred inflation target, which is the core PCE [Personal Consumption Expenditures] deflator, has averaged about 1.5 percent. Their target for it is 2 percent. Despite all these programs, the Fed itself hasn't been able to generate the inflation that it wants. What's the explanation behind that?

ALLAN: Yes. Way back when they started all that stuff, I said, "We're going to have an inflation." I was wrong. The reason I was wrong [is] because, like the Fed, I missed the fact that the reserves were piling up on the bank's balance sheet and that M2, or whatever monetary growth measure you prefer, none of them were rising very rapidly.

M2 growth stayed between 5 and 6 percent throughout the thing. It's picking up now. I was wrong about that. I recognized it when I saw the reserves piling up instead of going into creating money. Why do we have this slow recovery? The answer is because we have, as I said, real problems in the American economy, but they're not monetary problems. The same is true of the ECB.

They have real problems, and the same is true of Japan. Japan has real problems in it.

DAVID: Are you worried that any of these experiments will go awry, like Japan's balance sheet is growing so much that they might lose control of the monetary base?

ALLAN: No. Japan has increased its debt enormously, but then, it's all bought by the central bank, so net, it isn't [laughs] increasing all that much.

DAVID: Well, let's move forward to the election and talk about that just a bit. President-elect Donald Trump is now with us. You mentioned earlier the market response to his election. Bond yields have shot up, which suggests more spending, higher inflation possibly, maybe higher real growth. Stock prices are up.

Do you see the market saying that he may be a net plus for the economy? What do you think the market's saying about that?

ALLAN: I think just what you said. They see it as a net plus. What seems to me to be the lesson that the Democrats and the elites refuse to learn is what this election was about. For the last four or five, seven years maybe, I've been working on something called Regulation and the Rule of Law.[9]

Out of that experience, I learned that there's a great deal of unhappiness in the country because they believe that their sovereignty has been taken away; that they have nothing to say about the regulations, the rules, and the policies that affect them; that all those things are done by the administrative agencies and the courts.

That our government, the US government, the American Revolution, was founded on the idea of popular sovereignty. You just have to read the history of that period. You'll see that just comes popping out at you: popular sovereignty. Who is going to rule? It wasn't going to be an elite. It wasn't going to be the administrative agencies. It was going to be the public.

That's what Lincoln said. He described in the Gettysburg Address— he said "government of the people, by the people." "By the people": popular sovereignty. The public elected a Congress. The Congress made the laws. That doesn't describe the beginnings of what we do in this country. What happens is the rules are made by the administrative agencies. Congress doesn't do anything about them.

Congress doesn't even have a veto power over those rules. It's discussed something called the REINS Act over and over again and never passed it. They abdicate responsibility. That's what the public here is objecting to, and it's what the public that voted for Brexit was objecting to.

They didn't like the idea that their rules were made by unelected individuals in Brussels.

That's what people in Germany who are part of the Alternative für Deutschland, that's what people all over Europe are complaining about: that they do not have sovereignty. They want to get back their sovereignty. That's what they voted for when they voted for Trump. You may like Trump, you may not like Trump, but you have to recognize that that is a fundamental issue in our country.

He was on the side which said, "I'm going to give you back your sovereignty." We'll see whether he does.

DAVID: Well, it'll be interesting to see who he appoints to the Fed. We've got several board positions that are open, as well as Janet Yellen's term as chair is coming to an end in 2017.

ALLAN: He has a couple before that.

DAVID: Yes. What is your forecast for the shape of the board to come?

ALLAN: Oh, he's going to appoint more people who are going to be in favor of rules.

DAVID: All right, so maybe John Taylor?

ALLAN: John Taylor will probably be a candidate for chairman.

DAVID: Yes. You mentioned a minute ago the prospects of new legislation coming out that would make the Fed adopt some rule, at least as a benchmark. So that's the FORM Act, I think, you're referring to.

It sounds like you're favorable of something like the FORM Act, which, just to be clear—it would require the Fed to pick a benchmark rule, and the Fed could violate that rule as long as it explained itself. It's not truly a binding constraint. It's just a benchmark that would facilitate conversation and understanding. But you're sympathetic towards that legislation?

ALLAN: I worked on that. Carpenter and I, way back, began to talk about uncertainty, and I'll tell you a little story. We wrote a paper that said, "No matter what model you have, that model may make mistakes." You want to have an idea as to something else like the money growth rate or something—credit growth rate, real GDP—something which tells you, "Are you on track or is something happening? The model is giving you bad advice."

We had a conference, and Franco Modigliani, Larry Klein, all the model builders came to the conference. They absolutely refused to believe there was anything like uncertainty. They said, "No, no. When we have a model, we will have the model. The right model will be exactly right."

[laughter]

ALLAN: Well, hooray for that. I don't think anyone would say that anymore. The author—the person who was taking notes and wrote them up—Bill Dewald writes in his essay that Brunner and I, and half a dozen other people who were at the conference, accepted the idea that there was uncertainty in the world.

That uncertainty meant that you just could never have a model that was going to tell you what happened. There were always going to be events that you can't forecast, and that Modigliani, Klein, others just didn't believe that. Well, I think now economists have finally gotten on to the idea that there is such a thing as uncertainty.

Tom Sargent and people like that are working diligently on trying to build models in which uncertainty is an important element.

DAVID: You've mentioned some recent writings. You'd also like to reform the structure of the Fed. I believe I've read that you would like to see all twelve regional presidents vote at the FOMC [Federal Open Market Committee]. Can you speak about that proposal?

ALLAN: Yes. From the very first of the Fed, it was considered unalterable truth that the Washington Fed was political and that the regional Fed represented economic ideas and, at that time, bankers. They're no longer bankers, but the banks are run by economists and business people.

I think the perspective of the bankers and the business people is much better than the political pressures which come up on the board. I would like to see more of that view in the deliberations and in the policy making.

[background conversation]

ALLAN: I said, "Originally, all the open market decisions were made by the regional banks. The 1933 and '35 act transferred the power to Washington." One of the anomalies of the time was that one of the authors of the Federal Reserve Act was the chairman of the committee in 1935 that changed the rules and strengthened . . . and he was against the idea of having a central bank.

He never wanted a central bank, but somehow he got hoodwinked or buffaloed into creating one.

DAVID: All right. That ends the interview part of the podcast. We're now going to turn to our Q&A. As was mentioned before, please raise your hand. Please state a question. Not a strong view, just a question . . .

[laughter]

DAVID: . . . for Professor Meltzer. Keep it brief. Please stand up and share with us.

AUDIENCE MEMBER: Professor, could you comment on the folly of negative interest rates in Japan and Europe?

ALLAN: Yes. Let me preface my remark about that because I want to say that what guides me in thinking of doing these things is that I'm an economist. I'm an economist, so I try to think about the economics of the problem. I am certainly very much aware that politics plays a role. I have certainly done my bit to create models of political economy, but I'm an economist first and foremost.

I try to think about, "What does the economics tell us?" When it comes to negative interest rates, here's what it boils down to in my mind. People—you see this in Europe—rush to hold currency. In Germany they buy safes to store the currency at home, so the currency has a fixed price. If you really want negative interest rates, you want to loosen that restriction.

You want to float the value of the currency. Now, if you float the value of the currency, you put uncertainty, risk, right into the consumer's market basket. Do you really want to do that? I don't think that's a very good idea, but that's what seems to me to be involved. Otherwise, the present business with negative interest rates has this interesting result.

The Swiss have very negative interest rates. That's because they want to discourage the movement of European currency into Switzerland because they want to control inflation. They have very negative interest rates applied to these inflows. The idea is, that slows down the Swiss economy because the exchange rate has gone up.

DAVID: OK, next.

ALLAN: Wait, wait.

[laughter]

ALLAN: In the ECB, they want negative interest rates because they think it's going to be expansive. That is, they don't look across the border and say, "The Swiss are doing this to slow their economy." They say, "We're going to do it to expand ours." It can't do both. [laughs] My guess is the ECB is probably right, that it would be a mildly expansive thing.

How many people are going to lend on the supply side where they have to pay the borrower for the privilege of taking a loan from them? I don't think you're going to get much increase in credit under those circumstances. I believe that the increases in credit are what we need to see to see recovery. What would I do instead?

I would do what they need to do badly, which is to make nonmonetary reforms in their countries. That's what's hurting them. It's what's hurting us. We have taken a step which I believe will move us in that direction. The market seems to think that's the case. The Europeans cannot or don't seem to be capable of doing similar things.

The Japanese? My old friend Governor Kuroda tells me that the government of Japan has agreed that it will change the rules in the labor and commodity market. We'll see whether they finally do that.

DAVID: Next question.

AUDIENCE MEMBER: Dr. Meltzer, if I'm not mistaken, earlier David said that expansionary monetary policy in the mid-2000s fueled the boom, and contractionary monetary policy shortly thereafter exacerbated the economic downturn. I believe you agreed with that. In late 2008, early 2009, Anna Schwartz expressed a similar position.

Dr. Sumner described her as breaking from her monetarist position as stated in her work with Friedman and referred to her, instead, as a neo-Austrian. I'm curious whether you would characterize yourself as a monetarist or a neo-Austrian.

ALLAN: I don't really care about those titles.

[laughter]

ALLAN: People have called me many things.

[laughter]

AUDIENCE MEMBER: Very recently I heard Lawrence Summers saying that monetary policy applies to people whose savings is a choice. Now, in [the United States], with this acute income inequality and savings is no longer a choice, he's trying to say that only fiscal ways we can reach these people. Do you agree with this?

ALLAN: Do I agree with him about what?

AUDIENCE MEMBER: About that fiscal policy . . . the monetary policy is losing its shine because a lot of people, savings is not a choice, so interest rate movements really does not affect them.

ALLAN: No. I don't agree with him. The reason monetary policy is said to be losing its power is because we don't have a monetary problem. You can print money from now to doomsday and not get much effect from it if the banks just hold the excess reserves. In order to get monetary policy to work, you have to have a monetary problem that you're solving.

The monetary problem we're solving isn't there. The problems that we have are, we get the first effect of monetary expansion—namely, asset prices rise—so the stock market booms. That creates a large constituency that is a big claque for continuing that policy even though it doesn't have much effect on the output.

If you ask me do I think that that policy of the Fed has had important increases in output, my answer is, I don't see it. Why I don't see it? Because I don't see the increase in credit that would be required. The demand for credit would have to increase.

The fact that we're getting recovery probably has very little to do with what the Fed has done because the asset prices rose, but there hasn't been the follow-through on the real side. That's very important. As far as I'm concerned, that's where the transmission takes place. The reason I've given for why there isn't a follow-through is because the businessmen are very pessimistic, and rightly so.

How do I know they're pessimistic? Well, I look at what they do. What they do is they make profits, and they use them to buy back their stock at very high equity prices. I can't think of anything that is more discouraging than that. They don't want to invest, so the only thing that they do these days is, they buy up their competitors and reduce competition, which is . . . Is that great?

Look what's happened to the insurance industry. Look what this administration has allowed to happen to hospitals. You go to almost any city now, there's only one or at most two hospitals. Competition is really being reduced. Is that good? I don't consider it good. I consider it bad.

[clears throat] We would be much better off if we didn't allow all those mergers.

DAVID: All right. One last question, in the back there.

AUDIENCE MEMBER: Earlier this evening, Professor Sumner gave a very conciliatory address on the relationship between market monetarism and classical monetarism, but at other times he's emphasized the differences.

I wonder if, as somebody who has been instrumental in the development of both strands, do you see market monetarism as the rightful heir to monetarism as far as monetary theory goes, or do you think there's some reason to adhere, still, to classical monetarism?

ALLAN: I worry very little about those distinctions. If they do the right thing, which is have a rule controlling money growth, I really don't [laughs] care what they call it—or a rule controlling monetary policy that's like the Taylor rule. I don't care what they call it.

DAVID: All right, our guest today has been Allan Meltzer. Allan, thank you for being on the show.

[applause]

ALLAN: Thank you, and thank all the viewers. Been a pleasure to be with you. I have spent almost sixty years working as an economist. I love economics, and I have enjoyed having the privilege of doing what I did.

[applause]

NOTES

1. For more on Allan Meltzer's relationship with Karl Brunner, see Allan H. Meltzer, "Karl Brunner, Scholar: An Appreciation" (Economics Working Paper 15116, Hoover Institution, Stanford University, Stanford, CA, October 2015).

2. Karl Brunner, "The Report of the Commission on Money and Credit," *Journal of Political Economy* 69, no. 6 (1961): 605–20.

3. James Tobin, "A General Equilibrium Approach to Monetary Theory," *Journal of Money, Credit and Banking* 1, no. 1 (1969): 15–29.

4. Allan H. Meltzer, *Keynes's Monetary Theory: A Different Interpretation* (Cambridge: Cambridge University Press, 1988).

5. Abba Lerner, *The Economics of Control: Principles of Welfare Economics* (New York: Macmillan, 1944).

6. Milton Friedman, "Inflation: Causes and Consequences," in *Dollars and Deficits: Living with America's Economic Problems* (Englewood Cliffs, NJ: Prentice-Hall, 1970), 39.

7. John B. Taylor, "Housing and Monetary Policy" (paper presented at the Symposium on Housing, Housing Finance, and Monetary Policy, Federal Reserve Bank of Kansas City, Jackson Hole, WY, August 30–September 1, 2007), 463–76.

8. Robert Hetzel, *The Great Recession: Market Failure or Policy Failure?* (New York: Columbia University Press, 2012).

9. "Regulation and Rule of Law Initiative." Hoover Institution, Economic and Policy Working Group. https://www.hoover.org/regulation-and-rule-law-initiative.

Published Works of Allan H. Meltzer

T his bibliography presents the published works authored, coauthored, edited, or coedited by Allan Meltzer. The publications are grouped by type and, within these groups, are arranged in order of publication year. While every attempt has been made to render this list as complete as possible, omissions surely remain given Meltzer's prolific energies. Testimony, conference proceedings, committee reports, speeches and keynote addresses, memoranda, and unpublished papers have been excluded from this list.

The Carnegie Mellon University library maintains the largest archive of Meltzer's published and unpublished work.

BOOKS

David J. Ott and Allan H. Meltzer. *Federal Tax Treatment of State and Local Securities*. Westport, CT: Greenwood, 1980.

Thomas Romer, Peter Ordershook, and Allan H. Meltzer, eds. *The Carnegie Papers on Political Economy*. The Hague, Netherlands: Martinus Nijhoff, 1981–1986.

Allan H. Meltzer, Alan Reynolds, and Edwin J. Feulner Jr. *Towards a Stable Monetary Policy: Monetarism vs. the Gold Standard; A Debate between Allan Meltzer and Alan Reynolds*. Fiscal Issues 3. Washington, DC: Heritage Foundation and Institute for Research on the Economics of Taxation, 1982.

Allan H. Meltzer, ed. *International Lending and the IMF: A Conference in Memory of Wilson Schmidt*. The Heritage Lectures 21. Washington, DC: Heritage Foundation, 1983.

Allan H. Meltzer and Karl Brunner, eds. *Theory, Policy, Institutions: Papers from the Carnegie-Rochester Conferences on Public Policy*. Amsterdam: North-Holland, 1983.

Allan H. Meltzer. *De onzekere wereldeconomie* [Uncertain world economy]. Rotterdamse monetaire studies 14. Rotterdam: Stichting Rotterdamse Monetaire Studies, 1984.

Allan H. Meltzer. *Monetarism and Contemporary Monetary Policy in the US.* [In Japanese.] Tokyo:
Committee of International Programs, Meiji University, 1985.

Allan H. Meltzer. *Keynes's Monetary Theory: A Different Interpretation.* Cambridge: Cambridge
University Press, 1988.

Karl Brunner and Allan H. Meltzer. *Monetary Economics.* Oxford: Basil-Blackwell, 1989.

Marvin H. Kosters and Allan H. Meltzer. *International Competitiveness in Financial Services.*
New York: Springer, 1991.

Allan H. Meltzer, Alex Cukierman, and Scott F. Richard. *Political Economy.* New York: Oxford
University Press, 1991.

Karl Brunner and Allan H. Meltzer. *Money and the Economy: Issues in Monetary Analysis.*
Cambridge: Cambridge University Press, 1993.

Allan H. Meltzer, Mark Perlman, and Mark Blaug. *Money, Credit and Policy.* Cheltenham, UK:
Edward Elgar, 1995.

Allan H. Meltzer. *A History of the Federal Reserve.* Vol. 1, *1913–1951.* Chicago: University of
Chicago Press, 2002.

George P. Shultz, Allan H. Meltzer, Peter R. Fisher, Donald L. Kohn, James D. Hamilton, John B. Taylor,
Myron S. Scholes et al. *The Road Ahead for the Fed.* Stanford, CA: Hoover Institution Press, 2009.

Allan H. Meltzer. *A History of the Federal Reserve.* Vol. 2, *1951–1986.* Chicago: University of
Chicago Press, 2010.

Allan H. Meltzer. *Why Capitalism?* London: Oxford University Press, 2012.

ACADEMIC ARTICLES AND BOOK CHAPTERS

Allan H. Meltzer. Comment on "Market Structure and Stabilization Policy," by John Kenneth
Galbraith. *Review of Economics and Statistics* 40, no. 4 (November 1958): 413–15.

Allan H. Meltzer. "The Behavior of the French Money Supply: 1938–54." *Journal of Political
Economy* 67, no. 3 (June 1959): 275–96.

Geoffrey P. Clarkson and Allan H. Meltzer. "Portfolio Selection: A Heuristic Approach." *Journal of
Finance* 15, no. 4 (December 1960): 465–80.

Allan H. Meltzer. "Mercantile Credit, Monetary Policy and Size of Firm." *Review of Economics and
Statistics* 42, no. 4 (November 1960): 429–37.

Karl Brunner and Allan H. Meltzer. "The Place of Financial Intermediaries in the Transmission of
Monetary Policy." *American Economic Review* 53, no. 2 (May 1963): 372–82.

Karl Brunner and Allan H. Meltzer. "Predicting Velocity: Implications for Theory and Policy."
Journal of Finance 18, no. 2 (May 1963): 319–54.

Allan H. Meltzer. "The Demand for Money: A Cross-Section Study of Business Firms." *Quarterly
Journal of Economics* 77, no. 3 (August 1963): 405–22.

Allan H. Meltzer. "The Demand for Money: The Evidence from the Time Series." *Journal of Political
Economy* 71, no. 3 (June 1963): 219–46.

Allan H. Meltzer. "Monetary Policy and the Trade Credit Practices of Business Firms." In
Stabilization Policies, by the Commission on Money and Credit, 471–97. Englewood Cliffs,
NJ: Prentice-Hall, 1963.

Allan H. Meltzer. "A Weekly New Issue Yield Curve for Municipal Bonds." *National Banking
Review,* December 1963, 167–76.

Allan H. Meltzer. "Yet Another Look at the Low Level Liquidity Trap." *Econometrica* 31, no. 3 (July 1963): 545–49.

David J. Ott and Allan H. Meltzer. "Issues in the Tax Treatment of State and Local Securities." Brookings Research Report No. 8, Brookings Institution, Washington, DC, 1963.

Karl Brunner and Allan H. Meltzer. "Comments on Federal Reserve Policy." *Banking Journal of the American Bankers' Association*, April 1964.

Karl Brunner and Allan H. Meltzer. "Some Further Investigations of Demand and Supply Functions for Money." *Journal of Finance* 19, no. 2 (May 1964): 240–83.

Allan H. Meltzer. Comment on "Financial Markets in Business Cycles: A Simulation Study," by Frank De Leeuw, and on "Longer Waves in Financial Relations: Financial Factors in the More Severe Depressions," by Hyman Minsky. *American Economic Review* 54, no. 3 (May 1964): 340–43.

Allan H. Meltzer. "A Little More Evidence from the Time Series." *Journal of Political Economy* 72, no. 5 (October 1964): 504–8.

Allan H. Meltzer. "Public and Private Financial Institutions: A Review of Reports from Two Presidential Committees." *Review of Economics and Statistics* 46, no. 3 (August 1964): 269–78.

Allan H. Meltzer. "Rejoinder to Professor West." *National Banking Review* 4 (1964): 261–62.

Karl Brunner and Allan H. Meltzer. "Auerbach's Defense of Defensive Operations." *Journal of Finance* 20, no. 3 (September 1965): 500–502.

Karl Brunner and Allan H. Meltzer. Reply to "Should Federal Reserve Float Be Abolished and Its Check Activities Curtailed?," by Irving Auerbach. *Journal of Finance* 22, no. 3 (September 1965): 496–98.

Allan H. Meltzer. "Improvements in the Balance of Payments: A Response to Monetary Policy or to Ad Hoc Fiscal Policies." *Journal of Business* 38, no. 3 (July 1965): 267–76.

Allan H. Meltzer. "Monetary Theory and Monetary History." *Swiss Journal of Economics and Statistics* 101, no. IV (December 1965): 404–22.

Allan H. Meltzer. Reply to G. S. Maddala, Robert C. Vogel, and Eduard Whalen's comments on "The Demand for Money: A Cross-Section Study of Business Firms," by Allan H. Meltzer. *Quarterly Journal of Economics* 79, no. 1 (February 1965): 162–65.

Allan H. Meltzer. "What Should We Teach in a Money and Banking Course: Discussion." *Journal of Finance*, May 1965.

Karl Brunner and Allan H. Meltzer. "A Credit Market Theory of the Money Supply and an Explanation of Two Puzzles in US Monetary Policy." *Rivista internazionale di scienze economiche e commerciali* 13, no. 5 (May 1966): 405–32. Reprinted in *Studi in onore di Marco Fanno: Ricerche di metodologia e di teoria economica* [Essays in honor of Marco Fanno: Investigations in economic theory and methodology], edited by Tullio Bagiotti, 2:151–76. Padua, Italy: CEDAM, 1966.

Allan H. Meltzer. "The Money Managers and the Boom." *Challenge* 14, no. 4 (March–April 1966): 4–7.

Allan H. Meltzer. "The Regulation of Bank Credits Abroad: Another Failure for the Government's Balance of Payments Program." In *Guidelines, Informal Controls and the Market Place*, edited by George Shultz and Robert Z. Aliber. Chicago: University of Chicago Press, 1966.

Karl Brunner and Allan H. Meltzer. Comment on Daniel Brill's commentary on "Predicting Velocity: Implications for Theory and Policy," by Karl Brunner and Allan H. Meltzer. In *Monetary Process and Policy: A Symposium*, edited by George Horwich. Homewood, IL: Richard D. Irwin, 1967.

Karl Brunner and Allan H. Meltzer. "Economies of Scale in Cash Balances Reconsidered." *Quarterly Journal of Economics* 81, no. 3 (August 1967): 422–36.

Karl Brunner and Allan H. Meltzer. "The Meaning of Monetary Indicators." In *Monetary Process and Policy: A Symposium*, edited by George Horwich, 187–217. Homewood, IL: Richard D. Irwin, 1967.

Karl Brunner and Allan H. Meltzer. "Rejoinder to Chase and Hendershott." In *Monetary Process and Policy: A Symposium*, edited by George Horwich. Homewood, IL: Richard D. Irwin, 1967.

Allan H. Meltzer. Comment on "Blend of Fiscal and Monetary Policies," by Richard Musgrave. In *Fiscal Policy and Business Capital Formation*, 187–93. Washington, DC: American Enterprise Institute, 1967.

Allan H. Meltzer. Comment on "Some Implications of Money Supply Analysis," by David I. Fand, and on "Keynes and the Keynesians: A Suggested Interpretation," by Axel Leijonhufvud. *American Economic Review* 57, no. 2 (May 1967): 426–27.

Allan H. Meltzer. "Irving Fisher and the Quantity Theory of Money." *Orbis Economicus* 10, no. 9 (March 1967).

Allan H. Meltzer. "Is Secular Inflation Likely in the U.S.?" In *Monetary Problems of the Early 1960s: Review and Appraisal*, 29–42. Proceedings of the Third Annual Conference on Economic Affairs, Atlanta, May 1967.

Allan H. Meltzer. "Major Issues in the Regulation of Financial Institutions." Supplement, *Journal of Political Economy* 75, no. 4, part II (August 1967): 482–500.

Allan H. Meltzer. "Money Supply Revisited: A Review Article." *Journal of Political Economy* 75, no. 2 (April 1967): 169–82.

Allan H. Meltzer. "On Human Wealth and the Demand for Money." *Journal of Political Economy* 75, no. 1 (February 1967): 96–97.

Karl Brunner and Allan H. Meltzer. "Comment on the Long-Run and Short-Run Demand for Money." *Journal of Political Economy* 76, no. 6 (November–December 1968): 1234–40.

Karl Brunner and Allan H. Meltzer. "Liquidity Traps for Money, Bank Credit, and Interest Rates." *Journal of Political Economy* 76, no. 1 (January–February 1968): 1–37.

Karl Brunner and Allan H. Meltzer. "What Did We Learn from the Monetary Experience of the United States in the Great Depression?" *Canadian Journal of Economics* 1, no. 2 (May 1968): 334–48.

Allan H. Meltzer. "Introduction." *Journal of Political Economy* 76 (1968): 661.

Allan H. Meltzer. "Predicting the Effects of Monetary Policy." *Business Economics* 3, no. 2 (Spring 1968): 7–13.

Karl Brunner and Allan H. Meltzer. "The Nature of the Policy Problem." In *Targets and Indicators of Monetary Policy*, edited by Karl Brunner, 1–26. San Francisco: Chandler, 1969.

Allan H. Meltzer. "The Appropriate Indicators of Monetary Policy." In *Savings and Residential Financing: Conference Proceedings*, edited by D. P. Jacobs and R. T. Pratt, 11–31. Chicago: United States Savings and Loan League, 1969.

Allan H. Meltzer. Comment on "Financial Disintermediation and Policy," by Donald D. Hester. *Journal of Money, Credit and Banking* 1, no. 3 (August 1969): 618–24.

Allan H. Meltzer. "Controlling Money." *Review* (Federal Reserve Bank of St. Louis), May 1969, 16–24. Reprinted in *Ensaios em economia política* [Essays in political economy], edited by A. M. Silveira. Rio de Janeiro: Edições Multiplic, 1982.

Allan H. Meltzer. "Money, Intermediation, and Growth." *Journal of Economic Literature* 7, no. 1 (March 1969): 27–56.

Allan H. Meltzer. "On Efficiency and Regulation of the Securities Industry." In *Economic Policy and the Regulation of Corporate Security*, edited by Henry Manne, 217–38. Washington, DC: American Enterprise Institute, 1969.

Allan H. Meltzer. Panelist for "The Role of Money in National Economic Policy." In *Controlling Monetary Aggregates: Proceedings of a Conference Held in June, 1969*, 25–30. Conference Series No. 1. Boston: Federal Reserve Bank of Boston, 1969.

Allan H. Meltzer. "Tactics and Targets: Discussion." In *Controlling Monetary Aggregates: Proceedings of a Conference Held in June, 1969*, 96–103. Conference Series No. 1. Boston: Federal Reserve Bank of Boston, 1969.

Judith Gertler and Allan H. Meltzer. "Selecting Creative Ph.D. Candidates for Admission." *Journal of Experimental Education* 38, no. 3 (Spring 1970): 15–18.

Allan H. Meltzer. "Is There an Optimal Money Supply? A Discussion." *Journal of Finance* 25, no. 2 (May 1970): 450–53.

Allan H. Meltzer. "Public Policies as Causes of Fluctuations." *Journal of Money, Credit and Banking* 2, no. 1 (February 1970): 45–55.

Allan H. Meltzer. Review of *Documentary History of Banking and Currency*, by Herman E. Krooss. *Journal of Economic Literature* 8, no. 1 (March 1970): 55–57.

Karl Brunner and Allan H. Meltzer. "Inflation, Output and the Role of Monetary and Fiscal Policy." In "The Monetary Fiscal Approach to Inflation: A Multi Country Study," by Karl Brunner, Michael Fratianni, Jerry Jordan, and Manfred J. M. Neumann. Discussion Paper No. 9a, University of Konstanz, Department of Economics, 1971.

Karl Brunner and Allan H. Meltzer. "The Uses of Money: Money in the Theory of an Exchange Economy." *American Economic Review* 61, no. 5 (December 1971): 784–805.

Allan H. Meltzer. "Regulation Q: The Money Markets and Housing." In *Housing and Monetary Policy*, 41–51. Conference Series No. 4. Boston: Federal Reserve Bank of Boston, 1971.

Allan H. Meltzer. "Restoring a Healthy Economic Environment." In *Proceedings of the American Insurance Association*. May 1970. Reprinted in *Kredit und Kapital*, no. 2 (1971).

Karl Brunner and Allan H. Meltzer. "Friedman's Monetary Theory." *Journal of Political Economy* 80, no. 5 (September–October 1972): 837–51.

Karl Brunner and Allan H. Meltzer. "A Monetarist Framework for Aggregative Analysis." In *Proceedings of the First Konstanzer Seminar on Monetary Theory and Monetary Policy*, edited by Karl Brunner, 31–88. Berlin: Duncker & Humblot, 1972.

Karl Brunner and Allan H. Meltzer. "Money, Debt, and Economic Activity." *Journal of Political Economy* 80, no. 5 (September–October 1972): 951–77.

Karl Brunner and Allan H. Meltzer. "Relative Prices and Tax Policies: Some Preliminary Implications and Results." In *Scritti in memoria di Antonio de Viti de Marco* [Written in memory of Antonio de Viti de Marco], edited by Ernesto D'Albergo. Bari, Italy: Cacucci, 1972.

Allan H. Meltzer. "Aggregative Consequences of Removing Restrictions." *Journal of Bank Research* 3, no. 2 (Summer 1972): 72–83.

Allan H. Meltzer. "What the Commission Didn't Recommend." *Journal of Money, Credit and Banking* 4, no. 4 (November 1972): 1005–9.

Francisco Arcelus and Allan H. Meltzer. "The Markets for Housing and Housing Services." *Journal of Money, Credit and Banking* 5, no. 1, part 1 (1973): 78–89.

Francisco Arcelus and Allan H. Meltzer. Reply to Craig Swan's comment on "The Markets for Housing and Housing Services," by Francisco Arcelus and Allan H. Meltzer. *Journal of Money, Credit and Banking* 5, no. 4 (November 1973): 973–78.

Karl Brunner, Michele Fratianni, Jerry L. Jordan, Allan H. Meltzer, and Manfred J. M. Neumann. "Fiscal and Monetary Policies in Moderate Inflation: Case Studies of Three Countries." *Journal of Money, Credit and Banking* 5, no. 1 (February 1973): 313–53.

Karl Brunner and Allan H. Meltzer. "Mr. Hicks and the 'Monetarists.'" *Economica* 40, no. 157 (February 1973): 44–59.

Allan H. Meltzer. "The Dollar as an International Money." *Banca Nazionale del Lavoro Quarterly Review* 26, no. 104 (March 1973): 21–28.

Stephen M. Goldfield and Allan H. Meltzer. Discussion of "Session Topic: The Flow of Funds and Interest Rates—I: U.S. Financial Models." *Journal of Finance* 29, no. 2 (May 1974): 358–63.

Allan H. Meltzer. "Credit Availability and Economic Decisions: Some Evidence from the Mortgage and Housing Markets." *Journal of Finance* 29, no. 3 (June 1974): 763–78.

Allan H. Meltzer. Discussion of "Policy Implications of a Flow-of-Funds Model," by James S. Duesenberry and Barry Bosworth, and on "Short Term Financial Models at the Federal Reserve Board," by James L. Pierce and Thomas T. Thomson. *Journal of Finance* 29, no. 2 (May 1974): 360–64.

Francisco Arcelus and Allan H. Meltzer. "Aggregate Economic Variables and Votes for Congress: A Rejoinder." Reply to Saul Goodman and Gerald H. Kramer's comment on "The Effect of Aggregate Economic Variables on Congressional Elections," by Francisco Arcelus and Allan H. Meltzer. *American Political Science Review* 69, no. 4 (December 1975): 1266–69.

Francisco Arcelus and Allan H. Meltzer. "The Effect of Aggregate Economic Variables on Congressional Elections." *American Political Science Review* 69, no. 4 (December 1975): 1232–39.

Allan H. Meltzer. "Commentary on the Papers." In *The Phenomenon of Worldwide Inflation*, edited by David I. Meiselman and Arthur B. Laffer, 53–56. Washington, DC: American Enterprise Institute, 1975.

Allan H. Meltzer. "Housing and Financial Policy." *Challenge* 18, no. 5 (November–December 1975): 61–64.

Allan H. Meltzer. "Inflation, Energy and the World Economy, Prospects for International Cooperation." In *Selected Papers on Inflation, Recession, Energy and the International Financial Structure*, edited by Penelope Hartland-Thunberg, 53–66. Washington, DC: Center for Strategic and International Studies, Georgetown University, 1975.

Allan H. Meltzer and Marc Vellrath. "The Effects of Economic Policies on Votes for the Presidency: Some Evidence from Recent Elections." *Journal of Law and Economics* 18, no. 3 (December 1975): 781–98.

Allan H. Meltzer and Marc Vellrath. Reply to George J. Stigler and Gerald H. Kramer's comments on "The Effects of Economic Policies on Votes for the Presidency: Some Evidence from Recent Elections," by Allan H. Meltzer and Marc Vellrath. *Journal of Law and Economics* 18, no. 3 (December 1975): 803–5.

Karl Brunner and Allan H. Meltzer. "An Aggregative Theory for a Closed Economy." In *Monetarism*, edited by Jerome L. Stein, 69–103. Amsterdam: North-Holland, 1976.

Karl Brunner and Allan H. Meltzer. "The Economics of Price and Wage Controls: An Introduction." *Carnegie-Rochester Conference Series on Public Policy* 2 (1976): 1–6.

Karl Brunner and Allan H. Meltzer. "Government, the Private Sector and 'Crowding Out.'" *Banker*, July 1976, 765–69.

Karl Brunner and Allan H. Meltzer. "Institutional Arrangements and the Inflation Problem." *Carnegie-Rochester Conference Series on Public Policy* 3 (1976): 1–13.

Karl Brunner and Allan H. Meltzer. "Institutions, Policies and Economic Performance." *Carnegie-Rochester Conference Series on Public Policy* 4 (1976): 1–14.

Karl Brunner and Allan H. Meltzer. "Introduction to the Series." *Carnegie-Rochester Conference Series on Public Policy* 1 (1976).

Karl Brunner and Allan H. Meltzer. "Introduction to the Series." *Carnegie-Rochester Conference Series on Public Policy* 3 (1976).

Karl Brunner and Allan H. Meltzer. "Monetarism: The Principal Issues, Areas of Agreement and the Work Remaining." In *Monetarism*, edited by Jerome L. Stein, 150–82. Amsterdam: North-Holland, 1976.

Karl Brunner and Allan H. Meltzer. "Monetary and Fiscal Policy in Open, Interdependent Economies with Fixed Exchange Rates." In *Recent Issues in International Monetary Economics*, edited by Emil-Maria Claassen and Pascal Salin, 328–59. Amsterdam: North-Holland, 1976.

Karl Brunner and Allan H. Meltzer. "The Phillips Curve." *Carnegie-Rochester Conference Series on Public Policy* 1 (1976): 1–18.

Allan H. Meltzer. "Monetary and Other Explanations of the Start of the Great Depression." *Journal of Monetary Economics* 2, no. 4 (November 1976): 455–71.

Allan H. Meltzer. "The Monetary Approach to Inflation and the Balance of Payments: Theoretical and Empirical Contributions at the Leuven Conference." In *Bank Credit, Money and Inflation in Open Economics*, edited by Michele Fratianni and Karel Tavernier, 579–617. Berlin: Duncker & Humblot, 1976.

Karl Brunner and Allan H. Meltzer. "The Explanation of Inflation: Some International Evidence." *American Economic Review* 67, no. 1 (February 1977): 148–54. Simultaneously published in *Transaction-Society* 14 (March–April 1977): 35–40.

Karl Brunner and Allan H. Meltzer. "International Organization, National Policies and Economic Development." *Carnegie-Rochester Conference Series on Public Policy* 6 (1977): 1–16.

Karl Brunner and Allan H. Meltzer. "Introduction to the Series." *Carnegie-Rochester Conference Series on Public Policy* 6 (1977).

Karl Brunner and Allan H. Meltzer. "Optimal Policies, Control Theory and Technology Exports." *Carnegie-Rochester Conference Series on Public Policy* 7 (1977): 1–11.

Karl Brunner and Allan H. Meltzer. "Stabilization of the Domestic and International Economy." *Carnegie-Rochester Conference Series on Public Policy* 5 (1977): 1–6.

Allan H. Meltzer. "Anticipated Inflation and Unanticipated Price Change: A Test of the Price-Specie Flow Theory and the Phillips Curve." *Journal of Money, Credit and Banking* 9, no. 1, part 2 (February 1977): 182–205.

Allan H. Meltzer. "The Decline of the Liberal Economy." *Vie et sciences economiques* 72 (January 1977): 1–77. Reprinted as "A decadência da economia liberal" in *Revista brasileira de economia* 31, no. 1 (January–March 1977): 205–20. Also reprinted in *Ensaios em economia política* [Essays in political economy], edited by A. M. Silveira. Rio de Janeiro: Edições Multiplic, 1982.

Allan H. Meltzer. "Monetarist, Keynesian and Quantity Theories." *Kredit und Kapital* 10, no. 2 (1977): 149–82. Reprinted in *The Structure of Monetarism*, edited by Thomas Mayer, 145–75. New York: W. W. Norton, 1978.

Allan H. Meltzer. "Too Much Government?" In *The Economy in Transition*, edited by R. Blattberg. New York: New York University Press, 1977.

Allan H. Meltzer, Edy Luiz Kogut, and Élcio Giestas. "Leilão de redescontos" [Rediscount auction]. *Revista brasileira de economia* 31, no. 3 (July/September 1977): 541–45.

Karl Brunner and Allan H. Meltzer. "Introduction to the Series." *Carnegie-Rochester Conference Series on Public Policy* 8 (1978).

Karl Brunner and Allan H. Meltzer. "The Problem of Inflation." *Carnegie-Rochester Conference Series on Public Policy* 8 (1978): 1–15.

Karl Brunner and Allan H. Meltzer. "Public Policies in Open Economies." *Carnegie-Rochester Conference Series on Public Policy* 9 (1978): 1–4.

Pieter Korteweg and Allan H. Meltzer. "Inflation and Price Changes: Some Preliminary Estimates and Tests of Alternative Theories." *Carnegie-Rochester Conference Series on Public Policy* 8 (1978): 325–53.

Allan H. Meltzer. "The Conduct of Monetary Policy under Current Monetary Arrangements." *Journal of Monetary Economics* 4, no. 2 (April 1978): 371–88.

Allan H. Meltzer. "The Effects of EFT on the Instruments of Monetary Policy." *Journal of Contemporary Business* 7, no. 2 (Spring 1978): 101–25.

Allan H. Meltzer. "The Effects of Financial Innovation on the Instruments of Monetary Policy." *Economies et sociétés: Cahiers de l'ISMEA* 12, no. 10-11-12 (October 1978): 1889–916.

Allan H. Meltzer. "Princípios que orientam a política monetária brasileira" [Principles guiding Brazilian monetary policy]. *Debate economico* 1, no. 3 (September 1978). Reprinted in *Edições Multiplic*, April 1981, 73–82.

Allan H. Meltzer and Scott F. Richard. "Why Government Grows (and Grows) in a Democracy." *Public Interest*, no. 52 (Summer 1978): 111–18.

Karl Brunner and Allan H. Meltzer. "Policies for Employment, Prices, and Exchange Rates." *Carnegie-Rochester Conference Series on Public Policy* 11 (1979): 1–7.

Karl Brunner and Allan H. Meltzer. "Three Aspects of Policy and Policymaking: Knowledge, Data and Institutions." *Carnegie-Rochester Conference Series on Public Policy* 10 (1979): 1–7.

Allan H. Meltzer. "Europe Enters the Eighties." *Banca Nazionale del Lavoro Quarterly Review* 32, no. 129 (June 1979): 117–32.

Allan H. Meltzer. "Perspekteren in Sicherung der Unternehmungsautonomie" [Aspects in securing enterprise autonomy]. In *Proceedings of the International Management Symposium*, 115–22. Bern, Switzerland: Verlag Paul Haupt, 1979.

Allan H. Meltzer. Review of *Curing Chronic Inflation*, edited by Arthur M. Okun and George L. Perry, and *Microeconomic Effects of Monetary Policy: The Fallout of Severe Monetary Restraint*, by Ervin Miller with Alasdair Lonie. *Journal of Economic Literature* 17, no. 3 (September 1979): 1038–43.

Allan H. Meltzer. "The Spending Limitation Approach." In *Balancing the Budget*, edited by P. Trulock, 7–13. Washington, DC: Heritage Foundation, 1979.

Allan H. Meltzer. "Washington." *Challenge* 22, no. 4 (September 1979): 60–62.

Karl Brunner, Alex Cukierman, and Allan H. Meltzer. "Stagflation, Persistent Unemployment and the Permanence of Economic Shocks." *Journal of Monetary Economics* 6, no. 4 (October 1980): 467–92.

Karl Brunner and Allan H. Meltzer. "Monetary Institutions and the Policy Process." *Carnegie-Rochester Conference Series on Public Policy* 13 (1980): 1–8.

Karl Brunner and Allan H. Meltzer. "On the State of Macroeconomics." *Carnegie-Rochester Conference Series on Public Policy* 12 (1980): 1–5.

Allan H. Meltzer. "Appropriate Monetary Policy Guidelines for 1980 and Beyond." In *Issues in Financial and Monetary Policy*, edited by Michael J. Hamburger, 13–14. New York: New York University, 1980.

Allan H. Meltzer. "The Case for Gradualism in Policies to Reduce Inflation." In *Stabilization Policies: Lessons from the '70s and Implications for the '80s*, 127–54. Center for the Study of American Business, April 1980.

Allan H. Meltzer. "Central Bank Policy: Some First Principles." *Annual Monetary Review* (Centre for Banking and International Finance) 2 (December 1980): 27–33.

Allan H. Meltzer. Discussion of "A Consistent Characterization of a Near-Century of Price Behavior," by Robert J. Gordon. *American Economic Review* 70, no. 2 (May 1980): 258–59.

Allan H. Meltzer. "First Financial Forum, September 27, 1979: Allan Meltzer's Opening Statement." In *Issues in Monetary Policy: Three Financial Forums*, edited by Michael J. Hamburger, 13–14. New York: New York University, 1980.

Allan H. Meltzer. "Monetarism and the Crises in Economics." *Public Interest*, Special Issue (1980): 35–45. Reprinted in *The Crises in Economic Theory*, edited by Daniel Bell and Irving Kristol, 35–45. New York: Basic Books, 1981.

Karl Brunner and Allan H. Meltzer. "The Costs and Consequences of Inflation." *Carnegie-Rochester Conference Series on Public Policy* 15 (1981): 1–4.

Karl Brunner and Allan H. Meltzer. "Supply Shocks, Incentives and National Wealth." *Carnegie-Rochester Conference Series on Public Policy* 14 (1981): 1–8.

Karl Brunner and Allan H. Meltzer. "Time Deposits in the Brunner-Meltzer Model of Asset Markets." *Journal of Monetary Economics* 7, no. 1 (January 1981): 129–39.

Allan H. Meltzer. Comment on "Monetarist Interpretation of the Great Depression," by Robert J. Gordon and James A. Wilcox. In *The Great Depression Revisited*, edited by Karl Brunner, 148–64. Boston: Martinus Nijhoff, 1981.

Allan H. Meltzer. "Keynes's General Theory: A Different Perspective." *Journal of Economic Literature* 19, no. 1 (March 1981): 34–64. Reprinted in *Ensaios em economia política* [Essays in political economy], edited by A. M. Silveira. Rio de Janeiro: Edições Multiplic, 1982.

Allan H. Meltzer. "Tests of Inflation Theories from the British Laboratory." *Banker* 131, no. 665 (July 1981): 21–27.

Allan H. Meltzer and Scott F. Richard. "A Rational Theory of the Size of Government." *Journal of Political Economy* 89, no. 5 (October 1981): 914–27.

Karl Brunner and Allan H. Meltzer. "Economic Policy in a World of Change." *Carnegie-Rochester Conference Series on Public Policy* 17 (1982): 1–6.

Karl Brunner and Allan H. Meltzer. "Monetary Regimes and Protectionism." *Carnegie-Rochester Conference Series on Public Policy* 16 (1982): 1–10.

Allan H. Meltzer. Comment on "Exchange Rates, Interest Rates and the Mobility of Capital," by Andrew Britton and Peter Spencer. In *Exchange Rate Policy*, edited by Roy A. Batchelor and Geoffrey E. Wood, 226–31. London: Macmillan, 1982.

Allan H. Meltzer. Comment on "Federal Reserve Control of the Money Stock," by Ralph C. Bryant. *Journal of Money, Credit and Banking* 14, no. 4 (November 1982): 632–40.

Allan H. Meltzer. Comment on "Flexible Exchange Rates, Prices, and the Role of News: Lessons from the 1970s," by Jacob A. Frenkel. In *Exchange Rate Policy*, edited by Roy A. Batchelor and Geoffrey E. Wood, 94–98. London: Macmillan, 1982.

Allan H. Meltzer. Comment on "National Financial Policies in an Interdependent World: Background for Discussion," by Jacob S. Dreyer. In *The International Monetary System: A Time of Turbulence*, edited by Jacob S. Dreyer, Gottfried Habeler, and Thomas D. Willett, 513–19. Washington, DC: American Enterprise Institute, 1982.

Allan H. Meltzer. Comment on "Reserve Requirements on Eurocurrency Deposits: Implications for Eurodeposit Multipliers, Control of a Monetary Aggregate, and Avoidance of Redenomination Incentives," by Dale W. Henderson and Douglas G. Waldo, and on "Offshore Markets in Foreign Currencies and National Monetary Control: Britain, Singapore, and the United States," by Ronald I. McKinnon. In *The International Monetary System: A Time of Turbulence*, edited by Jacob S. Dreyer, Gottfried Habeler, and Thomas D. Willett, 364–71. Washington, DC: American Enterprise Institute, 1982.

Allan H. Meltzer. Discussion of "External Pressures and Operations of the Federal Reserve," by E. Kane. In *Political Economy and International Domestic Monetary Relations*, edited by Raymond Lombra and Willard E. Witte. Iowa City: University of Iowa Press, 1982.

Allan H. Meltzer. "Epistle to the Gold Commission." *Report to the Congress of the Commission on the Role of Gold in the Domestic and International Monetary Systems* 2 (March 1982): 459–60.

Allan H. Meltzer. "Rational Expectations, Risk, Uncertainty, and Market Responses." In *Crises in the Economic and Financial Structure*, edited by Paul A. Wachtel, 3–22. Lexington, MA: Lexington Books, 1982.

Allan H. Meltzer. "The Thrift Industry in the Reagan Era." In *Managing Interest Rate Risk in the Thrift Industry: Proceedings of the Seventh Annual Conference*, 5–14. San Francisco: Federal Home Loan Bank of San Francisco, 1982.

Allan H. Meltzer, Peter Ordeshook, and Thomas Romer. "Introduction." *Public Choice* 39, no. 1 (January 1982): 1–3.

Robert H. Rasche, Allan H. Meltzer, Peter D. Sternlight, and Stephen H. Axilrod. "Is the Federal Reserve's Monetary Control Policy Misdirected?" Money, Credit, and Banking Debate. *Journal of Money, Credit and Banking* 14, no. 1 (February 1982): 119–47.

Karl Brunner, Alex Cukierman, and Allan H. Meltzer. "Money and Economic Activity, Inventories and Business Cycles." *Journal of Monetary Economics* 11, no. 3 (1983): 281–319.

Karl Brunner and Allan H. Meltzer. "Introduction to the Series." *Carnegie-Rochester Conference Series on Public Policy* 18 (1983).

Karl Brunner and Allan H. Meltzer. "Money, Monetary Policy, and Financial Institutions." *Carnegie-Rochester Conference Series on Public Policy* 18 (1983): 1–7.

Karl Brunner and Allan H. Meltzer. Reply to Stephen H. Axilrod's comment on "Strategies and Tactics for Monetary Control," by Karl Brunner and Allan H. Meltzer. *Carnegie-Rochester Conference Series on Public Policy* 18 (1983): 113–16.

Karl Brunner and Allan H. Meltzer. "Strategies and Tactics for Monetary Control." *Carnegie-Rochester Conference Series on Public Policy* 18 (1983): 59–103.

Karl Brunner and Allan H. Meltzer. "Variability in Employment, Prices, and Money." *Carnegie-Rochester Conference Series on Public Policy* 19 (1983): 1–4.

Angelo Mascaro and Allan H. Meltzer. "Long- and Short-Term Interest Rates in a Risky World." *Journal of Monetary Economics* 12, no. 4 (November 1983): 485–518.

Allan H. Meltzer. "Deficits and Inflation." In *Toward a Reconstruction of Federal Budgeting: A Public Policy Research Program Conducted by the Conference Board*, 46–51. New York: Conference Board, 1983. Reprinted in *Reconstructing the Federal Budget: A Trillion Dollar Quandary*, edited by Albert T. Sommers, 117–29. New York: Praeger, 1984.

Allan H. Meltzer. "Five Reasons for Opposing the IMF Quota Increase." In *Constructive Approaches to the Foreign Debt Dilemma*, edited by Mark Hulbert and Eric Meltzer. Washington, DC: Taxpayers' Foundation, 1983.

Allan H. Meltzer. "Interpreting Keynes." Review of "Keynes's General Theory: A Different Perspective," by Allan H. Meltzer. *Journal of Economic Literature* 21, no. 1 (March 1983): 66–78.

Allan H. Meltzer. "Introduction." *Public Choice* 41, no. 1 (January 1983): 1–5.

Allan H. Meltzer. "Monetary Reform in an Uncertain Environment." *Cato Journal* 3, no. 1 (Spring 1983): 93–112. Reprinted in *The Search for Stable Money: Essays on Monetary Reform*, edited by James A. Dorn and Anna Jacobson Schwartz, 201–20. Chicago: University of Chicago Press, 1987.

Allan H. Meltzer. "On Keynes and Monetarism." In *Keynes in the Modern World: Proceedings of the Keynes Centenary Conference*, edited by David Worswick and James Trevithick, 49–77. Cambridge: Cambridge University Press, 1983.

Allan H. Meltzer. "Present and Future in an Uncertain World." In *The Interest Rate Dilemma*, edited by Terry Sanford, 37–55. ITT Key Issues Lecture Series. New York: KCG Productions, 1983.

Allan H. Meltzer. "Tests of a Rational Theory of the Size of Government." *Public Choice* 41, no. 3 (January 1983): 403–18.

Allan H. Meltzer and Scott F. Richard. "Rejoinder to Gordon Tullock." Comment on "Further Tests of a Rational Theory of the Size of Government," by Gordon Tullock. *Public Choice* 41, no. 3 (January 1983): 423–26.

Karl Brunner and Allan H. Meltzer. "Essays on Macroeconomic Implications of Financial and Labor Markets and Political Processes." *Carnegie-Rochester Conference Series on Public Policy* 21 (1984): 1–8.

Karl Brunner and Allan H. Meltzer. "Introduction to the Series." *Carnegie-Rochester Conference Series on Public Policy* 20 (1984).

Karl Brunner and Allan H. Meltzer. "Monetary and Fiscal Policies and Their Application." *Carnegie-Rochester Conference Series on Public Policy* 20 (1984): 1–5.

Allan H. Meltzer. Comment on "Financial Innovation and Financial Instability: Observations and Theory," by Hyman P. Minsky. In *Financial Innovations*, by the Federal Reserve Bank of St. Louis. Boston: Kluwer Academic, 1984.

Allan H. Meltzer. "The Cure for Monetary Madness." *Policy Review* 27 (Winter 1984): 72–74.

Allan H. Meltzer. "The Fight against Inflation: A Comment." In *Monetarism in the United Kingdom*, edited by Brian Griffiths and Geoffrey E. Wood, 61–66. London: Macmillan, 1984.

Allan H. Meltzer. "The International Debt Problem." *Cato Journal* 4, no. 1 (Spring–Summer 1984): 63–69.

Allan H. Meltzer. "Keynes's Labor Market: A Reply." *Journal of Post Keynesian Economics* 6, no. 4 (July 1984): 532–39.

Allan H. Meltzer, Thomas Romer, and Howard Rosenthal. "Introduction to the Series." *Public Choice* 44, no. 1 (January 1984): 1.

Karl Brunner and Allan H. Meltzer. "Introduction to the Series." *Carnegie-Rochester Conference Series on Public Policy* 22 (1985).

Karl Brunner and Allan H. Meltzer. "Introduction to the Series." *Carnegie-Rochester Conference Series on Public Policy* 23 (1985).

Karl Brunner and Allan H. Meltzer. "The 'New Monetary Economics,' Fiscal Issues, and Unemployment." *Carnegie-Rochester Conference Series on Public Policy* 23 (1985): 1–12.

Karl Brunner and Allan H. Meltzer. "Understanding Monetary Regimes." *Carnegie-Rochester Conference Series on Public Policy* 22 (1985): 1–8.

Allan H. Meltzer. "The Case for a Monetary Rule." In *Modern Concepts in Macroeconomics*, edited by Thomas M. Havrilesky. Arlington Heights, IL: Harlan Davidson, 1985.

Allan H. Meltzer. Comment on "Economic Stabilization and Liberalization in Korea, 1980–84," by Yung-Chul Park. *Monetary Policy and the Changing Financial Environment: Proceedings of Seminar Commemorating the 35th Anniversary of the Bank of Korea*, 141–47. June 1985.

Allan H. Meltzer. "Financial Failures and Financial Policies." Report of the Technical Committee, Global Action Institute, New York, September 1985. Reprinted in *Deregulating Financial Services: Public Policy in Flux*, edited by George Kaufman and Roger Kormendi, 79–96. Cambridge, MA: Ballinger, 1986.

Allan H. Meltzer. "Policies for Growth with Low Inflation and Increased Efficiency." In *Monetary Policy and the Changing Financial Environment: Proceedings of Seminar Commemorating the 35th Anniversary of the Bank of Korea*, 1–22. June 1985.

Allan H. Meltzer. "A Positive Theory of In-Kind Transfers and the Negative Income Tax." *Public Choice* 47, no. 1 (January 1985): 231–65.

Allan H. Meltzer. "Rules for Price Stability: An Overview and Comparison." *Price Stability and Public Policy* (Federal Reserve Bank of Kansas City), 1985, 209–22.

Allan H. Meltzer. "Variability of Prices, Output and Money under Fixed and Fluctuating Exchange Rates: An Empirical Study of Monetary Regimes in Japan and the United States." *Bank of Japan Monetary and Economic Studies* 3, no. 3 (December 1985): 1–46.

Karl Brunner and Allan H. Meltzer. "Introduction to the Series." *Carnegie-Rochester Conference Series on Public Policy* 24 (1986).

Karl Brunner and Allan H. Meltzer. "Introduction to the Series." *Carnegie-Rochester Conference Series on Public Policy* 25 (1986).

Karl Brunner and Allan H. Meltzer. "The National Bureau Method, International Capital Mobility, and Other Essays." *Carnegie-Rochester Conference Series on Public Policy* 24 (1986): 1–10.

Karl Brunner and Allan H. Meltzer. "Real Business Cycles, Real Exchange Rates, and Actual Policies." *Carnegie-Rochester Conference Series on Public Policy* 25 (1986): 1–10.

Alex Cukierman and Allan H. Meltzer. "The Credibility of Monetary Announcements." In *Monetary Policy and Uncertainty*, edited by Manfred J. M. Neumann, 39–67. Baden-Baden, Germany: Nomos Verlagsgesellschaft, 1986.

Alex Cukierman and Allan H. Meltzer. "A Positive Theory of Discretionary Policy, the Cost of Democratic Government and the Benefits of a Constitution." *Economic Inquiry* 24, no. 3 (July 1986): 367–88.

Alex Cukierman and Allan H. Meltzer. "A Theory of Ambiguity, Credibility, and Inflation under Discretion and Asymmetric Information." *Econometrica* 54, no. 5 (September 1986): 1099–128.

Allan H. Meltzer. Commentary on "Increasing Indebtedness and Financial Stability in the United States," by Benjamin M. Friedman. In *Debt, Financial Stability, and Public Policy: A Symposium Sponsored by the Federal Reserve Bank of Kansas City*, 55–61. Federal Reserve Bank of Kansas City, 1986.

Allan H. Meltzer. Comment on "Money, Credit, and Interest Rates in the Business Cycle," by Benjamin M. Friedman. In *The American Business Cycle: Continuity and Change*, edited by Robert J. Gordon, 441–50. Chicago: University of Chicago Press and National Bureau of Economic Research, 1986.

Allan H. Meltzer. "Comment on Real and Pseudo-financial Crises." In *Financial Crises and the World Banking System*, edited by Forrest Capie and Geoffrey E. Wood, 32–37. London: Macmillan, 1986.

Allan H. Meltzer. "Lessons from the Experience of Japan and the United States under Fixed and Fluctuating Exchange Rates." *Bank of Japan Monetary and Economic Studies* 4, no. 2 (October 1986): 129–45.

Allan H. Meltzer. "Money and Exchange Rate Regimes: A Comparison of Japan and the United States." *Cato Journal* 6, no. 2 (Fall 1986): 667–83.

Allan H. Meltzer. "Size, Persistence and Interrelation of Nominal and Real Shocks: Some Evidence from Four Countries." *Journal of Monetary Economics* 17, no. 1 (January–February 1986): 161–94.

Allan H. Meltzer. "Some Evidence on the Comparative Uncertainty Experience under Different Monetary Regimes." In *Alternative Monetary Regimes*, edited by Colin D. Campbell and William R. Dougan, 122–53. Baltimore: Johns Hopkins University Press, 1986.

Karl Brunner and Allan H. Meltzer. "Bubbles and Other Essays." *Carnegie-Rochester Conference Series on Public Policy* 26 (1987): 1–8.

Karl Brunner and Allan H. Meltzer. "Empirical Studies of Velocity, Real Exchange Rates, Unemployment, and Productivity." *Carnegie-Rochester Conference Series on Public Policy* 27 (1987): 1–8.

Karl Brunner and Allan H. Meltzer. "Introduction to the Series." *Carnegie-Rochester Conference Series on Public Policy* 26 (1987).

Karl Brunner and Allan H. Meltzer. "Introduction to the Series." *Carnegie-Rochester Conference Series on Public Policy* 27 (1987).

Allan H. Meltzer. "Debt-Equity Swaps." Paper presented at the Euromoney-Mexico Debt to Equity Conversion and Investment Conference, Mexico City, May 1987.

Allan H. Meltzer. "International Debt Problems." *Contemporary Economic Policy* 5, no. 1 (January 1987): 100–105.

Allan H. Meltzer. "Limits of Short-Run Stabilization Policy: Presidential Address to the Western Economic Association, July 3, 1986." *Economic Inquiry* 25, no. 1 (January 1987): 1–14.

Allan H. Meltzer. "Notes on the Problem of International Debt." In *International Debt and Central Banking in the 1980s*, edited by Zannis Res and Sima Motamen, 21–29. London: Macmillan, 1987.

Allan H. Meltzer. "On Monetary Stability and Monetary Reform." *Bank of Japan Monetary and Economic Studies* 5, no. 2 (September 1987): 13–34. Reprinted in *Toward a World of Economic Stability: Optimal Monetary Framework and Policy*, edited by Yoshio Suzuki and Mitsuaki Okabe, 51–73. Tokyo: University of Tokyo Press, 1988. Also reprinted in *Dollars, Deficit & Trade*, edited by James A. Dorn and William A. Niskanen, 63–85. Boston: Kluwer Academic, 1989.

Allan H. Meltzer. "Who Should Bail Out the Banks?" In *What Are All Those Deficits About?*, edited by Martin Geisel and Svetozar Pejovich, 35–52. Studies in Political Economy 2. College Station: Texas A&M University, 1987.

Allan H. Meltzer, Keith Poole, and Thomas Romer. "Introduction." *Public Choice* 55, no. 1 (September 1987): 1–3.

Karl Brunner and Allan H. Meltzer. "Money and Credit in the Monetary Transmission Process." *American Economic Review* 78, no. 2 (May 1988): 446–51.

Karl Brunner and Allan H. Meltzer. "Stabilization Policies and Labor Markets." *Carnegie-Rochester Conference Series on Public Policy* 28 (1988): 1–8.

Allan H. Meltzer. "De Stabiliteit van de Wereldeconomie" [The stability of the world economy]. *Rotterdamse Montaire Studies* (Erasmus Universiteit), no. 33 (1988).

Allan H. Meltzer. "Economic Policies and Actions in the Reagan Administration." *Journal of Post Keynesian Economics* 10, no. 4 (July 1988): 528–40.

Allan H. Meltzer. "Economic Priorities for the Next President." *Policy Review* 44 (Spring 1988): 18–19.

Allan H. Meltzer. "Overview." In *Black Monday and the Future of Financial Markets*, edited by Robert W. Kamphuis Jr., Roger C. Kormendi, and J. W. Henry Watson, 1–33. Homewood, FL: Dow Jones-Irwin, 1988.

Allan H. Meltzer. "The Policy Proposals in the AEI Studies." In *Restructuring Banking and Financial Services in America*, edited by William S. Haraf and Rose Marie Kushmeider, 440–47. Washington, DC: American Enterprise Institute, 1988.

Allan H. Meltzer. "Reaganomics im Urteil der Wirtschaftswissenschaft" [Reaganomics in the judgment of economics]. *Steuersystem und Wirthshaftswachstum* (Frankfurter Institut), 1988, 27–33.

Karl Brunner and Allan H. Meltzer. "International Debt, Federal Reserve Operations, and Other Essays." *Carnegie-Rochester Conference Series on Public Policy* 30 (1989): 1–6.

Alex Cukierman and Allan H. Meltzer. "A Political Theory of Government Debt and Deficits in a Neo-Ricardian Framework." *American Economic Review* 79, no. 4 (September 1989): 713–32.

Allan H. Meltzer. "Efficiency and Stability in World Finance." *Bank of Japan Monetary and Economic Studies* 7, no. 2 (August 1989): 1–14.

Allan H. Meltzer. "Eliminating Monetary Disturbances." Comment on "Can Monetary Disequilibrium Be Eliminated?," by Leland B. Yeager and Robert L. Greenfield. *Cato Journal* 9, no. 2 (Fall 1989): 423–28.

Allan H. Meltzer. "IMF Policy Advice, Market Volatility, Commodity Price Rules, and Other Essays." *Carnegie-Rochester Conference Series on Public Policy* 31 (1989): 1–6.

Allan H. Meltzer. "Keynes on Monetary Reform and International Economic Order." In *Monetary Economics in the 1980s*, edited by Forrest Capie and Geoffrey E. Wood, 101–50. London: Macmillan, 1989.

Allan H. Meltzer. "Some Lessons on Monetary Management." *Kredit und Kapital* 22, no. 1 (1989): 43–65.

Allan H. Meltzer. "Tobin on Macroeconomic Policy: A Review Essay." *Journal of Monetary Economics* 23, no. 1 (January 1989): 159–73.

Allan H. Meltzer and Jeremy P. Fand. "International Monetary Coordination." *AEI Economist*, July 1989.

Allan H. Meltzer and Saranna Robinson. "Stability under the Gold Standard in Practice." In *Money, History, and International Finance: Essays in Honor of Anna J. Schwartz*, edited by Michael D. Bordo, 163–202. Cambridge, MA: National Bureau of Economic Research, 1989.

Karl Brunner and Allan H. Meltzer. "Money Supply." In *Handbook of Monetary Economics*, edited by B. M. Friedman and F. H. Hahn, 1:357–98. Amsterdam: North-Holland, 1990.

Allan H. Meltzer. Commentary on "Monetary Policy and the Control of Inflation," by John W. Crow. In *Central Banking Issues in Emerging Market-Oriented Economies: A Symposium Sponsored by the Federal Reserve Bank of Kansas City*, 105–111. Federal Reserve Bank of Kansas City, 1990.

Allan H. Meltzer. Commentary on "The Financial System and Economic Performance," by Robert C. Merton. *Journal of Financial Services Research* 4 (1990): 301–5.

Allan H. Meltzer. "Comment from the Floor." In *Central Banking Issues in Emerging Market-Oriented Economies: A Symposium Sponsored by the Federal Reserve Bank of Kansas City*, 139. Federal Reserve Bank of Kansas City, 1990.

Allan H. Meltzer. Comment on "What Washington Means by Policy Reform," by John Williamson. In *Latin American Adjustment: How Much Has Happened?*, edited by John Williamson. Washington, DC: Institute for International Economics, 1990.

Allan H. Meltzer. "Diritti di voto e redistribuzione: Implicazioni per le democrazie" [Voting rights and redistribution: Implications for liberal, democratic governments]. *Biblioteca della liberta* 109 (April 1990): 27–47.

Allan H. Meltzer. "Japanese Competition Is No Threat." *Water*, Spring 1990, 24–25.

Allan H. Meltzer. "Karl Brunner, 1916–1989." *Economic Inquiry* 28, no. 1 (1990): R7–8.

Allan H. Meltzer. "My Life Philosophy." *American Economist* 34, no. 1 (March 1990): 22–32. Reprinted in *Reflections of Eminent Economists*, edited by Michael Szenberg and Lall Ramrattan, 308–24. Cheltenham, UK: Edward Elgar, 2004.

Allan H. Meltzer. "Productivity Perplex." Review of "Productivity in American Leadership," by William J. Baumol, Sue Ann Batey Blackman, and Edward N. Wolff. *Public Interest* 101 (Fall 1990): 139–45.

Allan H. Meltzer. "Some Empirical Findings on Differences between EMS and Non-EMS Regimes: Implications for Currency Blocs." *Cato Journal* 10, no. 2 (Fall 1990): 455–83.

Allan H. Meltzer. "Unit Roots, Investment Measures and Other Essays." *Carnegie-Rochester Conference Series on Public Policy* 32 (1990): 1–6.

Allan H. Meltzer. "Walter Oi at 60." *Carnegie-Rochester Conference Series on Public Policy* 33 (1990): 1–2.

Allan H. Meltzer. "What Should Be Done about Exchange Rates?" *Wirtschaftspolitische Blatter* 37, no. 4 (1990).

Allan H. Meltzer. "The Fed at Seventy Five." In *Monetary Policy on the 75th Anniversary of the Federal Reserve System*, edited by M. T. Belongia, 3–65. Boston: Kluwer Academic, 1991.

Allan H. Meltzer. "Folgenschwerer Irrtum" [Serious error]. *Wirtschaftswoche* 17 (April 19, 1991).

Allan H. Meltzer. "The Growth of Government Revisited." In *Perspectives on an Economic Future: Forms, Reforms, and Evaluations*, edited by Shripad Gopal Pendse, 131–43. New York: Greenwood, 1991.

Allan H. Meltzer. "Introduction." *Carnegie-Rochester Conference Series on Public Policy* 35 (1991): 1–5.

Allan H. Meltzer. "U.S. Leadership and Postwar Progress." In *Policy Implications of Trade and Currency Zones: A Symposium Sponsored by the Federal Reserve Bank of Kansas City*, 237–74. Federal Reserve Bank of Kansas City, 1991.

Allan H. Meltzer. "U.S. Policy in the Bretton Woods Era." *Review* (Federal Reserve Bank of St. Louis) 73, no. 3 (May 1991): 54–83.

Allan H. Meltzer, H. Erich Heinemann, Jerry L. Jordan, Mickey D. Levy, Charles I. Plosser, William Poole, Robert H. Rasche, and Anna Jacobson Schwartz. "Shadow Open Market Committee (SOMC): Policy Statement and Position Papers." IP 91-01, Industry Policy Studies Working Paper Series, Bradley Policy Research Center, March 1991.

Allan H. Meltzer and Charles I. Plosser. "Introduction." *Carnegie-Rochester Conference Series on Public Policy* 34 (1991): 1–5.

Allan H. Meltzer and Charles I. Plosser. "Introduction." *Carnegie-Rochester Conference Series on Public Policy* 35 (1991): 1–5.

Allan H. Meltzer. Commentary on "Macroeconomic Policy and Long-Run Growth," by J. Bradford De Long and Lawrence H. Summers. In *Policies for Long-Run Economic Growth: A Symposium Sponsored by the Federal Reserve Bank of Kansas City*, 141–48. Federal Reserve Bank of Kansas City, 1992.

Allan H. Meltzer. "Introduction." *Carnegie-Rochester Conference Series on Public Policy* 36 (July 1992): 1–4.

Allan H. Meltzer. "Karl Brunner: In Memoriam." *Cato Journal* 12, no. 1 (Spring/Summer 1992): 1–5.

Allan H. Meltzer. "Measurement, Economic, and Political Issues of Debt and Deficits." In *Fiscal Politics and the Budget Enforcement Act*, edited by Marvin H. Kosters, 60–76. Washington, DC: AEI Press, 1992.

Allan H. Meltzer. "Open Market Committee of the Federal Reserve System." In *The New Palgrave Dictionary of Money and Finance*, edited by John Eatwell, Murray Milgate, and Peter Newman, vol. 3. Palgrave Macmillan, 1992.

Allan H. Meltzer. "Patinkin on Keynes and Meltzer." *Journal of Monetary Economics* 29, no. 1 (February 1992): 151–62.

Allan H. Meltzer. "Who Failed? The Press, the Regulators and Other Contributors to S&L Losses." In *Rebuilding Public Confidence through Financial Reform*, edited by Peter Dickson, 107–8. Columbus: Ohio State University College of Business, 1992.

Jerry L. Jordan, Allan H. Meltzer, Anna Jacobson Schwartz, and Thomas J. Sargent. "Symposium and Articles in Honor of Milton Friedman's 80th Birthday." *Economic Inquiry* 31, no. 2 (April 1993): 197–212.

Allan H. Meltzer. "Benefits and Costs of Currency Boards." *Cato Journal* 12, no. 3 (Winter 1993): 707–10.

Allan H. Meltzer. "The Deficit: A Monetarist's Perspective." *Choices: The Magazine of Food, Farm, and Resource Issues* 8, no. 1 (1993): 1–2.

Allan H. Meltzer. "Inflation and Stabilization in Brazil." In *Proceedings of a Conference on Currency Substitution and Currency Boards*, edited by Nissan Liviatan, 77–83. World Bank Discussion Paper 207. Washington, DC: World Bank, 1993.

Allan H. Meltzer. "Is the Deficit a Friendly Giant after All?" *Harvard Business Review* 71, no. 4 (July/August 1993): 144.

Allan H. Meltzer. "Monetarism." In *The Fortune Encyclopedia of Economics*, edited by David R. Henderson. New York: Warner Books, 1993.

Allan H. Meltzer. "Monetary Policy: Some Theory and Evidence." In *Economic Policy, Financial Markets, and Economic Growth*, edited by Benjamin Zycher and Lewis C. Solmon, 167–88. Boulder, CO: Westview, 1993.

Allan H. Meltzer. "Real Exchange Rates: Some Evidence from the Postwar Years." *Review* (Federal Reserve Bank of St. Louis), March 1993, 103–17.

Allan H. Meltzer. "Socialist Economic Transformation: Correspondence." *Journal of Economic Perspectives* 7, no. 1 (Winter 1993): 199–201.

Allan H. Meltzer. "Some Lessons from the Great Inflation." In *Price Stabilization in the 1990s: Domestic and International Policy Requirements*, edited by Kumiharu Shigehara, 7–29. London: Macmillan, 1993.

Allan H. Meltzer. "Transition to a Market Economy: Some First Principles." *Human Systems Management* 12, no. 4 (1993): 281–88.

Allan H. Meltzer. "Heterodox Policy and Economic Stabilization." *Journal of Monetary Economics* 34, no. 3 (December 1994): 581–600.

Allan H. Meltzer. "Regulatory Arrangements, Financial Stability, and Regulatory Reform." *Monetary and Economic Studies* 12, no. 1 (July 1994): 1–15.

Allan H. Meltzer. Commentary on "What Do Budget Deficits Do?," by Laurence Ball and N. Gregory Mankiw. In *Budget Deficits and Debt: Issues and Options; A Symposium Sponsored by the Federal Reserve Bank of Kansas City*, 129–37. Federal Reserve Bank of Kansas City, 1995.

Allan H. Meltzer. "Information, Sticky Prices and Macroeconomic Foundations." *Review* (Federal Reserve Bank of St. Louis), May/June 1995, 101–18.

Allan H. Meltzer. "Introduction to the Series." *Carnegie-Rochester Conference Series on Public Policy* 42 (June 1995).

Allan H. Meltzer. "Monetary, Credit and (Other) Transmission Processes: A Monetarist Perspective." *Journal of Economic Perspectives* 9, no. 4 (Fall 1995): 49–72.

Allan H. Meltzer. Reply to commentary by Randall Wright on "Information, Sticky Prices and Macroeconomic Foundations," by Allan H. Meltzer. *Review* (Federal Reserve Bank of St. Louis), May/June 1995, 125–26.

Allan H. Meltzer. "What Is Money?" *Economic Affairs* 15, no. 4 (September 1995): 8–14. Reprinted in *Money, Prices and the Real Economy*, edited by Geoffrey E. Wood, 8–18. Cheltenham, UK: Edward Elgar, 1998.

Allan H. Meltzer. "Carl Christ." *Carnegie-Rochester Conference Series on Public Policy* 45 (December 1996): 1.

Allan H. Meltzer. "The Choice of the Monetary Regime." In *The Quest for Monetary Stability*, edited by Carlos Geraldo Langoni, James Ferrer, and Márcio Valério Ronci. Washington, DC: Getulio Vargas Foundation and George Washington University, 1996.

Allan H. Meltzer. "The General Theory after Sixty Years." *Journal of Post Keynesian Economics* 19, no. 1 (September 1996): 35–45.

Allan H. Meltzer. "Introduction to the Series." *Carnegie-Rochester Conference Series on Public Policy* 44 (June 1996).

Allan H. Meltzer. "On Making Monetary Policy More Effective Domestically and Internationally." *Monetary and Economic Studies* 14, no. 1 (July 1996): 1–27.

Allan H. Meltzer. "Supervisión bancaria y seguro de depósitos" [Banking supervision and deposit insurance]. *Cuestiones económicas* (Banco Central del Ecuador), no. 29 (June 1996): 27–41.

Allan H. Meltzer. "An American Perspective on Monetary Union." In *A Single European Currency?*, edited by Jeffrey Gedmin, 13–21. Washington, DC: AEI Press, 1997.

Allan H. Meltzer. Comment on "Debt-Deflation: Theory and Evidence," by Mervyn King. In *Asset Prices and the Real Economy*, edited by Forrest Capie and Geoffrey E. Wood, 228–35. London: Palgrave Macmillan, 1997.

Allan H. Meltzer. Comment on "Deposit Insurance: Do We Really Need It?," by Larry A. Sjaastad. In *Preventing Banking Sector Distress and Crises in Latin America: Proceedings of a Conference Held in Washington, D.C., April 15–16, 1996*, edited by Suman K. Bery and Valeriano F. Garcia, 56–58. World Bank Discussion Paper 360. Washington, DC: World Bank, 1997.

Allan H. Meltzer. "Keynes on the Interest Rate and Redistribution: Reply." *Journal of Post Keynesian Economics* 20, no. 2 (December 1997): 315–19.

Allan H. Meltzer. "Money and the European Union." In *European Monetary Policy*, edited by Stefan Collignon. London: Pinter, 1997.

Allan H. Meltzer. "Asian Problems and the IMF." *Cato Journal* 17, no. 3 (Winter 1998): 264–74.

Allan H. Meltzer. "Monetarism: The Issues and the Outcome." *Atlantic Economic Journal* 26, no. 1 (March 1998): 8–31.

Allan H. Meltzer. "Monetary Policy and the Quality of Information." *Monetary and Economic Studies* 16, no. 2 (December 1998): 1–18.

Allan H. Meltzer. "Commentary: Monetary Policy at Zero Inflation." Commentary on "How Should Monetary Policy Be Conducted in an Era of Price Stability?," by Lars E. O. Svensson. In *New Challenges for Monetary Policy: A Symposium Sponsored by the Federal Reserve Bank of Kansas City*, 261–76. Federal Reserve Bank of Kansas City, 1999.

Allan H. Meltzer. "Recent Crises in Post-crisis Perspective." Paper presented at the 35th Annual Conference on Bank Structure & Competition, Federal Reserve Bank of Chicago, Chicago, May 1999.

Allan H. Meltzer. "What's Wrong with the IMF? What Would Be Better?" *Independent Review: A Journal of Political Economy* 4, no. 2 (Fall 1999): 201–15.

Allan H. Meltzer. "Introduction to a Symposium on Central Banks after the European Monetary Union." *Atlantic Economic Journal* 28, no. 3 (September 2000): 295–96.

Allan H. Meltzer. "Lessons from the Early History of the Federal Reserve." *Atlantic Economic Journal* 28, no. 3 (September 2000): 269–78.

Allan H. Meltzer. "Monetary Policy in the New Global Economy: The Case of Japan." *Cato Journal* 20, no. 1 (Spring/Summer 2000): 69–72.

Allan H. Meltzer. "The Report of the International Financial Institution Advisory Commission: Comments on the Critics; Reform of the International Architecture." *CESifo Forum* (Ifo Institute) 1, no. 4 (October 2000): 9–17.

Allan H. Meltzer. "Response to Professor Bird." Reply to "Sins of the Commission: The Meltzer Report on International Financial Institutions," by Graham Bird. *World Economics* 1, no. 3 (July–September 2000): 31–37.

Allan H. Meltzer. "The Shadow Open Market Committee: Origins and Operations." *Journal of Financial Services Research* 18, no. 2 (December 2000): 119–28.

Allan H. Meltzer. "Financial Collapse: 1933." *Atlantic Economic Journal* 29, no. 1 (March 2001): 1–19.

Allan H. Meltzer. "IFI Reform: A Plan for Financial Stability and Economic Development." *Economic Perspectives* (US Department of State) 6, no. 1 (February 2001): 9–12.

Allan H. Meltzer. "Monetary Transmission at Low Inflation: Some Clues from Japan in the 1990s." *Monetary and Economic Studies* 19, no. S1 (February 2001): 13–34.

Allan H. Meltzer. "Money and Monetary Policy: An Essay in Honor of Darryl Francis." *Review* (Federal Reserve Bank of St. Louis) 83, no. 2 (July 2001): 23–32.

Allan H. Meltzer. "The Transmission Process." In *The Monetary Transmission Process: Recent Developments and Lessons for Europe*, edited by Deutsche Bundesbank, 112–30. London: Palgrave, 2001.

Allan H. Meltzer. "International Economic Policies of the Clinton Administration." In *American Economic Policy in the 1990s*, edited by Jeffrey A. Frankel and Peter R. Orszag, 265–70. Cambridge, MA: MIT Press, 2002.

Allan H. Meltzer. "Japan's Monetary and Economic Policy." *World Economics* 3, no. 3 (July 2002): 85–103.

Allan H. Meltzer. "New International Financial Arrangements." *Monetary and Economic Studies* 20, no. S1 (December 2002): 11–22.

Kunio Okina, Allan H. Meltzer, Maurice Obstfeld, Roger W. Ferguson Jr., Pierre van der Haegen, and Yutaka Yamaguchi. "Concluding Panel Discussion: The Role of Central Banks in Exchange Rate Regimes in the 21st Century." *Monetary and Economic Studies* 20, no. S1 (December 2002): 241–74.

Stanley Fischer, Allan H. Meltzer, Jeffrey D. Sachs, and Nicholas Stern. "The Future of the IMF and World Bank: Panel Discussion." *American Economic Review* 93, no. 2 (May 2003): 45–50.

Adam Lerrick and Allan H. Meltzer. "Blueprint for an International Lender of Last Resort." *Journal of Monetary Economics* 50, no. 1 (January 2003): 289–303.

Allan H. Meltzer. "Argentina 2002: A Case of Government Failure." *Cato Journal* 23, no. 1 (Spring/Summer 2003): 29–31.

Allan H. Meltzer. "Choosing Freely: The Friedmans' Influence on Economic and Social Policy." *Proceedings* (Federal Reserve Bank of Dallas), October 2003, 191–205.

Allan H. Meltzer. Comment on "Full Employment in Japan: Domestic and International Policy Considerations," by Takashi Omori. In *Japan's Economic Recovery: Commercial Policy, Monetary Policy, and Corporate Governance*, edited by Robert M. Stern. Cheltenham, UK: Edward Elgar, 2003.

Allan H. Meltzer. "Leadership and Progress." *World Economics* 4, no. 3 (July 2003): 15–26.

Allan H. Meltzer. "What Future for the IMF and the World Bank?" *Quarterly International Economics Report*, July 2003, 1–3.

Allan H. Meltzer. "Monetarism Revisited." *World Economics* 5, no. 3 (July 2004): 161–64.

Allan H. Meltzer. "A Monetary History as a Model for Historians." *Cato Journal* 23, no. 3 (Winter 2004): 357–60.

Allan H. Meltzer. Commentary on "Understanding the Greenspan Standard," by Alan S. Blinder and Ricardo Reis. In *The Greenspan Era: Lessons for the Future; A Symposium Sponsored by the Federal Reserve Bank of Kansas City*, 97–105. Federal Reserve Bank of Kansas City, 2005.

Allan H. Meltzer. "New Mandates for the IMF and World Bank." *Cato Journal* 25, no. 1 (Winter 2005): 13–16.

Allan H. Meltzer. "Origins of the Great Inflation." *Review* (Federal Reserve Bank of St. Louis) 87, no. 2, part 2 (March/April 2005): 145–75.

Allan H. Meltzer and C. A. E. Goodhart. "A History of the Federal Reserve." *Macroeconomic Dynamics* 9, no. 2 (April 2005): 267–75.

Allan H. Meltzer. "From Inflation to More Inflation, Disinflation, and Low Inflation." *American Economic Review* 96, no. 2 (May 2006): 185–88.

Allan H. Meltzer. Reply to Anne Krueger's commentary on "Reviving the Bank and Fund," by Allan H. Meltzer. *Review of International Organizations* 1, no. 1 (March 2006): 65–67.

Allan H. Meltzer. "Reviving the Bank and Fund." *Review of International Organizations* 1, no. 1 (March 2006): 49–59.

Allan H. Meltzer. "A Blueprint for IMF Reform: What Is Worth Retaining?" *International Finance* 10, no. 2 (July 2007): 177–82.

Allan H. Meltzer. "End of the American Century." *World Economics* 9, no. 4 (October 2008): 1–12.

Allan H. Meltzer. "Reflections on the Financial Crisis." *Cato Journal* 29, no. 1 (Winter 2009): 25–30.

Allan H. Meltzer. "Learning about Policy from Federal Reserve History." *Cato Journal* 30, no. 2 (Spring 2010): 279–309.

Allan H. Meltzer. "The IMF Returns." *Review of International Organizations* 6, no. 3 (September 2011): 443–52.

Allan H. Meltzer. "Milton Friedman: Non-research Activities 1976–89." Economics Working Paper WP11102, Hoover Institution, Stanford, CA, January 2011.

Allan H. Meltzer. "Politics and the Fed." *Journal of Monetary Economics* 58, no. 1 (January 2011): 39–48.

George P. Shultz, Michael J. Boskin, John F. Cogan, Allan H. Meltzer, and John B. Taylor. "An End to the Quick Fixes." *Hoover Digest*, no. 1 (January 2011).

Allan H. Meltzer. "The Federal Reserve (Almost) 100." *Journal of Macroeconomics* 34, no. 3 (2012): 626–30.

Allan H. Meltzer. "Federal Reserve Policy in the Great Recession." *Cato Journal* 32, no. 2 (Spring/Summer 2012): 255–63.

Allan H. Meltzer. Review of *The New Lombard Street: How the Fed Became the Dealer of Last Resort*, by Perry Mehrling. *Economic History Review* 65, no. 2 (May 2012): 826–27.

Allan H. Meltzer. "How and Why the Fed Must Change in Its Second Century." *Forefront*, Spring 2013, 9–12.

Allan H. Meltzer. Review of *Making the European Monetary Union*, by Harold James. *Business History Review* 87, no. 4 (December 2013): 803–5.

Allan H. Meltzer. "What's Wrong with the Federal Reserve: What Would Restore Independence?" *Business Economics* 48, no. 2 (April 2013): 96–103. Reprinted as "What's Wrong with the Fed? What Would Restore Independence?" in *Cato Journal* 33, no. 3 (Fall 2013): 401–16.

George P. Shultz, Gary S. Becker, Michael J. Boskin, John F. Cogan, Allan H. Meltzer, and John B. Taylor. "How to Ignite Economic Growth (It's Not a Mystery)." *Hoover Digest*, no. 3 (Summer 2013): 9–14.

Charles W. Calomiris and Allan H. Meltzer. "'Too Big to Fail'? The Problem Is Still with Us." *Hoover Digest*, no. 3 (Summer 2014): 46–50.

Allan H. Meltzer. "Current Lessons from the Past: How the Fed Repeats Its History." *Cato Journal* 34, no. 3 (Fall 2014): 519–39.

Allan H. Meltzer. "Federal Reserve Independence." *Journal of Economic Dynamics and Control* 49, no. C (2014): 160–63.

Allan H. Meltzer. "A Slow Recovery with Low Inflation." In *Across the Great Divide: New Perspectives on the Financial Crisis*, edited by Martin Neil Baily and John B. Taylor, 145–61. Stanford, CA: Hoover Institution Press, 2014.

Allan H. Meltzer. "The United States of Envy." *Hoover Digest*, no. 4 (Fall 2014): 42–46.

Allan H. Meltzer. "Congress vs. Cronyism." *Hoover Digest*, no. 1 (Winter 2015): 57–60.

Allan H. Meltzer. "Die Politik der Federal Reserve ist die schlechteste aller Zeiten—und kein Mensch kann sie aufhalten" [Federal Reserve policy is the worst of all times—and no one can stop it]. *Perspectives of Economic Policy* 16, no. 2 (June 2015): 151–63.

Allan H. Meltzer. "Karl Brunner, Scholar: An Appreciation." Economics Working Paper 15116, Hoover Institution, Stanford University, Stanford, CA, October 2015.

Allan H. Meltzer. "A Positive Theory of Economic Growth and the Distribution of Income." *Research in Economics* 69, no. 3 (2015): 265–90.

Allan H. Meltzer. "The QE Trap." *Intereconomics: Review of European Economic Policy* 50, no. 3 (May 2015): 171–72.

Charles W. Calomiris and Allan H. Meltzer. "Rules for the Lender of Last Resort: Introduction." *Journal of Financial Intermediation* 28, no. C (2016): 1–3.

Allan H. Meltzer. "Fail and Fail Again." *Hoover Digest*, no. 2 (Spring 2016): 27–32.

Allan H. Meltzer. "Myths of Redistribution." *Hoover Digest*, no. 1 (Winter 2016): 25–28.

Charles W. Calomiris, Douglas Holtz-Eakin, R. Glenn Hubbard, Allan H. Meltzer, and Hal S. Scott. "Establishing Credible Rules for Fed Emergency Lending." *Journal of Financial Economic Policy* 9, no. 3 (August 2017): 260–67.

Alex Cukierman, Thomas Lustenberger, and Allan H. Meltzer. "The Permanent-Transitory Confusion: Implications for Tests of Market Efficiency and for Expected Inflation during Turbulent and Tranquil Times." CEPR Discussion Paper 13187, Centre for Economic Policy Research, 2018.

Allan H. Meltzer. "Monetary and Other Policy Problems." In *Public Policy & Financial Economics: Essays in Honor of Professor George G. Kaufman for His Lifelong Contributions to the Profession*, edited by Douglas D. Evanoff, Anastasios G. Malliaris, and George G. Kaufman, 165–76. Singapore: World Scientific, 2018.

COMMENTARY

Allan H. Meltzer. "An Open Letter to Chairman Martin." *New York Times*, 1969.

Allan H. Meltzer. "Why Should Controls Work Now?" *Pittsburgh Post-Gazette*, September 25, 1971.

Allan H. Meltzer. "A Plan for Subduing Inflation." *Fortune*, September 1974.

Allan H. Meltzer. "Costs of Monetarism." *New York Times*, October 1975.

Allan H. Meltzer. "Floating Rates and Freedom to Choose." *Business Week*, September 29, 1975.

Allan H. Meltzer. "A Closet Capitalist Confesses." *Wall Street Journal*, April 1976.

Allan H. Meltzer. "The World Needs More Monetary Targets." *New York Times*, January 4, 1976.

Allan H. Meltzer. "It Takes Long-Range Planning to Lick Inflation." *Fortune*, December 1977.

Allan H. Meltzer. "Some Prescriptions for Government Bloat." *Fortune*, January 1977.

Allan H. Meltzer. "Money, Growth and Inflation." *Wall Street Journal*, May 17, 1978.

Allan H. Meltzer. "Avoiding the Monetary Shoals." *Wall Street Journal*, May 9, 1979.

Allan H. Meltzer. "A Monetarist Looks at the Federal Reserve." *New York Times*, October 14, 1979.

Allan H. Meltzer. "A Testing Time for Monetarism." *Fortune*, October 6, 1980.

Allan H. Meltzer. "The Result of the Fed's Failed Experiment." *Wall Street Journal*, July 29, 1982.

Allan H. Meltzer. "How to Cut Unemployment in the Next Five Years." *Financial Times*, May 25, 1983.

Allan H. Meltzer. "The International Debt Problem." *Financial Times*, December 1983.

Allan H. Meltzer. "A Way to Defuse the World Debt Bomb." *Fortune*, November 28, 1983.

Allan H. Meltzer and Karl Brunner. "Congress and the Administration Pass the Buck." *Wall Street Journal*, February 7, 1983.

Allan H. Meltzer. "Cures That Are Worse Than the Disease." *Financial Times*, August 22, 1984.

Allan H. Meltzer. "Monetary Reform." *Financial Times*, August 1984.

Allan H. Meltzer. "Time to Put an End to Tub-Thumping." *Financial Times*, March 12, 1984.

Allan H. Meltzer. "Will China Become Capitalist?" *Financial Times*, December 1984.

Allan H. Meltzer. "Baker Would Make Us Poorer." *Wall Street Journal*, December 13, 1985.

Allan H. Meltzer. "How to Cut the Trade Deficit." *Fortune*, November 25, 1985.

Allan H. Meltzer. "And We've Gone into Hock to the Rest of the World." *Washington Post*, April 5, 1987.

Allan H. Meltzer. "Rigid Exchange Rates Hurt Market." *Los Angeles Times*, December 13, 1987.

Allan H. Meltzer. "Trade Bill Is Hazardous to Consumer Health." *Los Angeles Times*, October 11, 1987.

Allan H. Meltzer. "A Wary Look at Volcker's Legacy." *Los Angeles Times*, August 11, 1987.

Allan H. Meltzer. "British Economy a Textbook Case." *Los Angeles Times*, April 3, 1988.

Allan H. Meltzer. "What Really Happened in the Crash." *Wall Street Journal*, 1988.

Allan H. Meltzer. "What the Country Needs Is More Discipline, Less Talk about Tax Hike." *Los Angeles Times*, February 7, 1988.

Allan H. Meltzer. "Worry Less about Foreign Debt." *Los Angeles Times*, November 13, 1988.

Allan H. Meltzer. "Brady's Treasure Needs Fixing." *New York Times*, December 11, 1989.

Allan H. Meltzer. "Debt Crisis: A Familiar Fall Guy." *Los Angeles Times*, March 27, 1989.

Allan H. Meltzer. "The Great Deficit Debate." *National Review*, January 27, 1989.

Allan H. Meltzer. "Incentives Needed to Reform Debt." *Los Angeles Times*, March 5, 1989.

Allan H. Meltzer. "Inflation and Its Aftermath." *Los Angeles Times*, April 30, 1989.

Allan H. Meltzer. "The Model Is Market, Not Marxism." *Wall Street Journal*, January 8, 1989.

Allan H. Meltzer. "No Marshall Plan for the Soviet Union." *Los Angeles Times*, December 10, 1989.

Allan H. Meltzer. "Parkinson's Law Reigns at the IMF." *Los Angeles Times*, June 25, 1989.

Allan H. Meltzer. "S&L Regulatory System Still Flawed." *Los Angeles Times*, August 20, 1989.

Allan H. Meltzer. "Deposit Insurance System Was Culprit in S&L Mess." *Los Angeles Times*, September 16, 1990.

Allan H. Meltzer. "German Merger to Affect Economies around the World." *Los Angeles Times*, July 22, 1990.

Allan H. Meltzer. "The Persistent and Costly Myths about Trade Policy." *Los Angeles Times*, May 27, 1990.

Allan H. Meltzer. "Soviets Unlikely to Avert Stagnation and Inflation." *Los Angeles Times*, November 11, 1990.

Allan H. Meltzer. "Trade Policy: What Next?" *American Enterprise* (American Enterprise Institute), May–June 1990.

Allan H. Meltzer. "Uncle Sam Shouldn't Toss Money into R&D." *Los Angeles Times*, April 1, 1990.

Allan H. Meltzer. "Why Bashing the Fed Doesn't Pay." *Los Angeles Times*, February 4, 1990.

Allan H. Meltzer. "Fair Trade Policies Harm This Country's Consumers." *Los Angeles Times*, April 28, 1991.

Allan H. Meltzer. "If the Middle Class Is Falling Behind, Solution Lies in Higher Productivity." *Los Angeles Times*, December 8, 1991.

Allan H. Meltzer. "Is Monetarism Dead?" *National Review*, November 4, 1991.

Allan H. Meltzer. "Keynes war kein Keynesianer" [Keynes was not a Keynesian]. *Neue Zürcher Zeitung*, April 28, 1991.

Allan H. Meltzer. "No Need to Worry about a 1930s-Style Depression." *Los Angeles Times*, January 6, 1991.

Allan H. Meltzer. "No One but US Treasury Wants Interest Rate Cuts." *Los Angeles Times*, June 23, 1991.

Allan H. Meltzer. "Pointing Way to Prosperity for East European Countries." *Los Angeles Times*, August 18, 1991.

Allan H. Meltzer. "Road to Monetary Union in Europe Proving Bumpy." *Los Angeles Times*, March 3, 1991.

Allan H. Meltzer. "There Is No Credit Crunch." *Wall Street Journal*, February 8, 1991.

Allan H. Meltzer. "Western Loans Not Soviet Answer." *Los Angeles Times*, October 13, 1991.

Allan H. Meltzer. "Applying Market Principles to the Cause of Saving the Environment." *Los Angeles Times*, July 19, 1992.

Allan H. Meltzer. "The Attack on Central Banks." *Wall Street Journal*, December 18, 1992.

Allan H. Meltzer. "Exchange Rates Have Kept Tokyo Stock Woes from Reaching New York." *Los Angeles Times*, May 24, 1992.

Allan H. Meltzer. "Massive Aid Program for Russia, as Proposed by Nixon, Isn't the Answer." *Los Angeles Times*, March 29, 1992.

Allan H. Meltzer. "Prosperity May Not Have Arrived but an Economic Recovery Surely Has." *Los Angeles Times*, September 13, 1992.

Allan H. Meltzer. "A Quick Fix Not Likely to Lead to Long-Term Growth." *Los Angeles Times*, November 8, 1992.

Allan H. Meltzer. "Trade, Not Aid." *International Economy*, July/August 1992.

Allan H. Meltzer. "Why the Federal Reserve's Discount Rate Cut Will Bring On Inflation." *Los Angeles Times*, February 2, 1992.

Allan H. Meltzer. "Worry about Under-Investment, Not Deficits." *Wall Street Journal*, March 17, 1992.

Allan H. Meltzer. "Clinton Lost Chance to Boost Economy by Not Focusing on Productivity." *Los Angeles Times*, March 7, 1993.

Allan H. Meltzer. "Deficit Will Continue: History Teaches That New Taxes Will Be Spent." *Los Angeles Times*, May 30, 1993.

Allan H. Meltzer. "Failure of Uruguay Talks on Trade Would Be a Deficit for All Nations." *Los Angeles Times*, October 31, 1993.

Allan H. Meltzer. "Germany's Short-Term Difficulties Dwarfed by Long-Range Problems." *Los Angeles Times*, July 11, 1993.

Allan H. Meltzer. "Slight Tightening of Monetary Policy Needed to Keep Lid on Inflation." *Los Angeles Times*, February 14, 1993.

Allan H. Meltzer. "What the New Europe Needs: Adjustable Exchange Rates, Open Markets." *Los Angeles Times*, September 5, 1993.

Allan H. Meltzer. "Why Governments Make Bad Venture Capitalists." *Wall Street Journal*, May 5, 1993.

Allan H. Meltzer. "The Worst Kind of Short-Term Thinking." *Wall Street Journal*, February 22, 1993.

Allan H. Meltzer. "As Clinton Spends, the Dollar Weakens." *Wall Street Journal*, June 30, 1994.

Allan H. Meltzer. "End the IMF." *Wall Street Journal*, November 1994.

Allan H. Meltzer. "Still Too Easy." *Wall Street Journal*, February 9, 1994.

Allan H. Meltzer. "A Costly Mistake: The Flawed Logic of the Mexican Bailout." *Harvard International Review*, Winter 1995/1996.

Allan H. Meltzer. "Die EU ist nicht die Lösung" [The EU is not the solution]. *Finanz und Wirtschaft*, December 9, 1995.

Allan H. Meltzer. "Why It Is Time to Close Down the IMF." *Financial Times*, June 16, 1995.

Allan H. Meltzer. "Clinton's Bailout Was No Favor to Mexicans." *Wall Street Journal*, February 2, 1996.

Allan H. Meltzer. "Europas Probleme" [Europe's problems]. *Finanz und Wirtschaft*, April 3, 1996.

Allan H. Meltzer. "Is a Little Bit of Inflation OK?" *International Economy*, September/October 1996.

Allan H. Meltzer. "Pie-in-the-Sky Debt Relief." *Financial Times,* October 12, 1996.

Allan H. Meltzer. "Population Loss Should Be Wake-Up Call for Pittsburgh Region." *Tribune-Review* (Pittsburgh), February 11, 1996.

Allan H. Meltzer. "The Road to Botswana Britain." *New Labor Economics*, July 1996.

Allan H. Meltzer. "Asia Afloat." *National Review*, November 24, 1997.

Allan H. Meltzer. "Danger of Moral Hazard." *Financial Times*, October 27, 1997.

Allan H. Meltzer. "IMF Weakened by Lack of Enforcement." *Tribune-Review* (Pittsburgh), February 9, 1997.

Allan H. Meltzer. "Hohe Politik auf Kosten der Ökonomie" [High politics at the expense of the economy]. *Neue Zürcher Zeitung*, June 30, 1998.

Allan H. Meltzer. "The 'System' Is Still the Problem." *Los Angeles Times*, May 29, 1998.

Allan H. Meltzer. "Time to Print Money." *Financial Times*, July 17, 1998.

Charles W. Calomiris and Allan H. Meltzer. "Fixing the IMF." *National Interest*, June 1, 1999.

Allan H. Meltzer. "Communism's Fall Meant Little to Albania." *Tribune-Review* (Pittsburgh), April 25, 1999.

Allan H. Meltzer. "Liquidity Claptrap." *International Economy*, November/December 1999.

Allan H. Meltzer. "A Better Way to Help the World." *Financial Times*, April 28, 2000.

Allan H. Meltzer. "What the World Bank Ought to Be Doing." *Washington Post*, April 11, 2000.

Allan H. Meltzer and Adam Lerrick. "Slow Progress in Prague." *Financial Times*, October 10, 2000.

Allan H. Meltzer. "Default without Disruption." *Financial Times*, May 10, 2001.

Allan H. Meltzer. "IFI Reform: A Plan for Economic Development." *The Independent*, September 21, 2001.

Allan H. Meltzer. "The World Bank Is Wrong to Oppose Grants." *Wall Street Journal*, July 26, 2001.

Allan H. Meltzer and Adam Lerrick. "Beyond IMF Bailouts." *Financial Times*, May 9, 2001.

Allan H. Meltzer and Adam Lerrick. "World Bank: The Wrong Answers for the Wrong Reasons." *National Post*, July 27, 2001.

Allan H. Meltzer. "Back to Bailouts." *Wall Street Journal*, August 7, 2002.

Allan H. Meltzer. "Depreciate the Yen." *Financial Times*, April 16, 2002.

Allan H. Meltzer and Adam Lerrick. "A Solution for Argentina." *Financial Times*, January 24, 2002.

Allan H. Meltzer. "A Jobless Recovery?" *Wall Street Journal*, September 26, 2003.

Allan H. Meltzer. "New IMF Loan Will Not Solve Argentine Crisis." *Financial Times*, January 13, 2003.

Allan H. Meltzer. "A Reality Check for the Conventional Wisdom." *Financial Times*, August 17, 2003.

Allan H. Meltzer and Bruce Rich. "World Bank Drain." *Washington Times*, January 13, 2003.

Allan H. Meltzer. "Why the Collapse of the Dollar Is Just a Myth." *Financial Times*, April 5, 2004.

Allan H. Meltzer. "Banking on Paul Wolfowitz." *Wall Street Journal*, May 17, 2005.

Allan H. Meltzer. "Regime Change at the World Bank." *Wall Street Journal*, March 18, 2005.

Allan H. Meltzer. "An Appreciation: Milton Friedman, 1912–2006." *On the Issues* (American Enterprise Institute), December 2006.

Allan H. Meltzer. Commentary in "A Symposium of Views: Is the IMF Obsolete?" *Magazine of International Economic Policy*, Spring 2007, 12.

Allan H. Meltzer. "The Fed Should Hold Firm." *Wall Street Journal*, September 15, 2007.

Allan H. Meltzer. "Let 'Em Fail." *Wall Street Journal*, July 21, 2007.

Allan H. Meltzer. "The Epic of Finance." *National Review*, December 15, 2008.

Allan H. Meltzer. "Grading Bernanke: A Symposium." *The American* (American Enterprise Institute), May 27, 2008.

Allan H. Meltzer. "Keep the Fed Away from Investment Banks." *Wall Street Journal*, July 16, 2008.

Allan H. Meltzer. "A Plan to Rebuild the Housing Market." *Financial Times*, November 11, 2008.

Allan H. Meltzer. "Regulatory Overkill." *Wall Street Journal*, March 27, 2008.

Allan H. Meltzer. "That '70s Show." *Wall Street Journal*, February 28, 2008.

Allan H. Meltzer. "Why the Crisis?" *The American* (American Enterprise Institute), February 21, 2008.

Allan H. Meltzer and Desmond Lachman. "Yes, It's a Wreck, but We Can Fix It." *Newsweek*, October 20, 2008.

Allan H. Meltzer. "A Broken Record on Deflation." *AEIdeas* (American Enterprise Institute), June 1, 2009.

Allan H. Meltzer. "Can the Fed Control Inflation? Yes. Will It? Unlikely." *AEIdeas* (American Enterprise Institute), June 30, 2009.

Allan H. Meltzer. "A History Lesson for Paul Krugman." *AEIdeas* (American Enterprise Institute), May 5, 2009.

Allan H. Meltzer. "Inflation Nation." *New York Times*, May 3, 2009.

Allan H. Meltzer. "Preventing the Next Financial Crisis." *Wall Street Journal*, October 23, 2009.

Allan H. Meltzer. "Regulation Usually Fails." *The American* (American Enterprise Institute), February 11, 2009.

Allan H. Meltzer. "What Happened to the 'Depression'?" *Wall Street Journal*, September 1, 2009.

Allan H. Meltzer. "Will the Fed Play Politics?" American Enterprise Institute, August 17, 2009.

Allan H. Meltzer and Desmond Lachman. "If Barack Obama Could Achieve Only One Financial Reform, What Should It Be?" American Enterprise Institute, April 13, 2009.

Allan H. Meltzer and Desmond Lachman. "Neglected Stimulus Ideas." *AEIdeas* (American Enterprise Institute), January 5, 2009.

Michael J. Boskin, George P. Shultz, John F. Cogan, Allan H. Meltzer, and John B. Taylor. "Principles for Economic Revival." *Wall Street Journal*, September 16, 2010.

Michael Greve, Adam Lerrick, Allan H. Meltzer, Alex J. Pollock, and Peter Wallison. "Transatlantic Law Forum: Regulating Financial Institutions in a Global Economy." American Enterprise Institute, October 19, 2010. Video.

Allan H. Meltzer. "Europe Jumps Off the Keynesian Bus." *Wall Street Journal*, August 12, 2010.

Allan H. Meltzer. "The Fed Compounds Its Mistakes." *Wall Street Journal*, October 11, 2010.

Allan H. Meltzer. "The Fed's Anti-inflation Exit Strategy Will Fail." *Wall Street Journal*, January 28, 2010.

Allan H. Meltzer. "Focus on the Long Term." American Enterprise Institute, September 9, 2010.

Allan H. Meltzer. "Market Failure or Government Failure?" *Wall Street Journal*, March 18, 2010.

Allan H. Meltzer. "Milton Friedman vs. the Fed." *Wall Street Journal*, November 4, 2010.

Allan H. Meltzer. "Privatization Can Help Greece." *Wall Street Journal*, May 21, 2010.

Allan H. Meltzer. "Why Obamanomics Has Failed." *Wall Street Journal*, June 30, 2010.

Allan H. Meltzer. "Ben Bernanke's '70s Show." *Wall Street Journal*, February 5, 2011.

Allan H. Meltzer. "The Fed Should Consider a 'Bad Bank.'" *Wall Street Journal*, April 7, 2011.

Allan H. Meltzer. "The Folly of Economic Short-Termism." *Wall Street Journal*, August 11, 2011.

Allan H. Meltzer. "Four Reasons Keynesians Keep Getting It Wrong." *Wall Street Journal*, October 28, 2011.

Allan H. Meltzer. "Gold Fever Is a Symptom." *New York Times*, August 4, 2011.

Allan H. Meltzer. "Leave the Euro to the PIGS." *Wall Street Journal*, September 14, 2011.

Allan H. Meltzer. "Meltzer: Solve Long-Term Problems." *Tribune-Review* (Pittsburgh), August 13, 2011.

Allan H. Meltzer. "A Welfare State or a Start-Up Nation?" *Wall Street Journal*, June 15, 2011.

Allan H. Meltzer. "Banks Need More Capital, Not More Rules." *Wall Street Journal*, May 17, 2012.

Allan H. Meltzer. "Growth or Redistribution." Letter to the editor. *Wall Street Journal*, March 20, 2012.

Allan H. Meltzer. "A Look at the Global One Percent." *Wall Street Journal*, March 9, 2012.

Allan H. Meltzer. "What's Wrong with the Federal Reserve?" *Wall Street Journal*, July 10, 2012.

George P. Shultz, Michael J. Boskin, John F. Cogan, Allan H. Meltzer, and John B. Taylor. "The Magnitude of the Mess We're In." *Wall Street Journal*, September 16, 2012.

Allan H. Meltzer. "Quantitative Quicksand." *Project Syndicate*, June 6, 2013.

Allan H. Meltzer. "What's Stopping Europe?" *Project Syndicate*, April 17, 2013.

Allan H. Meltzer. "When Inflation Doves Cry." *Project Syndicate*, August 13, 2013.

George P. Shultz, Gary S. Becker, Michael J. Boskin, John F. Cogan, Allan H. Meltzer, and John B. Taylor. "A Better Strategy for Faster Growth." *Wall Street Journal*, March 24, 2013.

George P. Shultz, Michael J. Boskin, John F. Cogan, Allan H. Meltzer, and John B. Taylor. "Start Now." *Wall Street Journal*, January 25, 2013.

Charles W. Calomiris and Allan H. Meltzer. "How Dodd-Frank Doubles Down on 'Too Big to Fail.'" *Wall Street Journal*, February 13, 2014.

Allan H. Meltzer. "Avoid Ethnocentrism on Hong Kong." Letter to the editor. *Wall Street Journal*, October 13, 2014.

Allan H. Meltzer. "Cronyism vs. the Constitution." *Wall Street Journal*, August 25, 2014.

Allan H. Meltzer. "How the Fed Fuels the Coming Inflation." *Wall Street Journal*, May 6, 2014.

Allan H. Meltzer. "Meltzer on Santelli Exchange: Our Crystal Ball Is Not Very Good." CNBC, May 9, 2014. Video.

Allan H. Meltzer. "Ronald Reagan Is Alive in India." *Defining Ideas* (Hoover Institution), May 29, 2014.

Allan H. Meltzer. "The United States of Envy." *Defining Ideas* (Hoover Institution), April 17, 2014.

Allan H. Meltzer. "The Follies of Income Redistribution." *Defining Ideas* (Hoover Institution), July 17, 2015.

Allan H. Meltzer. "The GOP's Tea Party Problem." *Defining Ideas* (Hoover Institution), November 4, 2015.

Allan H. Meltzer. "Keynes Was No Keynesian." *Defining Ideas* (Hoover Institution), December 8, 2015.

Allan H. Meltzer. "Three Strikes against the Fed." *Defining Ideas* (Hoover Institution), January 15, 2015.

Allan H. Meltzer and Kenneth E. Scott. "The Magna Carta at 800." *Defining Ideas* (Hoover Institution), June 15, 2015.

Milton Friedman, David Davenport, Allan H. Meltzer, and Thomas Sowell. "Socialism's Empty Promises." PolicyEd.org, October 17, 2016. Video.

Allan H. Meltzer. "College Students Flunk Economics." *Defining Ideas* (Hoover Institution), January 14, 2016.

Allan H. Meltzer. "The EU's Path Forward." *Defining Ideas* (Hoover Institution), July 7, 2016.

Allan H. Meltzer. "Fed Failures." *Defining Ideas* (Hoover Institution), March 9, 2016.

Allan H. Meltzer. "Fed Up with the Fed." *Defining Ideas* (Hoover Institution), February 17, 2016.

Allan H. Meltzer. "Lessons from the European Welfare State." *Defining Ideas* (Hoover Institution), May 25, 2016.

Allan H. Meltzer. "Lies Politicians Tell Us." *Defining Ideas* (Hoover Institution), July 27, 2016.

Allan H. Meltzer. "Mortgaging Our Low Interest Future." *Defining Ideas* (Hoover Institution), September 1, 2016.

Allan H. Meltzer. "The Power and Independence of the Federal Reserve." American Enterprise Institute, May 11, 2016.

Allan H. Meltzer. "Reform the Federal Reserve." *Defining Ideas* (Hoover Institution), October 12, 2016.

Allan H. Meltzer. "Restoring Liberty to the States." *Defining Ideas* (Hoover Institution), April 8, 2016.

Allan H. Meltzer. "The Sullen Leftists." *Defining Ideas* (Hoover Institution), December 14, 2016.

Allan H. Meltzer. "Worst Election Ever." *Defining Ideas* (Hoover Institution), November 10, 2016.

Allan H. Meltzer. "A Humane Reduction in Healthcare Costs." *Defining Ideas* (Hoover Institution), February 23, 2017.

Allan H. Meltzer. "Three Democrat Errors." *Defining Ideas* (Hoover Institution), April 25, 2017.

About the Contributors

David Beckworth is a senior research fellow at the Mercatus Center at George Mason University and a former international economist at the US Department of the Treasury. He is the author of *Boom and Bust Banking: The Causes and Cures of the Great Recession* (Independent Institute, 2012). His research focuses on monetary policy, and his work has been cited by the *Wall Street Journal*, the *Financial Times*, the *New York Times*, *Bloomberg Businessweek*, and the *Economist*. He has advised congressional staffers on monetary policy and has written for *Barron's*, *Investor's Business Daily*, the *New Republic*, the *Atlantic*, and *National Review*. He also hosts the popular podcast *Macro Musings*, where he and his guests discuss the important macroeconomic issues of the past, present, and future.

Michael D. Bordo is a professor of economics and the director of the Center for Monetary and Financial History at Rutgers University–New Brunswick in New Jersey. He has held previous academic positions at the University of South Carolina and at Carleton University in Ottawa, Canada. He has been a visiting professor at the University of California, Los Angeles; Carnegie Mellon University; Princeton University; Harvard University; and Cambridge University—where he was the Pitt Professor of American History and Institutions—as well as a visiting scholar at the International Monetary Fund and the Federal Reserve Banks of St. Louis and Cleveland, the Federal Reserve Board of Governors, the Bank of Canada, the Bank of England, and the Bank for International Settlement. He also is a research associate of the National Bureau of Economic Research in Cambridge, Massachusetts. He has a BA from McGill University, a MSc (econ) from the London School of Economics, and a PhD from the University of Chicago. He has published many articles in leading journals and authored or coedited 14 books on monetary economics and monetary history. He is editor of a series of books for Cambridge University Press: Studies in Macroeconomic History.

James Bullard is the president and CEO of the Federal Reserve Bank of St. Louis. He oversees the activities of the Eighth Federal Reserve District, including operations in the St. Louis headquarters and its branches in Little Rock, Arkansas; Louisville, Kentucky; and Memphis, Tennessee. He also participates on the Federal Reserve's Federal Open Market Committee. Bullard is a noted economist and scholar, and his positions are founded on research-based thinking and an intellectual openness to new theories and explanations. In addition, he makes public outreach and dialogue a priority to help build a more transparent and accessible Federal Reserve. He is an honorary professor of economics at Washington University in St. Louis, where he also sits on the advisory council of the economics department. Bullard received his doctorate in economics from Indiana University in Bloomington and holds bachelor of science degrees in economics and in quantitative methods and information systems from St. Cloud State University in St. Cloud, Minnesota.

Joshua R. Hendrickson is an associate professor at the University of Mississippi. His work primarily centers on issues related to monetary theory, history, and policy. He has written extensively on nominal GDP targeting and the political economy of Bitcoin. His work has appeared in the *Journal of Money, Credit and Banking*, the *Journal of Economic Dynamics and Control*, *Macroeconomic Dynamics*, the *Journal of Economic Behavior & Organization*, *Economics & Politics*, *Economic Inquiry*, the *Journal of Macroeconomics*, and the *Southern Economic Journal*. He received his PhD in economics from Wayne State University and his MA and BA in economics from the University of Toledo.

Robert L. Hetzel is a retired economist from the Federal Reserve Bank of Richmond. He received an AB and a PhD from the University of Chicago. While at Chicago, he was in the Money and Banking workshop and did his thesis work under Milton Friedman. He joined the research department at the Federal Reserve Bank of Richmond in 1975, where, as senior economist and research advisor, he counseled the bank's president on matters concerning his participation in meetings of the Federal Open Market Committee. His research agenda is the evolution of central banking in the modern regime of fiat money. He regularly writes articles on monetary policy in which he continues the Friedman monetarist tradition. His two recent books, both published by Cambridge University Press, are *The Monetary Policy of the Federal Reserve: A History* (2008) and *The Great Recession: Market Failure or Policy Failure?* (2012).

Peter N. Ireland is the Murray and Monti Professor of Economics at Boston College, a research associate in the Monetary Economics Program at the National Bureau of Economic Research, and a member of the Shadow Open Market Committee. Before joining the faculty at Boston College, Ireland held positions at Rutgers University and at the Federal Reserve Bank of Richmond. He received his PhD in economics from the University of Chicago. Ireland's teaching and research focus on macroeconomics and monetary economics, particularly Federal Reserve policy and its effects on the United States economy. His work has appeared in the *Journal of Monetary Economics*, the *Journal of Money, Credit and Banking*, and the *International Journal of Central Banking*.

Robert E. Lucas Jr. is the John Dewey Distinguished Service Professor of Economics at the University of Chicago. He is a fellow of the Econometric Society, the American Academy of Arts and Sciences, and the American Philosophical Society, and a member of the National Academy of Sciences. He is a past president of the Econometric Society and the American Economic Association. In 1995, he received the Nobel Memorial Prize in Economic Sciences. Lucas received his BA in history and PhD in economics from the University of Chicago. He was a member of the faculty of the Graduate School of Industrial Administration at Carnegie Mellon University from 1963 until 1974. He joined the Chicago faculty in 1975. Among his books are *Studies in Business-Cycle Theory* (1981); *Rational Expectations and Econometric Practice* (1981), coedited with Thomas Sargent; *Models of Business Cycles* (1985); and *Recursive Methods in Economic Dynamics* (1989), with Nancy Stokey and Edward Prescott. His book *Lectures on Economic Growth* was published in 2002, and he published his *Collected Papers on Monetary Theory* in 2013.

Edward Nelson is a senior adviser at the Division of Monetary Affairs at the Federal Reserve Board in Washington, DC. As well as working previously at the Federal Reserve Board, he held prior positions at the Bank of England, the Federal Reserve Bank of St. Louis, and the University of Sydney. He has published many articles in the field of monetary economics and is author of the books *The U.K.'s Rocky Road to Stability* (2009), coauthored with Nicoletta Batini, and *Milton Friedman and Economic Debate in the United States, 1932–1972* (forthcoming). Nelson received his PhD from Carnegie Mellon University. Allan Meltzer was a member of Nelson's doctoral dissertation committee.

Gerald P. O'Driscoll Jr. is a senior fellow at the Cato Institute. Previously the director of the Center for International Trade and Economics at the Heritage Foundation, O'Driscoll was senior editor of the annual Index of Economic Freedom, copublished by Heritage and the *Wall Street Journal*. He has also served as vice president and director of policy analysis at Citigroup. Before that, he was vice president and economic adviser at the Federal Reserve Bank of Dallas. He also served as staff director of the congressionally mandated International Financial Institution Advisory Commission (the Meltzer Commission). O'Driscoll has taught at the University of California, Santa Barbara; Iowa State University; and New York University. He is widely published in leading publications, including the *Wall Street Journal*. He appears frequently on national radio and television, including Fox Business, CNBC, and Bloomberg Television. He is a member of the Mont Pelerin Society, and is president of the Association of Private Enterprise Education. O'Driscoll holds a BA in economics from Fordham University and an MA and PhD in economics from the University of California, Los Angeles.

Charles I. Plosser served as president and CEO of the Federal Reserve Bank of Philadelphia from 2006 until his retirement in 2015. He is currently a visiting fellow at the Hoover Institution at Stanford University and a member of the Board of Governors of the Financial Industry Regulatory Authority (FINRA). Before coming to Philadelphia, Plosser was the John M. Olin Distinguished Professor of Economics and Public Policy and director of the Bradley Policy Research Center at the William E. Simon Graduate School of Business Administration at the University of Rochester. His research interests include macroeconomics, monetary theory and policy, econometrics, and finance. He has published articles in the major economic journals and served as coeditor with Robert King of the *Journal of Monetary Economics* for twenty years. Plosser has been a visiting scholar at the Bank of England and the Federal Reserve Bank of Minneapolis. He also has served as a research associate at the National Bureau of Economic Research in Cambridge, Massachusetts.

He earned a BA from Vanderbilt University and an MBA and PhD in economics from the University of Chicago.

George Selgin is a senior fellow and director of the Center for Monetary and Financial Alternatives at the Cato Institute, and professor emeritus of economics at the University of Georgia. He is the author of *The Theory of Free Banking* (1988), *Bank Deregulation and Monetary Order* (1996), *Less Than Zero: The Case for a Falling Price Level in a Growing Economy* (1997), *Good Money: Birmingham Button Makers, the Royal Mint, and the Beginnings of Modern Coinage* (2008), and *Money: Free and Unfree* (2017). Selgin holds a BA in economics and zoology from Drew University and a PhD in economics from New York University.

John B. Taylor is the George P. Shultz Senior Fellow in Economics at the Hoover Institution and the Mary and Robert Raymond Professor of Economics at Stanford University. He chairs the Hoover Working Group on Economic Policy and is director of Stanford's Introductory Economics Center. Taylor served as senior economist on the Council of Economic Advisers under President Ford and President Carter, as a member of President George H. W. Bush's Council of Economic Advisers, and as an economic adviser to multiple presidential campaigns. From 2001 to 2005, Taylor served as undersecretary of the Treasury for international affairs where he was responsible for currency markets and international development, oversight of the International Monetary Fund and the World Bank, and coordinating policy with the G-7 and G-20. Taylor formerly held positions as professor of economics at Princeton University and Columbia University. Taylor received a BA in economics summa cum laude from Princeton University and a PhD in economics from Stanford University.

Index

Page numbers in *italics* indicate figures; n indicates a note.